A Universal History of the Destruction of Books

Atlas & Co.
New York

A Universal
History of the
Destruction of Books

From Ancient Sumer
to Modern Iraq

Fernando Báez

Translated from the Spanish by
Alfred MacAdam

Interior design by Yoshiki Waterhouse
Typesetting by Wordstop Technologies
Map © Adrian Kitzinger

Originally published as *Historia universal de la destrucción de libros:
De las tablillas sumerias a la Guerra de Irak,* Ediciones Destino, S.A.,
Barcelona, 2004.

Atlas & Co.
15 West 26th Street, 2nd floor
New York, NY 10010
www.atlasandco.com

Distributed to the trade by W. W. Norton & Company

Printed in the United States

Atlas & Company books may be purchased for educational, business,
or sales promotional use. For information, please write to
info@atlasandco.com.

Library of Congress Cataloging-in-Publication Data is available upon
request.

ISBN-13: 978-1-934633-01-4
13   12   11   10   09   08   2   3   4   5   6

Contents

Acknowledgments

This has been a twelve-year labor. No one could write such a history without a group of friends willing to rewrite and correct—bringing all their severity to bear—each of its historical or literary mistakes. I must therefore mention Napoleón de Armas, Rafael Rattia, Enrique García de la Garza, Giovanny Márquez, and Jorge Chacín, whose comments on the original manuscript decidedly enriched this work. My most heartfelt thanks go to Osmán Gómez, a distinguished physician whose conversation I always miss.

I also want to take this opportunity to think my dear friend and agent Guillermo Schavelzon, who always believed in this book and told me of the talk he had with Julio Cortázar about books destroyed in Mexico. J. M. Briceño Guerrero, philosopher and philologist, teacher and friend, discussed with me the history of the transmission of Greek texts between the third century BCE and the third century CE. María González, in the preservation department of the library at the University of Texas at Austin, made wonderful comments I used in revising my work and sent me a copy of an old study by Cornelius Walford. I was extraordinarily lucky to have her help.

Professor William W. Fortenbaugh of Rutgers University generously sent me his compilations of the fragments of Theophrastus and Demetrius of Falero. Richard Janko, professor in the Department of Greek and Latin Classics at the University of London, gave me a copy of *Aristotle on*

Comedy containing the complete history of the loss of the second book of Aristotle's *Poetics*. We discussed extremely useful aspects of the case. My greatest thanks go to Charles Jones, researcher at the Oriental Institute in Chicago and creator of the IraqCrisis list.

Owen Gingerich of Harvard University, Donald Kerr, Special Collections Librarian at the University of Otago New Zealand, and Olivier Thill explained to me in detail the facts concerning the collection of the bibliophile Gian Vincenzo Pinelli. Ugo Rozzo, professor of the history of libraries at Udine, kindly explained how the library of Pico della Mirandola was destroyed. Francis Herbert, of the Royal Geographical Society of London, set aside time to study everything related to the burning of the workshop of the great Dutch cartographer Joan Blaeu, and I thank him with all my heart for his attention. Angela Nuovo supplied me with valuable information about book collections during the Italian Renaissance.

Paul Frank of Harvard University guided me in everything related to censorship and book destruction in China. I am in his debt for the transliteration of Chinese terms wherever they appear in this book. Julian Roberts explained the details of the looting of John Dee's library. Jay Dillon enumerated the reasons why Rimbaud could not have burned the copies of his first book and elucidated the versions of Edgar Allan Poe's *Tamerlane*. Luis Cuevas supplied me with facts and books that were of great help in the writing of this work: I am indebted to his disinterested service. The Argentine author Carina Maguregui sent me a book by Gérard Haddad, without which everything I say here would have been impoverished because of my ignorance of the theories of that prestigious psychiatrist. Marcus Billiamson gave me important information about certain unique books and about the destruction of the workshops of printers like Samuel Bagster.

Emiliano Bartolomé Domínguez and Arsenio Sánchez Hernampérez, librarians in Spain, splendid friends, set about revising and completing everything related to the Spanish Civil War and other aspects of Spanish history. Fred Schreiber told me all there is to know about the fate of the first edition of the Koran. Michael Chase, of the *Année Philologique*, supplied me with valuable facts about the most ancient Greek and Roman libraries. Samuel Ruiz Carmona, of the Archivo Documental del Centro de Humanidades of the CSIC, informed me about the famous Medinaceli fire of 2005 in Spain.

I would also like to express my most sincere thanks to Bárbara Graham, Mauricio Bach, Arístides Medina, Santos Himiob, Judith Hamilton, Luis Villafaña, René Teyggeler, specialist in library conservation, Jerry Morris, Deborah Brisset, Paolo Tinti, Clifford J. Scheiner, Alfonso Ruis Cagigal, Alexandra Mason, Martin Szinetar, María Teresa Delgado, Jesús Gascón, Silvia Cecilia Anselmi, Hans Mulder, Lázaro Civantos, Manuel Olivieri, Susana Ferrero, Benjamin Koch, Tamara Blanco, Ramón Araujo, Sergio Isquiza, Joseph Akl, Ramon Chacín, Natasha Alvarez, Malcolm Britt, Max Waddell, Juan Carlos Medina, Mauricio Bustamante, Alain Estévez, Saad Eskander, Muhamad Araim, and Blanche Ebeling-Koning.

I am indebted to antiquarian and used-book dealers from three continents who supplied me with facts. The aid provided by the staff of these libraries was invaluable: the Biblioteca Nacional de España, the Biblioteca Nacional de Buenos Aires, the Biblioteca de Ajuda Portugal, the Bibliothèque de l'Arsenal France, the British Library, the Biblioteca Nazionale Braidense Italy, the Biblioteca Nazionale Universitaria Italy, the Boston Public Library, the Bibliothèque Sainte-Geneviève Canada, the Biblioteca del Real Monasterio de El Escorial Spain, Herzog-August-Bibliothek Germany, Harvard's Houghton Library, the Hispanic Society of America the Bibliothèque de la Sorbonne France, Trinity College Ireland, the Biblioteca Apostolica Vaticana Italy, the Biblioteca

Nacional de Venezuela, the Biblioteca de la Universidad Central de Venezuela, the Biblioteca Simón Bolívar, the Biblioteca Tulio Febres Cordero, and the Sala de Libros Raros y Antiguos of the Universidad de los Andes Colombia.

I hold in my hands Fernand Drujon's *Dictionary of Destroyed Books*, and though it would be complicated to explain how this copy signed by the French author himself came to me, I must mention that it was a gift of Rafael Hurtado, a stupendous Spanish writer.

To Alejandro Padrón I owe having *Les unités perdues 2004* by Henri Lefebvre, a list of lost cultural artifacts; and to Lewis Ramírez I owe my information about lost Mexican codices.

I also wish to acknowledge Atlas & Co. and its staff for facilitating the English-language publication of this edition. Many thanks to John Oakes, a book lover.

And a message of respect and affection for all my friends on the mailing list Exlibris on the Internet.

Note for the English Translation

The term "universal" applied to this book confers upon it an almost magic condition while inevitably leaving it open to ambush by fragmentation. This English translation reveals that the work is condemned to permanent revision. Each new edition is an invitation to correction and amplification so that the book approaches the ideal, definitive history that perhaps will never exist. In any case, this miscellany owes much to Robert Burton's *Anatomy of Melancholy* and Julio Cortázar's novel *Hopscotch*. I suggest not reading it beginning-to-end because, in its way, this book is an anthology of possible books. The reader, with no remorse, can start reading anywhere. So, dear reader, you are invited to embark on a circular, but, I hope, intellectually stimulating adventure.

Where they have burned books, they will end in burning human beings.

—Heinrich Heine, *Almansor*, 1821

Every book burned enlightens the world.

—Ralph Waldo Emerson, *Essays: First Series*, 1841

Introduction

The Enigma of Baghdad

"Our memory no longer exists. The cradle of civilization, writing, and law, has been burned. Only ashes remain." These are the words of a professor of medieval history in Baghdad: a few days later he was arrested for belonging to the Baath Party. He spoke as he left the modern university building, where every single book in the library had been looted. He was alone, near the entrance, under a long, uninterrupted shadow. Perhaps he was merely thinking out loud. Or not thinking. Perhaps his voice was just part of that long, interminable murmur that is the Middle East. As he looked at me, he wept. I think he was waiting for someone, but whoever it was never came, and in a few minutes, I saw him walk off, aimlessly, threading his way around the enormous crater a missile had left beside the building.

Hours later, one of his history students unknowingly provided an explanation for the professor's comment. He stopped me with that air of authority suffering confers. He was wearing a brown robe, sandals, and glasses; despite his bristly beard, he was quite young, perhaps twenty or twenty-two, an excellent age for complaining. He didn't look me in the eye, but he wasn't looking to the side either. He asked me why man destroys so many books.

He asked his question calmly, continued with a quotation he didn't seem to remember correctly, finally ran out of adverbs, and said that for centuries Iraq had suffered despoilment and cultural destruction. "But aren't you the expert?" he asked, with a touch of bitterness. His name was Emad, and in his left hand he held up a worn volume by a Persian poet, with a dry palm leaf as a bookmark. I confess that I did not know what to say. So I left. Back in my hotel room, my confusion allowed me to ponder a few ideas, and my time shrank into a single space, where I took a narrow, necessary—even inevitable—step.

I don't know why I felt so impotent and why, after months passed, the incident still stuck in my memory. Perhaps it underscores the fact that I have understood nothing, and that whenever we try to exercise reason in the face of horror we make a futile mistake. But even so, I think I should outline a justification for that Baghdad student's question using my own experience. This introduction aims to do nothing more. And nothing less.

Suffice it to say, when I reached Baghdad in May of 2003, I met a new, indirect, oblique form of cultural destruction. After U.S. troops seized the city, a process of annihilation by omission began, contravening the 1954 Hague Convention and the Protocols of 1972 and 1999. The American soldiers did not burn Iraq's intellectual centers, but they didn't protect them, either. And that indifference gave carte blanche to criminal groups. To that professional vandalism was added another, more naïve kind of vandalism, perpetrated by mobs of looters who'd been spurred on by propaganda that triggered hatred for the symbols of Saddam Hussein's regime. We have to remember that museums and libraries were closely linked to the nation's power structure, so when they were burned to the ground, silence legitimized the catastrophe.

On April 12, 2003, the world learned about the looting of the Baghdad Archaeological Museum. Thirty objects of great value disappeared; more than 14,000 lesser pieces were stolen, and the galleries were destroyed. On April 14, a million books in the National Library were burned. The National Archive, with more than ten million registries from the republican and Ottoman periods, was also burned, and over the course of the following days the same took place at the libraries of the University of Baghdad, the Awqaf Library, and scores of university libraries all over the country.

In Basra, the Museum of Natural History was burned along with the Central Public Library, the university library, and the Islamic Library. In Mosul, the museum library fell victim to manuscript experts who removed specific texts. In Tikrit, when bombs fractured the structure of the museum, the security guards fled and looters walked in.

Added to this unexpected catastrophe, thousands of archaeological sites became endangered because they were no longer guarded. Illicit transnational trafficking in archaeological artifacts took place on an unprecedented scale. At the present time, despite the efforts of Italian troops, not one historical site in Iraq is safe. Gangs armed with AK-47s move through places like Hatra, Isin, Kulal, Jabr, Ninevah, Larsa, Tell el-Dihab, Tell el-Jbeit, Tell el-Zabul, Tell Jokha, Ur, Tell Naml, Umm el-Aqarib. . . . As soon as the helicopters and patrols leave, the thieves return, hastily and carelessly unearthing objects and destroying murals in the process. Some pieces are taken to Kuwait or Damascus, and from there they are transported to Rome, Berlin, New York, and London, where private collectors pay whatever price is asked.

Why should this murder of memory have occurred in the place where the book was born?

Among Destroyed Books

What I found in Iraq made me remember the first time I saw a destroyed book. I was four or five years old and lived in an honorable state of poverty, which had granted me as a last refuge the public library building in my hometown. My father was an honest—that is, unemployed—lawyer, and my mother, born in La Palma, in the Canary Islands, had to work all day in a notions shop weaving and unweaving, like the wife of that great traveler Odysseus. Which meant they had to leave me in the house that constituted the library in the old town of San Félix in Guayana, Venezuela. There my mother got discreet assistance from a widowed aunt related to her by marriage who for a time was the establishment's strict secretary. So I spent whole days under the indifferent protection of this kind woman in the moth-eaten stacks among scores of books.

There I discovered the value of reading: I found out I should read because I couldn't not read. I read because each good reading experience gave me an even stronger motive to keep reading. I read without following manuals, card catalogs, guides, critical anthologies, books labeled "classics," or recommendations for weekend reading. Books interested me so much because they were my only friends. I don't know if I was happy then, but I do know that as I turned those dearly beloved pages I forgot my hunger and misery, and that saved me from resentment and fear. As I learned to read, I forgot my tremendous loneliness. Like many other children, I learned to recognize the value of writers like Jules Verne, Emilio Salgari, Edgar Allan Poe, Rómulo Gallegos, Shakespeare, and Robert Louis Stevenson, and I was enchanted by the color pictures in an encyclopedia whose name I cannot quote today, but which had a great impact on me at the time because it showed me the moon as seen from a spaceship. I took it into my head that I too could be an astronaut. Anyone who could have seen me, with torn trousers, a stitched-up shirt, and that fantastic hairdo made for me by my pillow instead of a comb would have doubtlessly laughed out loud. But I believed it completely. I believed what books said: I wept when I saw Don Quixote on his deathbed.

That happiness was abruptly interrupted because the Caroní River, one of the Orinoco's tributaries, overflowed its banks without warning and flooded the town, carrying off with it the papers that constituted the object of my curiosity. It took away every volume. So I was left without my sanctuary and lost part of my childhood in that small library, all washed away by the dark waters. Sometimes, on the nights that followed, I dreamt Stevenson's *Treasure Island* sank, while one of Shakespeare's plays floated.

I never got over that terrible experience. Strangely enough, it wasn't the only one. Goethe says that when he was young he witnessed the burning of a book in Frankfurt, and that he became unhappy seeing "how an inanimate object is punished." When I was seventeen, I watched my classmates burn their schoolbooks at the end of the year. They were in a frenzy. There was no way to stop them, and they mocked my attempts to put out the fire. When I was nineteen and selling encyclopedias door-to-door, the nightmare recurred because a fire destroyed the secondhand bookstore I frequented. I still have a clear image of the owner, his hands burned, his eyes shut, and his face twisted in pain. In 1999, I went to Sarajevo with an investigating team and saw the ruins of the National Library, situated in the old town hall known as the Vijecnica. Prior to its deliberate firebombing, it housed 1.5 million volumes, including over 100,000 manuscripts. There I met a beautiful poet who said to me, "Each destroyed book is a passport to hell." That same year I saw how a landslide destroyed the libraries of coastal Venezuela. In 2000, I visited several cities in Colombia whose libraries had been destroyed by the civil war ravaging the country. . . .

Consciously or unconsciously, the subject came to obsess me, and one fine day I realized I was writing a book in which

I was telling about those events. In 2001, not without the kind of surprise you're supposed to feel in these instances, I received a heavy box that turned out to be the keystone of my investigation. The mailman, after handing me the receipt, warned me that it came from Caracas. Stuck to the outside was an envelope containing a simple letter signed in an illegible hand insinuating that the contents were books, my grandfather Domingo's only property. He'd willed them to me, but, as the letter explained, they were taken care of by an uncle who'd just died. The incredible thing is that I'd never met my paternal grandfather, a highly regarded shoemaker, and all I knew about him derived from a few family anecdotes.

In the box, which was stained with oil and ashes, I counted some forty volumes. I gave away the ones that didn't tempt me, but I kept William Blades's *The Enemies of Books* (1888) because it contained a charming exposition of the reasons books are destroyed. Still moved, and convinced this was a sign, I went to see my father, who was retired and living with my mother. He was suffering from Parkinson's disease. I told him about my strange inheritance, and as was usual with him, he showed no emotion. To the contrary, he told me that my grandfather was in the habit of conversing with him about the Library of Alexandria, his favorite historical enigma. When I left, he embraced me. I felt that gesture was definitive.

Ever since I began having memories, I've felt horror at the destruction of books. I've noted that words like "Alexandria," "Hypatia," or "censorship" tend to arouse my suspicion. The question asked by the young man at the University of Baghdad enabled me to understand that I should quickly finish this book and show the world one of its greatest cultural catastrophes. For fifty-five centuries books have been destroyed, and we barely have any idea why. There are hundreds of studies on the origin of books and libraries, but there is not a single history of their destruction. Isn't that a suspicious absence?

Apocalyptic Myths

While searching for a theory to explain book destruction, I coincidentally discovered that myriad myths deal with cosmic cataclysms, explanations of the origin of the world, or proclamations of its end. All civilizations, it seems, have postulated their origin and their end in a creation myth counterpoised to a destruction myth in a framework whose axis is the eternal return. Apocatastasis (from the Greek, meaning "hope in all things reconciled") has been the standard explanation for the end of history and the beginning of eternity. In ancient mythologies, hundreds of narratives describe how water, fire, or some other element has cleansed the world of human iniquity or will cleanse it in a constantly postponed future.

So destruction and creation are the only two alternatives for the universe. This belief was always present in Hebrew, Iranian, Greco-Roman, and Mesoamerican worldviews. In Zorastrianism, the end of the universe even has a date. Among the Aztecs, the gods sacrificed themselves to supply blood and hearts to the sun, and that ritual was maintained thanks to war, which conditioned men to repeat that sacrifice in perpetuity. The Germanic *Ragnarök*, or "grand conflagration," synthesized Asian and autochthonous myths. The Sibylline oracles constantly announced the end of Rome and the birth of a new world.

Christianity adopted that myth and added to the genesis of the Old Testament the apocalypse of the New Testament. The apocalypse is a cataclysm that will reveal the truth of things and salvage lost purity. The Greek word *apokalypsis* is translated as "destruction" but also as "revelation." Where there is apocalypse, there is revelation. The final message concerns the arrival of a new age.

Besides its cosmological and eschatological character, the myth of destruction was an essential trait of the gods, who are creators and destroyers at the same time. It was also assumed that the instrument of destruction was sacred. Fire was a god. Water was a god. The Cretans worshipped a bull because they attributed Crete's earthquakes and frequent tremors to its rage. Nergal, the Sumerian god of destruction, was presented as a youth with the power of a storm.

For humans, knowing the myth of every destructive element could result in salvation. In the Finnish epic the *Kalevala*, for example, it was only possible to help the seriously wounded and old Vainamoinen when the sacred origin of iron was recalled and its history recited. Also, a destructive man was seen as an illuminated being, a god or demon in potentia, capable of curing and omniscience. The Norse berserkers unleashed their fury so as to fuse themselves with the archetypal models of the gods' sacred fury. Even the good king was always a destroyer who repeated the actions of the gods.

Exploring this survival of annihilation myths is, in my opinion, the best way to introduce my speculations to the reader. In essence, I would dare to say that these extermination archetypes reflect a conviction about the most visible and painful aspect of humanity. The myths identify the scenario by linking events in the cosmic order and everyday life, thus consolidating the collective or individual behavior. They bring the macrocosm and the microcosm together. We may be living in a rationalist age, but thought and science are nothing more than disguised myths.

Those who attribute destructiveness to instinct are not so far from premodern men and women, who attributed it to a demon or an element in nature. The location of this instinct, according to recent neurological hypothesis, is either in the hypothalamus or in the limbic system in the prefrontal lobe. It therefore seems undeniable that human violence manifests itself refracted through social expectations: in the era of theological vision, the gods possessed us, and in the era of the atomic vision we are determined by minimal units whose genetic structure imposes on us an inheritance of reaction and struggle. The theory of instincts, it seems, is inscribed on a myth of liberation typical of our species, that is, the attempt to free ourselves from direct responsibility for destructive activity.

To the question of whether ancient myths contain an explanation of the human capacity for destruction I must say, yes, they do, even as I keep my distance from ideological or scientific reductionism. Myths transform both the human and the cosmos because we aspire to reconnect the sacred with actuality. Seen in this way, past, present, and future are articulated in a transparent and immediate chronology. Myth, from this point of view, presupposes the dynamic of expectations in the full exercise of foundation, normalization, and conservation. The apocalyptic narrative projects the human situation and its anguish: in each of us, the origin and the end interact in inevitable processes of creation and dissolution.

By destroying, we ratify this ritual of permanence, purification, and consecration; by destroying, we bring to the surface a behavior originating in the depths of personality, in a search for the restitution of an archetype of equilibrium, power, or transcendence. It might be a biological or a social system that is mobilized: the reaffirmation has only one purpose—continuity. The destructive ritual, like the constructive ritual applied to the building of temples, houses, or any work, fixes patterns that return the individual to the community, to shelter, or to the vertigo of purity.

Our affinity for restoring order by means of destroying threats has also grown. Autonomy has converged with the myth of destruction and resulted in a state of mind with dark and archaic motives, the core of which is death. To destroy is to assume the symbolic act of death by negating what is represented.

A Partial Theory of the Bibliocaust

Before explaining why books are destroyed, it's worth noting that the book is a relatively recent invention, made possible by the invention of writing. Anthropologists say that *Homo habilis*, our earliest ancestor, lived about 2.5 million years ago, and that *Homo sapiens sapiens*, from whom modern humans descend, developed writing just a few thousand years ago. Which means that humanity's existence is 99 percent prehistory and less than one percent written history.

The appearance of writing presupposes a complete transformation of our collective memory within a dozen founding civilizations. Of all the activities that distinguish culture, writing is one of the most important because it is a peerless tool for social organization and reaffirmation. Related to the Indo-European etymological root *skribh*, the act of enscribing, or writing, is to "cut, separate, make distinct." All complex species possess some form of communication—grunts, chemicals, gestures, scents. People, on the other hand, have managed to represent, using language, their most complex thought processes and in some way to convert signs and gestures into abstract, conventional visible signs that guarantee the protection of traditions.

Out of writing soon came the need for an ancillary object, the book. Jorge Luis Borges says:

Of all man's instruments, the most astonishing is, without any doubt, the book. The others are extensions of his body. The microscope, the telescope, are extensions of his eyes; the telephone an extension of his voice; then we have the plow and the sword, extensions of his arm. But the book is something else: the book is an extension of memory and imagination.

The book gives substance to human memory. The book, despite being portable, objectifies memory: it is a rational unity that uses audiovisual, printed, or electronic means to represent mnemonic and linguistic will. In the revolutionary step from orality to writing and, above all, in that significant process where the book triumphs as a cult object, what really takes center stage is a more certain model of permanence that codifies sensibility and translates it into uniform, legitimate states. The book is, then, a proposition that seeks to configure everything in terms of reason and not in terms of chaos. The idea that the book is something more than a physical structure that supports collective or individual memory has generated powerful metaphors.

> *The book as talisman*: Saint John Chrysostome recounts that in fourth-century Antioch, people hung codices around their necks to ward off the powers of evil.
> *The book of life.* Belief in a divine book that contains the names of those who will be saved in the Last Judgment, as Saint John testifies.
> *The book as nature.* Plotinus speaks of the stars as if they were letters eternally written in the heavens.
> *The book of the world.* It makes of the universe a bibliographic cosmos.
> *The world exists only to become a book.* This was the belief of the poet Stéphane Mallarmé.
> *The book as person.* As Walt Whitman proposes in his "Songs of Farewell."
> *The book as shared dream.*

Each of these metaphors, adopted and furthered by generations of readers who have understood that our souls persist only through language, accepts the idea that humanity and books are inseparable.

The book is an institution of memory for consecration and permanence, and for that reason should be studied as a key element in society's cultural patrimony. In itself, patrimony has the ability to stir a transmissible feeling of affirmation and belonging. It can reinforce or stimulate a people's awareness of identity in their territory. A library, an archive, or a museum are cultural patrimonies and all nations regard them as temples of memory.

It is for this reason, and for others that constitute the central thesis of this essay, that books are not destroyed as physical objects but as links to memory, that is, as one of the axes of identity of a person or a community. There is no identity without memory. If we do not remember what we are, we don't know what we are. Over the centuries, we've seen that when a group or nation attempts to subjugate another group or nation, the first thing they do is erase the traces of its memory in order to reconfigure its identity.

Instigators of the auto-da-fé—the public ritual of confession directed against books and their authors—recognize that to eradicate an idea it is not enough to murder a writer or even a people; only through the destruction of books can the murder of memory be accomplished. The ideologues behind these acts are moved by a radicalism that spurs cultural warfare of a political or religious nature.

There has never been a single cause for the destruction of a book or a library: there are dozens. Even so, and beyond the circumstantial anecdotes that exonerate or condemn, at the root of book destruction is the intent to induce historical amnesia that facilitates control of an individual or a society. In Greece, the partial elimination of the archives was authorized, as happened in 405 BCE, with Patrocleides' decree of amnesty. An attempt to unify Athenians in the wake of their defeat in the Peloponnesian War, the decree mandated the erasure of public records and established sanctions against those who kept copies or dared to recall the past with malice. The Romans called this *damnatio memoriae* or *abolitio memoriae*: the process by which the senate practiced the "damnation of memory," obliterating the memory of all those it classified as infamous. Among other things, *damnatio memoriae* erased the name of the affected person from all inscriptions, books, and monuments. Anyone who tears apart or burns a book repeats that classic pattern.

Public or private book destruction almost always takes place in alternating, melancholy phases: restriction, exclusion, censure, looting, and, finally, destruction. There is restriction in veto and emendation; there is censure in discriminatory suppression; there is looting in commercial theft. Extremist attacks, it seems, intend to destroy the principal cultural models that form part of the adversary's shared memories in order to manipulate the most resistant links and reconstruct everything by means of orthodoxy. This phenomenon is also known as acculturation and transculturation—when one culture imposes itself on another and transplants new memories in a society. We see this in cases of ethnic cleansing of the kind put into practice by the Nazis and despotic regimes like that of Mao in China. It is the triumph of Herostratus, who, in 356 BCE, on July 21, set fire to the Temple of Artemis at Ephesus, thus destroying one of the seven wonders of the world: he who destroys perseveres.

Books are burned and libraries bombed because they are symbols. A prime example is the National Library of Bosnia-Herzegovina in Sarajevo, opened in 1896. Beginning on the night of August 25, 1992, the building and its 1.5 million volumes, including 478 ancient manuscripts, was pounded into oblivion by artillery. Libraries are collateral victims of war and not usually military objectives, but the facts clearly show that their special condition as culturally agglutinating elements for a community puts them at risk.

It is unlikely that anyone has heard of a sacred computer or automobile, but we all know of sacred books. Aside from being mnemonic monuments, books for many societies come to be a divine manifestation of a superior spirit; we can see this in the rooms the Hebrews create in their synagogues called *geniza*, from a word whose root is "to hide," to store manuscripts containing verses or sacred texts such as the Torah (the Five Books of Moses). One of the most important of these is the Geniza in Cairo, which contained tens of thousands of texts in Hebrew. In Islam, as in Judaism, the remains of sacred texts are treated with the reverence accorded to human bodies: in fifty-six tunnels in the Chiltan mountains in the community of Quetta, Pakistan, a group of devotees watches over a cemetery with 70,000 sacks that contain damaged copies of the Koran. These deposits are called Jabal-e-Noor-ul-Quran.

"Bibliocaust," a neologism used to refer to the destruction of books, is an attempt to annihilate a memory considered to be a direct or indirect threat to another memory thought superior. Books are not destroyed because they are hated as objects. Enemies of pocketbooks, colophons, paper, typography, or gilt bindings are unknown. John Milton, in *Areopagitica* (1644), declared that what was destroyed in a book was rationality made manifest: "as good almost kill a man as kill a good book. Who kills a man kills a reasonable creature, God's image; but he who destroys a good book, kills reason itself, kills the image of God, as it were in the eye." The material part can only be associated with the book in a circumstantial way: at first it was a tablet among the Sumerians, a bone among the Chinese, a stone, a piece of skin, a plate of bronze or iron, a papyrus, a codex, a sheet of paper, and now it is a file stored on a compact disk or electronic device.

Umberto Eco describes three kinds of "biblioclasty," that is, book destruction: fundamentalist bibloclasty, biblioclasty through neglect, and biblioclasty out of interest. Fundamentalist biblioclasty does not hate books as objects, but fears them for their content and does not want others to read them.

While there are collector-destroyers who will mutilate a book to get an illustration or map, the collection destroyer is a totalitarian personality whose origins are rooted in apocalyptic myths of creation and destruction. In totalitarianism, politics and ideology are at the service of rituals that seek to reinvent history in the most brutal ways: the collectivist temptation, classism, the formation of millennial utopias, and precise, bureaucratic, servile despotism that manifests itself as the rejection of the other's memory. Even democratic societies can become totalitarian when they reduce their identity by accusations of sedition and become exclusionary. According to Rebecca Knuth, "libricide," a term she uses in her studies, is "the systematic destruction of books and libraries" oriented to "negation on the order of genocide and ethnocide."

Paradoxically, the destroyers are usually ingenious creators. The biblioclasts have their own book, which they judge eternal. As the ancient destructive ritual decrees it, destruction can remove the entity involved and return it to eternity. When aprioristic, extremist fervor assigns a categorical condition to a work (be it the Koran, the Bible, or the program for any religious, social, artistic, or political movement), it does so to legitimize its divine or permanent origin—God as author or, if not God, then a saint or a messiah. In *1984*, George Orwell describes a totalitarian state where an official branch of government is dedicated to finding and erasing the past. Books are rewritten, and the original versions destroyed in secret furnaces in order to save society from the enemy.

The destroyer of books is dogmatic, because s/he clings to a uniform, irrefutable concept of the world. This vision is absolute in nature, autarchic, self-founding, self-sufficient, infinite, atemporal, and simple and expresses itself as a pure, incorruptible present. That absolute implies an absolute reality. It doesn't explain itself: it comprehends directly through revelation.

When something or someone does not confirm the accepted point of view, an immediate, superstitious, and official condemnation ensues. The theological defense of a book considered definitive, irrefutable, and indispensable does not tolerate differences of opinion. This is in part because straying from the official line or reflecting critically is the same as rebellion, and in part because the sacred admits neither conjectures nor digressions. It supposes a heaven for its police force and a combustible nightmare for its transgressors.

There is one determining aspect here: control is not established unless there is a conviction involved. There is no religious, political, or military hegemony without cultural hegemony. Those who destroy books and libraries know what they are doing. Their objective has always been clear: intimidate, erase motivation, demoralize, enhance historical oblivion, diminish resistance, and, above all, foment doubt.

We should not forget that numerous fundamental human rights are violated in bibliocausts: the right to dignity, the right to a complete written memory for individuals and nations, the right to identity, and the right to information.

The Forms of Fire

Why has fire been the preeminent tool for destroying books? Are those who burn books merely pyromaniacs?

There are myriad explanations for this phenomenon. But psychiatrists tend to agree with the idea that while pyromaniacs may be biblioclasts, biblioclasts are not necessarily pyromaniacs. Some posit the problem is related to another kind of psychic manifestation, the cult of the sun. Fire was the essential element in the development of civilization, the first determining element in the life of humanity, for nutrition and collective security.

Fire is salvation, and for that reason, almost all religions dedicate fires to their respective divinities. This power to conserve life is also a destructive power. When man destroys with fire, he plays God, master of the fire of life and death. And in this way he identifies with a purifying solar cult and with the great myth of destruction that almost always takes place through fire.

The reason for using fire is obvious: it reduces the spirit of a work to matter. If you burn a man, he is reduced to his four principal elements—carbon, hydrogen, oxygen, and nitrogen; if you burn paper, the atemporal rationality stops being rationality and becomes ashes. There is also a visual element. Anyone who's seen something burned recognizes its undeniably black color. That which is light becomes dark.

And we destroy what we love: Sabbatai Zevi, a seventeenth-century Jewish mystic known as the "False Messiah," was a man of learning who told his followers that destroying the Holy Scriptures would bring about a new era. "We must destroy. All will be renewed. That which is forbidden is the good." The "People of the Book," as Jews are sometimes known, also endured the rise to prominence of Nachman of Bratislava, born in 1772. The sage's most remembered aphorism: "To burn a book is to bring light to the world."

Around 1935, Elias Canetti sentenced his character in *Auto-da-Fé* to be burned alive with his entire library. The last sentence in the book says: "Finally, when the flames reached him, he burst into laughter, as he'd never laughed before in his life." In 1953, Ray Bradbury imagined a future in *Farenheit 451* in which a team of firemen is in charge of burning books to keep them from disturbing the orthodoxy of the system in power.

The Roman poet Statius, at the death of his father, asked that his writings be exempted from the fire. That desire became a commonplace in poetry, but sometimes the desire to rewrite history was conflicting. Ovid, in the epilogue to the *Metamorphoses*, declares his interest in saving his work from fire, sword, divine hand, or time. Yet he also confessed to burning his poems because he'd become disillusioned with them.

The Culture of Destruction

It's a common error to attribute the destruction of books to ignorant men unaware of their hatred. After twelve years of study, I've concluded that the more cultured a nation or a person is, the more willing each is to eliminate books under the pressure of apocalyptic myths. In general, biblioclasts are well-educated people, cultured, sensitive, perfectionists, painstaking, with unusual intellectual gifts, depressive tendencies, incapable of tolerating criticism, egoists, mythomaniacs, members of the middle or upper classes, with minor traumas in their childhood or youth, with a tendency to belong to institutions that represent constituted power, charismatic, with religious and social hypersensitivity. To all that we would add a tendency to fantasy. In sum, we have to forget the stereotype of the savage book destroyer. Ignorant people are the most innocent.

There are abundant examples of philosophers, philologists, erudite individuals, and writers who vindicated biblioclasty. In Egypt, the governor and poet Akhenaton, a good monotheist, had all the religious books that preceded him burned in order to impose his own writings concerning the god Aton. In the fifth century BCE, the Athenian democrats prosecuted the sophist Protagoras for impiety and burned his book *On the Gods* in a public bonfire. According to his biographer Diogenes Laertius, Plato, not content with excluding the poets from his ideal republic, tried to burn the books of Democritus and even burned his own poems when he met Socrates.

In China, Li Si, one of the counselors of the emperor Shi Huang and the most original philosopher of the Legalist school, proposed the destruction of all books that defended a return to the past. His modest proposal took effect in 213 BCE. Unfortunately there was nothing new in that, because in the *Tao Te Ching*, Lao-Tzu had proposed, "Eliminate the wise, exile the geniuses, and that will be more useful to the people." He also wrote: "Suppress all study, and nothing will happen."

Spanish cardinal Jiménez de Cisneros, founder of the University of Alcalá and promoter of the Complutensian Polyglot Bible in Greek, Hebrew, and Chaldean, with a Latin translation, burned the Islamic books in Granada. In 1530, Fray Juan de Zumárraga, creator of the first library in Mexico, burned the Aztec codices. A man as tolerant as David Hume did not hesitate to demand the suppression of all books on metaphysics.

In 1910, the Futurists published a manifesto in which they called for the destruction of all libraries. Around 1967, the Colombian poets of the Nadaísta group burned copies of Jorge Isaacs's novel *María*, convinced that it was necessary to destroy the nation's literary past. Joseph Goebbels, a serious bibliophile, organized the Nazi burnings in 1933. In 1939, the librarians of the St. Louis Public Library rejected John Steinbeck's *The Grapes of Wrath* and publicly burned the book. Those who spoke at the event warned U.S. writers that they would not tolerate obscenity or communism. Borges, in his *Autobiographical Essay*, did not hide the fact that he burned his early books: "Until a few years ago, if the price wasn't too high, I would buy and burn them."

Until now, the premeditated destruction of books has occupied most of this chronicle of infamies. Whether it's the destruction of Sumerian tablets or the work of that French librarian who burned Hebrew books in 2002 is unimportant: the problem is that those who destroy books make manifest an attitude found in all cultures. All human beings divide the world into us and them. That "us," of course, is exclusive. Applying this criterion of negating the other, censorship has always been imposed along with the denial of the right to information.

Much book damage results from heterogeneous factors: natural disasters (fires, hurricanes, floods, earthquakes, tsunamis, cyclones, monsoons, etc.), accidents (fires, shipwrecks, etc.), animal life (bookworms, moths, rats, insects), cultural changes (the dying out of a language, shifts in literary fashion), and because of the very materials with which books are made (for example, the acid in paper is destroying millions of books). We should consider as well how many books have been destroyed because they weren't published, how many books in private editions were lost forever, how many books were left behind on the beach, in the subway, on a park bench. It's hard to respond to these disquieting thoughts, but the truth is that at this very moment, while you read these lines, at least one book disappears forever.

Part One

The Ancient World

Chapter 1

The Near East

In Sumer, once Mesopotamia and now southern Iraq, between the Tigris and Euphrates rivers, humanity's first books appeared. Oddly enough, no sooner had they come into being than they began to disappear. The clay they were made of was fragile: floods melted them and men smashed them.

No one knows how many books were destroyed in Sumer, but 100,000 is a plausible figure, given the number of military conflicts that ravaged the region. Archaeology reveals the existence of these ancient books. Excavations of the fourth level of the temple of the fearsome goddess Eanna, in the city of Uruk, uncovered tablets, some intact, others in fragments, pulverized or burned, that can be dated between 4100 and 3300 BCE. This discovery contains a great paradox of the Western world: the discovery of the earliest books also establishes the date of their earliest destruction.

This was neither accident nor nature at work. It was a premeditated act. Wars between city-states were always accompanied by fires, and in the literal heat of battle, the tablets fell off their wooden shelves, were smashed or damaged. The *Hymn to Ishbi-Erra* defines the objective of an attack: "By order of Enlil to reduce the country and the city to ruins . . . he had fixed as their destiny the annihilation of their culture." The tablets spared might also succumb to recycling: damaged tablets were used to make bricks or pave streets. But water was nature's principal means of destroying the first books. When the Tigris and Euphrates flooded, they eradicated entire towns and, of course, their archives and libraries. It is no coincidence that it was in Mesopotamia, where water was considered a capricious divinity, the enemy of the gods of memory, that the first myths of the universal flood appeared.

These factors accelerated the development of a durable means to preserve memory. The Sumerians, or Black Heads, believed in the supernatural origin of books and attributed their invention to Nidaba, the goddess of grain. We see how important writing was for them in the legend of Enmekar (ca. 2750 BCE), king of the city of Uruk, a respected and feared hero who was sentenced to drink putrid water in hell for not having had his deeds written down. Another myth speaks of a king of Uruk who invented writing because his principal messenger made such a long journey that he was too tired to recite his message when he arrived.

The scribes, a caste of hardworking palace functionaries, prayed to Nidaba before and after writing. They transmitted the secrets of the signs through a secondary religion, practiced magic, and endured a long apprenticeship. They knew by heart the flora, fauna, and geography of their time, along with mathematics and astronomy. No knowledge was alien to them, as the translation of the Nippur texts demonstrates. The first rank was *dub-sar* (scribe), and after various years of work, they rose to *ses-gal* (great brother). The highest rank was *um-mi-a* (master), a huge distinction. The scribe who reached that rank was above all laws.

Around 2800 BCE, the monarchs, not without apprehension, delegated absolute authority over the care of books to the scribes. In that way, the preservation of culture was protected from political shifts, and the archives became both a refuge and a guarantee of the nation's ontological continuity. When the Akkadians conquered the Sumerians, they reformed codes and customs and forced the scribes to teach them to write. The Assyrians, the Amorites, and the Persians did the same, with the result that the same written signs were used for the exposition of the most diverse languages.

The ziggurats of Sumer were built with the same clay used to make the first books: therefore, both combined the useful and the magical. The temples were storehouses and encouraged the careful administration of the city: the books were a metaphor for the temple. The clay used to make tablets was heated until it reached the ideal state for writing. Some tablets were so large that two scribes could work side by side on them. One held the tablet while the other wrote. The scribes wrote in cuneiform script, that is, using incisions made with a bone or a reed. At first this writing had strictly mnemotechnic functions and was pictographic, but it became overly complex. When the signs acquired phonetic attributes, they were reduced from two thousand to less than half that number. The text began in the upper right corner and was was usually written vertically.

Around 3300 BCE, when the Uruk III period began, the tablets became more elaborate. It was then that the first libraries were invented, their shelves holding economic registers and catalogs of flora, fauna, and minerals. In Ur and Adab, the remains of tablets from two libraries, active around 2800–2700 BCE, have been found. Between 2600 and 2500 BCE, several libraries existed in Fara, Abu Salabik, and Kis, all with the usual registers and lists but also with tablets containing poetry, magic spells, and proverbs. A tablet closely resembling a contemporary book derives from this era: scribes designed tablets with the names of the writer and the supervisor inscribed on the upper part.

The library of Lagas, fifty or a hundred years later, contained historical inscriptions, the so-called Vulture Stela, and historiographic documents. Around 2200 BCE, Prince

Gudea created a library containing historical texts and poems by Enkheduanna, the first woman writer known, daughter of the famous Sargon of Akkad. These poems were hymns to Inanna. There were also cylinders incised with texts, one of which was two "volumes"—the first cylinder indicated that it was the first half, while the second provided the end of the composition.

Around 2000–1000 BCE, there were libraries in Isin, Ur, and Nippur. In ancient Ur (modern-day Tell al-Muqayyar), tablets containing family archives from 1267 BCE were discovered in the ruins of houses. There were also archives and libraries from the Elamite period, particularly in Kabnak (Haft Tepe), as well as archives in a palace in Anshan (Tall-e-Malyan). Most of the tablets, which in the case of the Nippur discoveries number more than 30,000, repeated the traditional economic models. They also include the first texts in Akkadian and the first catalogs of the library itself, lists of titles and first lines. New genres also appear during this period: hymns dedicated to kings, lists of members of royal families, and letters. Even calligraphy underwent a transformation. Libraries were now called *é-dub-ba*, the house of the tablets. In the Nippur area to the south of Babylon (Niffer), thousands of tablets were discovered, either in pieces or completely destroyed.

There are many other libraries in that zone that are still buried, though, ironically, they were looted after the invasion of Iraq in 2003. The dominating factor is the same in all cases: the world's first libraries are in ruins, and more than half their books destroyed.

Buried in Syria

In 1964, Sabatino Moscati, an archaeologist at the University of Rome, began the excavation of an artificial hill in Tell Mardik, Syria, thirty-four miles south of Aleppo.

At first he found only a door, the remains of a city wall, some temples and houses, but in 1968 the torso of a king's statue appeared. Explicitly inscribed on it was "sovereign of Ebla," which identified the site as the ancient city of Ebla, perhaps the most important paleosemitic region of Syria. In 1975, archaeologists found thousands of tablets and a room used as a library.

The organization of the Ebla library suggests that its administrators used sophisticated classification techniques. One room contained 15,000 tablets, either whole or in pieces. Lexicographic tablets were on the north wall; commercial tablets were on the east wall. Wooden shelves held the tablets and were themselves supported by vertical beams: bookcases. The tablets were incised in a room next to the library.

The tablets, sometimes a foot long, have writing on two sides divided into vertical columns accompanied by register lines. They have a colophon at the end and a summary of the work's content. There are administrative texts of a surprising precision, as well as historical texts with treatises, lists of conquered cities, official communications, royal proclamations, and different legal statements. The first bilingual dictionaries also appear there, long lists with words in Sumerian and their meaning in Eblaite, which shows that by 2500 BCE philological research was being carried out in Ebla.

This library was abandoned when the Ebla palace was attacked and burned. The fire was devastating, and the looters removed the gold and precious objects, leaving only the broken tablets. This deed has been ascribed to the Akkadian king Naramsin (2254–2218 BCE).

The Libraries of Babylonia

About 4,000 years ago, the collapse of the Ur III dynasty signaled the establishment of a new political force on the plains south of what is today modern Baghdad. Between the years 1792 and 1750 BCE, Babylonia assumed dominance, and its king, Hammurabi, the sixth member of his family to rule, set about organizing his empire. He used each new conquest as an opportunity to loot archives and bring them to the great library in his palace. The language he adopted was a dialect of ancient Akkadian written in cuneiform.

To promote unity, Hammurabi composed a fearsome legal code. It is there we find one of the first references to the destruction of tablets: "If a man buys a field, garden, or house from a soldier, fisherman, or leaseholder, his tablet will be smashed, and he will lose his property." Quite a few tablets contained warnings to prevent their damage by imprudent users: "He who fears Anu and Antu will care for it and respect it." Hammurabi's legal code was stored along with thousands of literary, mathematical, astronomical, and historical texts in the king's library. The first interlinear translations date from this period, along with the first manuals for learning the Sumerian language.

In the year 689 BCE, Sennacherib's troops razed Babylon. His grandson, Asurbanipal, founded one of the most famous libraries of the period in Nineveh, itself devastated in 612 BCE. In each of these events, thousands of tablets disappeared, were stolen, confiscated, or simply reduced to rubble. Like our own, those were not good times for culture.

Asurbanipal's Grand Library

Asurbanipal, sovereign of Assyria from 668 to 627 BCE, was the first king to learn to write on tablets. To save his name from oblivion, he sponsored various cultural and religious projects, among them the library in his palace in the city of Nineveh (modern-day Kuyunjik). Starting in 1842, British archaeologists excavated the ruins of the library. They removed more than 20,000 whole tablets and many additional thousands of fragments, which they deposited in the British Museum. Some years later, the organization of the library became known, confirming the fact that Asurbanipal was the first great book collector in the ancient world. Before him, the only king known to have had the same interest was Tiglah Pileser I, king of Assyria between 1150 and 1077 BCE, though his holdings were smaller. About his passion, Asurbanipal boasted he owned "the best of scribal art, which none of my anteced-ants achieved."

The scribes must have worked night and day copying texts from all known cultures. For this reason, on some of his tablets we find the Code of Hammurabi, the *Enuma Elish* (a poem on the god Marduk), and *Gilgamesh*. His library also contained chronicles of voyages to hell and formulas for immortality. Today, the number of tablets discovered in that zone has reached 30,000, at least 5,000 of which are literary texts with colophons. Those figures tell us that the destruction of tablets had to be a common event, which explains why we have inscriptions like this one: "Anyone who breaks this tablet or puts it in water . . . Asur, Sin, Shamash, Adade Ishtar, Bel, Nergal, Ishtar of Nineveh, Ishtar of Arbela, Ishtar of Bit Kidmurri, the gods of heaven and earth and the gods of Assyria, can all curse him."

Before World War II, British archaeologists found the remains of Asurbanipal II's palace. Excavating a well, they found sixteen wooden tablets, approximately eighteen by eleven inches. Once the tablets were deciphered, it was possible to read the malignant oracle of *Enuma Anu Enlil*. What surprised the experts was that the Assyrians had books with left and right pages held together by metal hinges. Aside from Asurbanipal's celebrated library, there were two others in Nineveh, one of which was in King

Sennacherib's palace, and the other, probably, was in the temple of the god Nabu, the Assyrian god of writing and knowledge.

Unfortunately, around 612 BCE Babylonians and Medes destroyed Nineveh and its libraries, whose remains Sir James George Frazer eloquently described. During the years between 1500 and 300 BCE, in at least 51 Near Eastern cities, more than 233 libraries existed. Of those, twenty-five date from the period between 1500 and 100 BCE and thirty from the period 1000 to 300 BCE. All are in ruins.

The Books of the Mysterious Hittites

The Hittites, of the kingdom of Hatti, worshipped a god of fertility, Telepinus, who without warning would disappear from time to time. The followers of the god had to search for him to keep the world from perishing. Like their god, the Hittites themselves disappeared, and we know little of them.

The capital of the Hittite empire was Hattusa, today Bogazkoy, to the east of Ankara, Turkey. Between 1800 and 1200 BCE, for 600 years, this was one of the most important civilizations of Asia Minor. It possessed the most highly prized industrial secret of the ancient world: the manufacture of iron. In Hattusa, the Hittites created a library in the fortress, using the cuneiform script but writing in the Hittite language. Three tablets, one of which is lost, contained more than 200 laws. Two expeditions, between 1906 and 1912, found more than 10,000 tablets in at least eight different languages, legal documents, multilingual reproductions of the *Epic of Gilgamesh*, and prayers to combat witchcraft and sexual impotence.

The Burning of Persepolis

Darius the Great was one of the visionaries of the Persian world who compensated for a lack of military prowess by being organized. His most extraordinary project was Persepolis, about twenty-five miles south of Pasargadas, a residence begun in 518 BCE and enlarged by his successors Xerxes I and Artaxerxes I. Darius placed thousands of tablets in Persepolis, though some claim that the entire structure was created to contain one sacred book, the Avesta. King Vishtaspa supposedly ordered the creation of two copies of the text, intended as the only true sources: one he placed in Sasbigan and the other in the House of Archives, or *Diz i nibist*, in Persepolis.

In 331 BCE, Alexander the Great marched toward Babylon with 40,000 foot soldiers and 7,000 cavalry. He crossed the Tigris and the Euphrates and attacked Darius III's army of (according to some historians) a million men. Alexander triumphed in the battle of Gaugamela in 331 BCE. Darius fled and was later murdered by his own cohorts. Babylon surrendered after Gaugamela, as did Susa.

Legend has it that Thais, a beautiful Athenian hetaira, or courtesan, challenged Alexander to burn the palace at Persepolis to avenge insults to the Greeks. Alexander, drunk, set fire to the palace, which, since its beams were cedar, burned to the ground. The treasure of Persepolis was carried off on 20,000 mules and 5,000 camels. In the introduction to the *Arda viraf nahmhi*, or True Book of the Law, it states that "in order to make men lose faith and respect for law, the cursed [demon] Ahriman, the damned, inspired the damned Iskander the Greek [Alexander] to come to Iran to bring to it oppression, war, and devastation. He pillaged and ruined the Door of Kings, the capital. The Law, written in golden letters on ox hides, was kept in the fortress of texts in the capital. But the cruel Ahriman provoked the criminal

Iskander, and he burned the books of the Law and killed the prudent men, the legislators, and the wise."

Among the books burned was the Avesta, the holy book of Zoroastrianism. This loss meant that the Zoroastrians had to reconstruct the work from memory. By order of the Sassanid prince Ardasir I, during the third century BCE, it was called the Zendavesta. There were those who said the original book contained sentences that could confer immortality on believers.

The ruins of Persepolis were abandoned until several expeditions from the Oriental Institute of Chicago unlocked their mysteries. Between 1931 and 1934, 30,000 tablets in Elamite, the official language of the Persian Empire, were found. They had suffered serious damage in the fire, and many were merely mounds of clay. Most were registers of commercial transactions. A second group of 753 tablets was found in Xerxes' treasure room, those too accompanied by thousands of fragments.

Chapter 2

Egypt

Papyrus, the medium on which the first Egyptian documents and books were written, had been in use since 3000 BCE Because of its ephemeral nature, most of the texts have not survived and those that have, did so only in regions where the climate favored preservation. The very word "papyrus" is, according to one tradition, related to the Egyptian word *pa-pa-ra* (belonging to the king). The paper reed, *Cyperus papyrus*, is a plant of the Cyperaceae family. To make paper, the internal filaments are removed and, after a long drying process, turned into sheets. The technique is complicated: once forgotten, it was not again understood until the twentieth century.

The first papyrus with writing on it dates from 2500 BCE, during the Fifth Dynasty, and contains the accounts of the El-Gebelein temple during the reign of Neferirkare Kakai. Time and climate did not help many texts: the Westcar papyrus, for example, contains the stories of Khufu and the Magicians but has suffered serious damage. Only the final words of the first story remain and there is a huge lacuna in the second; the three final stories are in good condition, except for the end of the fifth, which is lost—the story of Dyedi the magician, possibly the first reference to a magician in literature. Other papyri have come down to us in bad condition. Those of Abusir, for example, an important group of administrative documents for the Old Kingdom, are completely ruined. Another alarming case is that of the 160 papyrus fragments known as the Canon of Turin, eleven sheets written during the era of Ramses II (1290–1224 BCE). Even though they are damaged and incomplete, these remains are the finest registry of Egyptian kings and pharoahs. The canon is exceedingly important because it also includes the exact number of years, months, and days of various reigns. When the canon was found, it was intact, but it was sent to Turin in a careless fashion and arrived in pieces. More than eighty percent of Egyptian literature and science has been lost.

The Ramesseum

The Greeks called Ramses II (ca. 1304–1237 BCE) Ozymandias and mythologized him; some have identified him as the pharaoh in the story of Moses and the exodus from Egypt. The Egyptians worshipped Ramses under the name User-maat-Re, thinking him the son of Amon, god of the occult. In fact, he was the bastard son of Seti I and Queen Tuya. But he became a larger-than-life monarch, lover of more than 200 women, father of one hundred sons and sixty daughters, and conqueror of the Hittites—a feat commemorated on hundreds of stelae. He governed for sixty-six years, but more importantly for this history, he was the founder of one of the first libraries composed entirely of papyri.

At the outset of the second year of his reign, Ramses II ordered the construction of a temple to house his remains. That temple, the Ramesseum, contained a library with dozens of papyrus rolls. Diodorus Siculus, in his *Bibliotheca historica*, mentions the description of it by Hecataeus of Abdera, emphasizing "the sacred library above whose entrance is written: 'Healing Place of the Soul.'" A beautiful term to describe a library, but the Egyptians used it for medical and not aesthetic reasons. Most of the papyri dealt with pharmacological subjects.

Inspired by Diodorus Siculus, several generations of archaeologists have tried, starting in the nineteenth century, to find Ramses' library. All have failed. J. F. Champollion, the man who deciphered hieroglyphic writing, thought he'd find it near the figures of Thoth and his sister Seshat, divinities connected with knowledge, but the absence of any other signs led him to conclude that the room had been demolished. Despite the conjectures of some scholars, I would suggest, after examining the plans of Quibell and Christian Leblanc (the current director of the French archaeological mission of the Centre National de la Recherche Scientifique [CNRS]) that the library was always in the last section of the temple, and that the inscription "Healing Place for the Soul" describes the room where doctors kept the *ka*, or soul, from leaving the body. The papyrus Anastasi I refers to the library, saying "the house of the books is hidden, not visible." The works in the temple of Ramses II, if we accept the papyrus just cited, were feared and venerated esoteric writings.

Unfortunately, after looting by Ethiopians, Assyrians, and Persians, the books disappeared. In the first century CE, the temple was taken over by Christians and made into a church. By then, the library no longer existed.

The Burning of Secret Papyri

The god Ra had a secret name. Isis caused him to be bitten by a scorpion, and if he refused to pronounce his true name, Ra would suffer terrible agonies. If he did say it, Isis would dominate his life. (Ra capitulated, and Isis reversed the effects of the scorpion's poison.) Knowing another's true name conferred power over that person. In some way, the papyri also possessed that power and could only be read by a group of priests whose fear of divine punishment was greater than their lust for power. The well-documented conspiracy against Ramses III was an apparent instance of deviation form this rule. After being murdered, the king sent a message from the afterworld, ordering an investigation to reveal the names of the conspirators. One of the rebels confessed to having achieved his goal by possessing a magic papyrus scroll, the recitation of which turned him into a god as powerful as the pharaoh.

The monotheist Akhenaton was one of the first to burn books. He had the secret texts destroyed in order to make his religion preeminent. As the historian A. Weigall observed: "Akhnaton threw all those formulas into the fire. Spirits, ghosts, monsters, demiurges, and even Osiris himself with his cohort, were consumed by the fire." To get their revenge, his successors erased even his face from the stones and restored from memory the content of many ancient papyri.

The Houses of Life

The library of the temple known as the House of Life was used to protect, copy, and interpret divine texts. One of the architects of the Temple of Luxor consulted the sacred texts there to ascertain the will of the gods. There was nothing exceptional in that: Ramses IV consulted the papyri before beginning the construction of his tomb, and, it seems, ordered one of the scribes of the House of Life to go on a mission to the Wadi Hammamat mines. The site remained active, because the Canopic Decree prepared during the reign of Ptolemy III put these daring words into the mouth of the priest: "I shall enter the House of Life to unroll the emanations of Ra and be guided by them."

It is possible that along with the Ramesseum, one of the antecedents for the Library of Alexandria was the House of Life, located in the temple dedicated to Horus at Edfu. The site was constructed by the pharaohs and reconstructed by Ptolemy Euergetes. The work of the librarian priests was not limited to medicine; they could supply practical or magical advice. According to the Vienna Papyrus 154, the people called the principal priest of Ptah in Memphis "Prophet of the Sacred Library, Scribe of the Sacred Library . . . who appreciates the content of the Sacred Library, he who restores what has fallen through the emanations of Ra."

One of the walls of the library at Edfu contains, along with the image of Seshat, the goddess of writing, thirty-seven fascinating titles, among them *The Book of the King's Magic Protection in His Palace*, *The Book of the Knowledge of Secrets*, and *The Book of the Knowledge of Secrets of the Forms of the God*. The Salt Papyrus 825 from the fourth century BCE speaks of the books as if they were emanations of Ra and considers these sacred texts the summa of all ancient wisdom. There were texts to which the public had access and others of a prohibited nature. The Bremner-Rhind Papyrus of the Ptolemaic period alludes to a secret book in the House of Life, never seen by anyone. We have no idea of the nature of the book because it was destroyed along with the other treasures of the library when Christians attacked Egypt's ancient monuments.

The Forbidden Writings of Thoth

Thoth was the inventor of writing, but he was also the secretary of the most obscure greater and lesser divinities. He established the first calendar and played the lyre. He accepted offerings of figs and honey, and his adepts identified one another by using the expression "Sweet is the truth" in their greetings. Naturally, at some moment people began to believe that Thoth was the author of a volume in which all things were explained. His book was a compendium of medicine, philosophy, and magic. It is thought that the papyrus used by the assassins of Ramses II was *The Book of Thoth*: the copy, it seems, was destroyed. Other copies caused disasters in several places in Egypt; they too have been destroyed. In Alexandria, Thoth became Hermes Trismegistus, inspiring more copies and, of course, more burnings.

Chapter 3

Greece

Our image of ancient Greek art is always linked to a sculptural fragment or a ruined temple. The same is true of Greek literature. Even the most optimistic estimates calculate that 75 percent of ancient Greek literature, philosophy, and science has been lost. K. J. Dover, by no means a nostalgic historian, notes: "Everything written by the Greeks has only been preserved to the slightest degree. We have the names of a hundred or so Greek historians, but we possess the works of only three from the classical period and a few more from later periods. In Athens, more than two thousand theatrical works were put on between 500 and 200 BCE, but we can barely read or put on forty-six."

The most ancient known fragment of a Greek work is the Derveni Papyrus, dated to the outset of the fourth century BCE. Partially burned, it is the remains of an extensive allegorical and philosophical interpretation of a poem attributed to Orpheus. The ramifications are horrifying: if the first Greek books, written on papyri imported from Egypt, were composed in the ninth century BCE, and we only have a fragmentary papyrus from the fourth century BCE, we have lost some 500 years of Greek culture.

It's equally important to understand we have also suffered enormous losses of works from the Hellenistic period (third to first century CE). *Die Fragmente der griechischen Historiker* (Fragments of the Greek Historians) by Felix

Jacoby illustrates this ideal: it contains fragments of more than 800 historians from the Hellenistic period whose writings have perished.

A "book" was a sheet of papyrus made into a roll. Its length varied, and when a work took up the equivalent of two volumes or tomes, it was said it had two rolls. The word used for books was *biblos*, in honor of the Phoenician city of Byblos. Reading was called *anagnosis*, which included the idea of "public reading." The reader unrolled the papyrus with his left hand while holding the roll in his right hand. The verb for the act of unrolling was *anelittoo*.

Before writing on papyrus and adopting the Phoenician alphabet, the Greeks of Crete, like the Sumerians, wrote on clay tablets. Their writing, called Linear B by its English rediscoverers in 1900, was syllabic. What was found was the king's archive, consisting of inventories and lists of foods and animals, but no literary texts.

In the fourth century BCE, the alphabet was transformed under the innovative pressure of Greek hexameter poetry and regular fluid vowels. Papyrus was accepted as the preferred medium for preserving memory. Reading and writing were common activities in cities. Of course, there were other materials for publishing texts—limited media, such as skins, wooden tablets, or stones. On Mount Helicon, Pausanias read a version of Hesiod's *Works and Days* that was inscribed on a sheet of lead. Of that, almost nothing remains.

In the organization of the Greek world, writing down laws was a decisive step. Aeschines praised the existence of public archives because they made it possible to detect lies. In fact, contracts or agreements between citizens were written down to keep the signers from changing their minds. There is a tablet from 500 BCE that contains an agreement between Elis and Heraia, where writing itself is taken into account and a warning made to the effect that anyone who tampers with the text will be subject to a fine.

The fifth century BCE was decisive in Greece: a revolution began when written culture dominated spoken culture. However, people generally read aloud, a residue from oral times, though there is proof of silent reading during the same period. Socrates mocked his judges by telling them that in the public marketplace the books of the atheist Anaxagoras could be purchased for a drachma. That bookselling went on in the market is a fact, as the writer of comedies Eupolis of Athens (ca. 445–411 BCE) notes: "I wandered around the market, garlic onions, incense and aromas, and the place where books are sold."

The erudite Julius Pollux called those bookstalls *bibliotheke*. Unlike the Egyptian scribes, Greek copyists, almost always slaves, had no prerogatives, but they were indispensable workers. Their writing method, unfaithful at times to the original manuscript, consisted in writing with a calamus, a reed sharpened at one end, using ink obtained by mixing gum with soot. At first, texts were written in columns without divisions, punctuation, or lowercase letters. A column of text in prose could measure three inches and, in the case of poetry, the meter used determined the width of the text. A lucky copyist would receive between one and four drachmas for ordinary works; exceptional texts could lift the copyist out of poverty. A book was considered published if it was read in public by a servant, called the reader, or by the author himself. Once the reading was over, the audience could ask questions.

The first illustrated Greek book that we know of was by Anaxagoras. There were also editions of great beauty. The *Vita Marciana*, unlike the three extant catalogs of Aristotle's works, included a luxurious edition of an *Iliad* made for Alexander the Great, possibly the copy he carried with him in his travels, in a coffer filled with jewelry stolen from Darius. Plutarch states that Aristotle was the author of that edition, which was either lost or buried with its owner—much the same thing, since Alexander's tomb has never been found.

"Lost" and "destroyed" often amount to the same thing in the history of books: sometimes works are lost because they have been destroyed and sometimes they are destroyed simply because they have disappeared. In any case, the texts no longer exist, and except for the miracle of a discovery in a tomb or a warehouse, there is little possibility that the hundreds of thousands of works lost in antiquity will ever be recovered.

Consider that 120 works are attributed to Sophocles, yet we only have seven complete titles and hundreds of fragments. Sappho left nine volumes, but all we have are two almost complete odes and fragments of others. The five books of Corinna of Tanagra, the second woman poet of record in Greek literature, are today reduced to a group of incoherent pieces. Of Euripides' eighty-two tragedies, we only possess eighteen, along with one satyr play and many quotations.

This horror only grows. The pre-Socratics and Sophists exist only in fragments. It always comes as a shock that we haven't preserved *On Not Being* or *On Nature* by Gorgias of Leontini, who proves that nothing exists. The loss of texts extends to all periods of Greek literature, science, and philosophy. Agathon of Athens, a tragic poet quoted by Plato and admired by Socrates, apparently wrote works of an almost irresistible perfection, but today we have nothing but weak fragments. The *Parthenion*, a collection of poems in six books written by Alcman of Sardis, has been lost. A delightful text by him (number 40 in Denys Page's anthology) and often quoted is "I know the song of every bird." Take the case of Aristophanes of Athens: of his forty comedies only eleven survive, along with a thousand fragments preserved thanks to the discovery of papyri and the quotations of lexicographers. The 101 comedies of Diphilus of Sinope, the 100 comedies of Eupolis of Athens, and the 250 comedies of Alexis of Turi have all been lost.

All the writings of the Cynics, the Pyrrhonists, the Skeptics, and the Stoics have been reduced to a miscellany of quotations. Zeno of Citium had a similar fate, and he wrote a *Republic* more widely read than Plato's. Only pieces remain of the 500 books of Crisipus of Solos. This list, as the reader may imagine, could go on and on: I myself have compiled three volumes of 2,000 pages each.

Chapter 4

The Library of Alexandria

Around 285 BCE in Lower Egypt, a Greek, Demetrius Phalereus, died after being bitten by an asp. None of the doctors consulted by local authorities could ascertain whether Demetrius's death was a suicide (the bite was on his wrist), accident, or murder. The death was hushed up, though at least two of the three possibilities were imaginable because the deceased had fallen into disfavor with the new king, Ptolemy II Philadelphus, and had been banished from Alexandria.

The cadaver, that of a man sixty or seventy years old, seemed older than Demetrius was supposed to be. He was buried without honors in the Busiris district, near Diospolis. The death was the talk of the town for weeks. Some writers and philosophers grieved because Demetrius was an exceptional character. He wrote scores of books and was considered a student of great thinkers and an influential political leader. But his most important contribution was to the founding of the most famous library of antiquity, the Library of Alexandria. After his death, the fate of the intellectual center was subject to the whims of royal policy and wars of conquest. For this reason, we must begin this chapter with a synopsis of Demetrius's life and the history of the library.

About Demetrius Phalereus we know little. He was born in 350 or 360 BCE in the port city of Phalerum, the son of Phanostraus, a slave of Conon, a general. He moved to Athens, studied first in the Lyceum with Aristotle of Stageira, and continued his education with Theophrastus. Because he made excellent speeches and had the support of the Peripatetic philosophers, Cassander named him despot of the city in 317 BCE, a post he held for ten years.

During his time in office, he carried out a census, promulgated laws, and established well-received fiscal and constitutional reforms. He was popular, a friend of philosophers, poets, and dramatists. He was so famous that 300 statues were erected in his honor. In 307 BCE, his government was dissolved when another Demetrius, nicknamed Poliorcetes ("Besieger of Cities") conquered Athens. The commemorative statues were destroyed and turned into urinals, and Demetrius's name was erased from all registers.

He was granted a safe-conduct pass to Thebes, where he wrote and constantly reread Homer. When he finally understood that he could never return to Athens, he moved to Alexandria. The city, named in honor of Alexander the Great, was built in 331 BCE west of the Nile Delta, next to Lake Mareotis. It was designed by the architect Dinocares of Rhodes, who decided to give it the form of a Macedonian chlamys, the mantle worn by horsemen. There were five districts, named for the first five letters of the Greek alphabet. Some saw in the five letters an acronym in Greek: "Alexander the King Born of God Founded It."

Demetrius presented himself at the royal palace, the Brucheion. It was 306 BCE, and Ptolemy I Soter had just taken the throne in Egypt. Ptolemy I was born in 367 BCE, the son of Lagus and Arsinoë. One of Alexander's generals, he had participated in the march to India, and his loyalty won him Alexander's esteem. He acquired the title Soter, or "Savior," in Rhodes, whose populace he aided during the wars of 304. He lived to be eighty-seven.

As Plutarch recounts it, Demetrius advised the king to collect and read books about monarchy because his friends would never dare to say to his face the things he'd find in books. Demetrius himself wrote a book on the art of politics, the *Ptolemy*, which he dedicated, oddly enough, to Ptolemy. He also advised Ptolemy to build a structure dedicated to the muses, the *Mouseion*, or Museum. This building, part of the royal palace, contributed to the displacement of the Egyptian culture in favor of the Greek at the same time that it brought Ptolomy prestige.

In a short time, the Museum contained an incredible library, and it was Demetrius who brought this about. According to the "Letter from Aristeas to Philocrates," a register of the second century BCE, "Demetrius of Phalerum, being in charge of the king's library, received huge sums of money in order to acquire, if possible, all the books in the world." The desire to reach half a million books also brought about a change in copying techniques. The letter goes on to tell how Demetrius, when he learned of the Jewish Torah, or Five Books of Moses, tried to have them translated into Greek. Ptolemy I, who had excellent relations with the Jewish community that resided in a zone on the eastern side of Alexandria, contacted the high priest Eleazer, who lived in Jerusalem, and asked for a team of translators. Seventy-two Jewish scribes came to Alexandria and were housed on the island of Pharos. For seventy-two days they worked under Demetrius's direction until their task was completed. The entire Torah, from Genesis to Malachi, was translated and copied onto papyrus. Their labors finished, the translators, laden with gifts, returned to Jerusalem.

The only description we have of the Museum suggests that it was part of the royal palace complex, that it had a hall, an exedra with seats, and interior patios (the final patio contained the private cabinets and shelves). There were allegorical murals and symbols painted on its walls, and annexed to it were a zoo and a botanical garden. The value of the place did not keep the sharp tongue of Timon of Philius from terming it "the cage of the Muses."

According to Galen of Pergamum, the Ptolemys spared no expense in augmenting their book collection. They habitually borrowed originals for a sum in order to copy them; but like many inveterate borrowers, they didn't always return what they had borrowed. Ptolemy I asked the Athenians if he could rent the official papyrus copies of the works of Aeschylus, Sophocles, and Euripides. The originals would be returned after they had been transcribed, or so the Athenians thought. But only the copies returned to Athens. Some seventy-nine official works of Aeschylus, 120 by Sophocles, and ninety-nine by Euripides took their place on the library's shelves. By law, all those who visited Alexandria were supposed to yield any manuscripts they might possess.

The copying and classification of texts was the labor of entire generations educated according to the methodical axioms of the Peripatetic school. The librarians, secluded in their chambers, responded to the growing demands of readers interested in ever more refined and annotated editions. For each commentary, they placed symbols to alert readers to issues in the text—but they didn't always use the best judgment: the *atétesis* (to indicate a missing verse); the *atétesis diplé* (to indicate a marvelous verse worthy of consideration); the asterisk (to indicate a verse repeated improperly); the *estigmé* (or dot to indicate dubious verses); an obelos (or horizontal line for spurious verses); and the antisigma (a reversed sigma, the eighteenth letter of the Greek alphabet, to mark a change in the order of verses).

Only the monarch could name the director of the library, and the director had to be a priest. He had to be closely guarded because of the jealousy of the indigenous population, outraged at the mere presence of the library, alien institution that it was. The director lived in the king's palace and received all sorts of economic inducements to prevent him from being bribed or betraying his master. He paid no taxes but was obliged to tutor the royal prince. In ancient times, librarians were rarely required to be members of the *tiasos*, the priesthood. In that sense, the Museum maintained the Eastern tradition of placing books in temples and thus making a place of learning a temple.

The first director was not Demetrius Phalereus but Zenodotus of Ephesus (325–260 BCE). His most frequently mentioned accomplishment was the editing of classics by such writers as Homer and Hesiod. A severe critic, he marked the dubious verses and oriented the reader by explaining difficult passages. Some think it was Zenodotus who divided the Homeric poems into twenty-four books. One of his most important works was a *Life of Homer*, in which he discusses all the legends about the epic poet.

The poet Apollonius Rhodius (ca. 295 BCE) succeeded Zenodotus and, like any good disciple, attacked him violently in his *Against Zenodotus*, in which he listed the conceptual and grammatical errors of the Homer edition. For unexplained reasons, Apollonius was stripped of his title despite having been tutor to Ptolemy III Euergetes, who named Eratosthenes director.

Eratosthenes (276–195 BCE) modified the image of the librarians by combining critical activity with scientific investigation. He was born in Cyrene and became a disciple of Zeno of Citium (Cyprus) in Athens, where he also heard the lectures of Ariston of Chios and Arcesilas of Pitane. Eager to learn, he studied mathematics in the Academy, the school founded by Plato. As director, Eratosthenes combined literary and scientific study. He measured Earth's circumference as 252,000 stadia, or about 29,000 miles. Today's scientists compute the distance as approximately 24,900 miles. Knowing he was not a grammarian, he called himself a philologist—a lover of words, someone who studies ancient languages and manuscripts.

Callimachus of Cyrene (310–240 BCE), chief librarian according to some, to others merely a collaborator, feuded with Apollonius and ridiculed him in dozens of ingenious epigrams. He also attacked Plato, whom he thought a terrible literary critic and enemy of true poetry. The *Lexicon of Suda* ascribes 800 rolls of papyrus to Callimachus, of which we have only six hymns, sixty-three epigrams, some elegies, and hundreds of fragments.

Callimachus was certainly a competent writer, but as a librarian he made an outstanding contribution to the history of bibliographic studies. Over the course of many months he compiled a bibliography of the most important classics in the library. The title of this work, which took up 120 volumes, was *Lists of Persons Eminent in Every Branch of Learning Together with a Text of Writers.* He conceived of eight types of author: rhetoricians, legislators, miscellaneous writers, philosophers, historians, doctors, epic poets, tragic poets, and comic poets. According to Athenaeus, Callimachus was in the habit of concluding his articles with the number of lines in the complete works of the authors he studied. He also left another catalog, the *List of Dramatic Writers Arranged Chronologically from the Earliest Times.* Callimachus had followers, the most famous of whom were Hermippus of Smyrna, a historian and philosopher; Istrus of Cirene, a compiler of historical material; and Philostephanus, a geographer.

Aristophanes of Byzantium (257–180 BCE) became director in 195 BCE. He created the Analogical school, edited Homer, and won the right to decree the obligatory classics for all of Greece. His lexicons of archaisms and his revision of Callimachus's *Lists* earned him a devoted following. Aristarchus of Samothrace (220–143 BCE) followed Aristophanes. For him, grammatical studies were a matter of honor. In 800 books he commented on the principal poets and delineated important problems with regard to Homer. With the exception of the work of Apollonius of Rhodes and Callimachus, nothing of Aristarchus, or of the others mentioned here, has survived.

The assassination of Ptolemy VII Neos Philopator, around 144 BCE, brought about a crisis. Aristarchus and his followers instantly fled Alexandria. A military man—possibly named Cidas, though we know nothing about him—was named director of the library. Around the year 88, a certain Onesandrus, a relative of the monarch, was director. After him, the names of the librarians are unknown.

The brilliant work carried out in the library was overshadowed by a series of attacks. During the war for the throne of Egypt, Julius Caesar supported Cleopatra. The ensuing civil war engulfed Alexandria: on November 9, 48 BCE, Egyptian troops commanded by Aquilus besieged Caesar in the royal palace and tried to capture the Roman ships in the port. Caesar launched an incendiary attack on the Egyptian fleet, reducing it to ashes in a few hours. Cassius Dio infers that the fire reached some warehouses in the port, where 40,000 books were burned. Seneca confirms the loss, which Orosius reiterates four centuries later: "When the flames invaded part of the city, they consumed forty thousand books that happened to be stored there." Seneca regarded such destruction as important principally because he was disgusted by the fact that there were "too many books." This seeming lack of interest in the book stems from the fact that it was an emerging phenomenon in those cultures, and authors were concerned only with specific cases of book destruction (the geographer Strabo's account of the disappearance of numerous writings by Aristotle, the commentaries of Ateneas of Naucratis about some lost books, or the observations of Aulus Gellius).

Did those 40,000 books belong to the Library of Alexandria? Scholars still argue. I would suggest that those volumes were in the warehouse after having reached Alexandria on different ships. That is, they were new acquisitions for the Museum library that never reached their final destination.

The destruction carried out by the Christians is still a hotly debated topic. Some historians accuse the patriarch Theophilus of inciting a mob to attack the Serapeum in 389 and the library in 391. In *The Decline and Fall of the Roman Empire* (1776–1787), Edward Gibbon states: "Theophilus proceeded to demolish the Temple of Serapis, with no other difficulties than those he found in the weight and solidity of its materials. . . . The valuable Library of Alexandria was looted or destroyed; and almost twenty years later, the appearance of the empty shelves aroused the fury and indignation of every spectator whose mind was not absolutely darkened by religious prejudice." When Theophilus seized the temple, the Christians filled it with crosses and demolished the walls. Theophilus was a resentful, small-minded opportunist. After having been a fanatical reader of Origen of Alexandria (185–232 CE), he became an enemy of everything he thought derived from that author's work and condemned Origen's writings in the Council of Alexandria in the year 400 CE.

The Serapeum was destroyed by order of Theophilus, but there is no unanimity among historians about who destroyed the books in the Museum. Romans? Christians? Arabs? According to Eutychius, once the conquest of Egypt was concluded, General Amr ibn al-Ass sent a letter to Mohammed's second successor, Omar I (586–644), providing an inventory of Alexandria: 400 palaces, 4,000 public baths, 400 theaters, 40,000 Jews, and 12,000 shops. The letter concluded: "The Muslims seem to be impatiently awaiting the right to enjoy the fruits of their victory."

The letter makes no reference to the Museum, though it was most certainly one of the monuments of Alexandria. According to the chronicler Ibn al-Qifti, an admirer of Aristotle, the commentator John Philoponus asked the general to make a decision about the future of the books in the Museum library, whose activities were temporarily suspended. Amr did not dare answer and instead sent another letter to find out what the monarch thought about those books. He read Omar's decision to Philoponus, not without some grief: "With regard to the books you mention, here is my answer. If the books contain the same doctrine as the Koran, they are useless because they merely repeat; if they are not in agreement with the doctrine of the Koran, there is no reason to conserve them."

Amr regretted that decision, but, according to the medieval Arab chronicler Abd al-Latif, he was obedient and did not hesitate to carry out his orders: "The Library of Alexandria was burned and totally destroyed." According to the twelfth-century scholar Ibn al-Qifti, the papyri were used to light the fires of the public baths: the works of Hesiod, Plato, Gorgias, Archilochus, Mateon, Sappho, Alceus, Alcman, and thousands more were used as fuel for six long months.

All of this appears coherent, but some scholars think these "facts" are apocryphal.

- There is no eyewitness account. Abd al-Latif and Ibn al-Qifti lived at least six or seven centuries after the event.
- The Museum library contained books by Aristotle, who was, for Arabs, the most famous philosopher

in the world. After all, the only Aristotle Europe knew during the Middle Ages came primarily from Arabic translations. Why would the Arabs destroy his books?

- It is quite possible that before the sixth century, when the Arabs conquered Egypt, the Christians destroyed the books in the Museum that they thought were heretical. If the monks of Cirilus had no scruples about murdering Hypatia, the daughter of the librarian Theon, if they destroyed the Serapeum, they would obviously have had no difficulty demolishing the library. This would explain why it isn't mentioned in the inventory sent to Omar I.

- John Philoponus could not converse with the representatives of Omar I because he lived in the sixth and not the seventh century.

At this point, matters become even more complicated, because no one can explain why the sources are all Arabic and not Greek, Christian, or Roman. Abd al-Latif and Ibn al-Qifti, the two historians, were well versed in Aristotelian thought. Some specialists think these two historians accused Omar I in order to discredit that caliph's dynasty and present Saladin (1137–1193), the hero of the Crusades, to the Arab world as a savior, a sultan who would be the opposite of Omar I.

It is true that Abd al-Latif and Ibn al-Qifti knew and admired Saladin. There is some controversy around Ibn al-Qifti, who was educated in Cairo and died in 1248: as A. Dietrich has pointed out, his book, titled *Tarikh al-hukama* (Chronicle of Wise Men), exists only in an epitome, or summary, made by al-Zawzani in 1249. Just as twenty-six of Ibn al-Qifti's books on medicine and philosophy were lost, important aspects of his chronicle not included in the epitome have also disappeared.

In any case, the notion that the Arabs destroyed the Library of Alexandria reached the West and grew stronger during the seventeenth century. The English Orientalist Edward Pococke (1604–1691) spread the idea in his 1649 translation of Bar Hebraeus's *Specimen Historiae Arabum*. In 1656, he again bolstered the theory when his edition of Eutychius's *Annals* appeared in Arabic and Latin. His son Edward (1648–1727) completed the puzzle of the burning of the library when he published Abd al-Latif's description of Egypt.

Edward Gibbon cast doubt on the accounts of the two Arab historians because of the years separating them from the event and because in the Muslim world it's more usual to preserve books than to destroy them. The polemic has gone on since the eighteenth century. The thesis that the Arabs destroyed the library has lost support, and new hypotheses have emerged. Here are three.

- The Romans did it. During a rebellion in Alexandria in 215, according to Cassius Dio, Caracalla's Roman troops sacked the Museum. In 272, when Queen Zenobia of Palmyra attacked Alexandria, librarians were persecuted and books were destroyed. The historian Ammianus, in describing this era, refers to the "now lost place called Brucheion, sturdy residence for prestigious men." The Brucheion comprised the royal palaces and the Museum. After the Zenobia episode, around 297, the emperor Diocletian set about purging the library of books about magic and alchemy. Apparently, he thought the Alexandrians might learn to transform metals into gold in order to buy arms. According to the librarian Anastasius, Diocletian also persecuted hundreds of Christians and burned the Scriptures. He even burned books on sale in the market. An ancient inventory points out that the *Acta Martyrum* was expensive because so many copies had disappeared.

- An earthquake did it. There were at least twenty-three earthquakes in Alexandria between 320 and 1303. In the summer of 365, an especially powerful tremor brought down numerous buildings. The team led by Franck Goddio of the Institut Européen d'Archéologie Sous-Marine has found hundreds of objects and pieces of columns in the port, proving that part of Alexandria sank.
- It was negligence. The various political and military conflicts cut off financial support for the library. The librarians moved to more peaceful cities—Rome, for example—and copying activity eventually disappeared. This hypothesis is not without merit.

According to the *Letter of Aristeas*, there were 20,000 papyrus rolls in the Library of Alexandria, and the king's plan was to raise the number to 500,000. Aulus Gellius and Ammiannus Mercellinus both speak of 700,000 rolls. Georgius Syncellus spoke of 100,000 books. John Tzetzes, the Byzantine commentator, placed 42,800 manuscripts in the Serapeum and 490,000 in the Museum, of which 90,000 were unedited.

Chapter 5

Other Ancient Libraries and Aristotle's Lost Books

The story of the Pergamum library and its mysterious disappearance is as fascinating as that of its rival in Alexandria. According to Strabo's *Geography*, King Eumenes created it in the second century BCE to challenge the monarchs of Alexandria. Vitruvius, in a less polemic comment, states that the Attalid monarchs were stimulated by their great love of philology to found a magnificent public library.

Eumenes managed to collect between two and three hundred thousand volumes copied onto vellum, a more flexible and less perishable material than papyrus. According to Lido, vellum was invented when Ptolemy V refused to export papyrus in order to stop the work of the Pergamum librarians. Pliny confirms this, and writes that thereafter, "the use of that material became common, to the point that it came to be mankind's means to achieve immortality."

Apparently, the haste to accumulate one of the most valuable collections in the world inspired philological indiscretions. One of the most serious examples was the discovery of a heretofore unknown speech by Demosthenes. In fact, it was nothing more than a little-known text already edited in Alexandria. And from time to time, according to Laertius, the Pergamum librarians censored books and expurgated passages they thought improper.

When Crates of Mallos became head of the library, he imposed philosophic guidelines, predominantly those of the Stoics. Allegorical conjectures about Homer were encouraged and etymology was used to reinforce epistemological theses. An example of the kind of research carried out by Crates relates to Homer's description of the shield of Achilles. Several generations of critics considered it a later interpolation, but Crates justified the passage by proposing an interpretation that takes the ten parts of the shield as references to the ten celestial spheres. Thus Homer becomes the father of astronomy.

Toward the third century BCE, Antigonus of Carystus worked in the library and distinguished himself as a biographer and historian. Unlike many of his contemporaries, Antigonus traveled and sought out testimonies about architectural works, legends, and characters.

The library-building effort stopped because of war in Asia Minor. It is thought that after the destruction of Pergamum, Mark Antony sent the manuscripts (about 200,000) to his beloved Cleopatra, with the intention of donating them to the Serapeum in Alexandria (it was his way of seeking pardon for the fire of 47 CE). Unfortunately this information comes from Plutarch and his only source is an unknown writer named Calvisius.

The rivalry became meaningless. It no longer matters whether the books ended up on the shelves in Alexandria or were destroyed in Pergamum: They all disappeared and the library today is a pile of ruins.

What we have today of Aristotle are merely class notes gathered together and preserved by bibliophiles or disciples. His first dialogues, miscellaneous writings, letters, and poems have all disappeared.

To understand why this happened, we would have to begin by quoting the geographer Strabo of Amasia: "[Aristotle], to my knowledge, was the first book collector we know of, and it was he who taught the kings of Egypt how to arrange a library." Aristotle of Stageira was the most renowned bibliophile in the Greek world and one of the first to be called the Reader. When the philosopher Speusippus, the nephew of Plato and director of the Academy, died, Aristotle acquired his works for three gold talents (a very rough approximation in today's currency would be $2.5 million: a talent weighed about as much as a person). His memorable collection of books was finally housed in the library of the Lyceum, a gymnasium where he began training students around the year 335 BCE.

Aristotle subjected his students to a regimen to stimulate reading.

- There were *acroátic* or *acroamátic* (oral) lessons, which were only for initiates and which consisted of talks where profound notions were discussed during a stroll.
- Then there were *exoteric* or *exterior* lessons for apprentices, where the popular works of the thinker—his dialogues, for example—were read or recited. It's likely that each student took a particular role and that Aristotle himself moderated the conversation.

Aristotle's writings today are classified along the lines of his lessons: *exoteric*, for dialogues in the Platonic mode—though these are all lost; or *esoteric*, that is, texts meant for internal use at the Lyceum.

Aristotle's world changed abruptly because of the sudden, inexplicable death of Alexander the Great in 323 BCE. Aristotle, who had been Alexander's tutor, adviser to the Macedonian regime, and probably a spy, was accused of impiety by the priest responsible for sacrifices in Athens. In reply, Aristotle published a poem composed in honor of the tyrant Hermias, a great friend of his in the region of

Assos who was assassinated by the Persians. Aristotle could have stayed and drunk hemlock like Socrates, but he fled. He went to the city of Chalcis on the island of Euboea, where his mother's family had land and a house. There he wrote his will and died in 322 BCE, leaving his library and the directorship of the Lyceum to young Theophrastus of Eresus.

Under Theophrastus, the Lyceum grew until it had more than 2,000 students (not all at the same time) from all parts of Greece. Theophrastus remained director for about thirty-five years. Unlike Aristotle, he owned the property on which the school stood, thanks to the exertions of Demetrius Phalereus, who helped him circumvent the law that forbade outsiders from owning property in Athens. Laertius credits Theophrastus with hundred of texts on an enormous variety of subjects. At the age of eighty-five, Theophrastus willed the library to a friend, a certain Neleus.

When Theophrastus died, Straton of Lampsacus became director. This in itself is surprising. Why did Theophrastus bequeath the books only to Neleus, and why was Neleus not named director? Historians speculate that Theophrastus did so because he wanted Neleus to prepare a catalog and edit his own works as well as those of Aristotle. Neleus was an expert on Aristotle as well as a respectable disciple of Theophrastus. He was also seventy years old and had a substantial relationship with that bibliographic bequest.

Another possibility is that the texts were in imminent danger in Athens because of the city's increasingly unstable political situation. Also, the Athenians were well aware of the connections between the Lyceum and the Macedonians. In 306 BCE, a leader proposed prohibiting the teaching of philosophy in Athens; this was a move to close the Lyceum. It is therefore possible that Neleus had been instructed by his teacher and friend to take the books to a more secure place, to Alexandria or his hometown. Theophrastus left in Neleus's hands the alarming number of 382 works by himself and Aristotle on over 1,005 rolls of papyrus. If we add the hundreds of originals or copies of other authors in the Lyceum library, we are talking about a library of more than 10,000 papyri. Incredibly, Neleus managed to transport those manuscripts from Athens to distant lands—which he did, according to the most reliable commentators.

But who was Neleus? We know that he was respected in the Lyceum and that he was born in Scepsis, in Asia Minor, sometime in the fourth century BCE. He was probably a contemporary of Theophrastus. His father, Coriscus, was a friend of Aristotle, his companion in Assos, where they lived under the protection of Hermias. This fact in itself is quite important: Plato, for instance, mentions Coriscus in his *Sixth Letter*, where he describes him as a studious man stimulated by political experiences. Aristotle names him in his works on logic and in the *Nicomachean Ethics*. With such a figure in his background and with his own intellectual formation in his favor, Neleus was a likely successor to Theophrastus. But it was not to be. When Straton, nicknamed "The Physicist," was named director of the Lyceum, Neleus packed up his books and departed for Scepsis, leaving the Peripatetics without the works of the master.

In one account, Neleus sold the books for a high price to the Library of Alexandria. In another, the books reached Scepsis and fell into the hands of Neleus's heirs, who hid them so they wouldn't be stolen by the Attalid kings. A prickly business: Did Neleus sell the books to make a fortune or did he give them to his family, renowned for its ignorance?

I think Neleus sold a good number of the books from the Lyceum library. However, he kept the unedited manuscripts, specifically the acroamatic writings—Aristotelian teachings intended only for disciples of the master, as opposed to the exoteric doctrines, meant for the masses—which, because they were notes either by the master or his disciples, were not ready for wide dispersal. Neleus kept the secret part, and his descendants hid them to prevent theft.

Proof that some of the books inherited by Neleus reached Alexandria appears in a document by a great Persian philosopher at the end of the tenth century, al-Farabi, who expressly points out that once Alexandria had been conquered, Emperor Augustus "inspected the libraries and the dates when books were produced, and found among them manuscripts of works by Aristotle written during his lifetime and that of Theophrastus." None of those manuscripts could have been in Alexandria unless Neleus sold them.

Two hundred years later, what could be salvaged of Aristotle's library was acquired by Apelicon of Teos from Neleus's descendants. Athanaeus confirms that Apelicon "practiced the theses of the Peripatetics and bought Aristotle's library and many other texts—he was a wealthy man."

Apelicon sent the books to his house in Athens, where he had new copies made (ones filled with errors). In 87–86 BCE, Sulla besieged and captured Athens. He did not want to destroy it, so he sanctioned limited looting, which won him the nickname "the Fortunate." The soldiers sacked house after house; they found Apelicon hiding in his library and killed him. Sulla ordered his books shipped to Rome, where he exhibited them in his villa to arouse the envy of all who mattered.

Another Roman general, Lucullus, found manuscripts and copies of the writings of Aristotle in Amiso and brought them to his house in Rome. Among his prisoners of war was a highly educated Greek named Tyranion. Tyranion, a man of great amiability and knowledge, lived in Rome starting in 67 BCE, and though he was a slave, he cultivated a deep friendship with Cicero, Atticus, and other educated figures of the empire. He wrote books on Homeric problems and grammatical texts. If we believe Cicero himself, he was a consummate geographer. He also created a school feared for its rigor. Strabo had him as a teacher in Rome, in all likelihood around the year 30 BCE, and that connection leads us to conclude that Strabo's account of the books of Aristotle and Theophrastus's books derives from a conversation with or lecture by Tyranion, whose greatest ambition was to become the editor of the legendary books.

Sulla and Lucullus opened their libraries to friends. Cicero, for example, frequented Lucullus's collection to revise some of Aristotle's texts. Tyranion always considered the manuscripts in Sulla's villa more interesting and craftily plotted ways to read and edit them. Strabo defined him as "a lover of Aristotelian things" and said that "he put his hands in the Library to flatter."

It seems Apelicon produced a terrible edition and ruined scores of books. Tyranion too failed to make a good edition, initiating a tradition of permanent misunderstandings in Aristotelian studies. Tyranion tried to finish off this colossal intellectual adventure, but death frustrated his intentions.

Andronicus, educated on the island of Rhodes and the supposed eleventh director of the Lyceum, made the definitive edition of the works of Aristotle and Theophrastus. Around 40 or 20 BCE, spurred on by the work of Tyranion, he edited the books and in the fifth volume included a catalog of titles now lost.There is no way to know what works Andronicus rewrote, but he did change the history of Aristotle's writings by causing his popular books to pass into oblivion. He may have created the term "metaphysics" to refer to Aristotle's works related to the first philosophy.

Cicero did not know Andronicus's edition because he died in 43 CE, but he did recognize, quite early, the differences between the exoteric and the acroamatic works. In *De finibus*, he states that the moral writings were "written in a popular style," as if they were exoteric, while the others were "more carefully shaped" and difficult. One of his letters reveals his taste for going to the villa of Sulla's son Faustus to read Aristotle. Faustus inherited all his father's wealth, including the library captured at Athens. At least for a time, that library was the center of attention for Rome's intellectuals. His spendthrift ways ruined him, and in a short time he had to publish a list of his possessions in order to auction them off. After the sale, the library was scattered, and then lost forever.

And then we have Emperor Caracalla (188–217), who in a fit of madness ordered many of Aristotle's books burned because he determined Aristotle had poisoned Alexander the Great.

In the history of the loss of Aristotle's writings, there is one lost book that has sparked intense discussion. It concerns the disappearance or destruction of the second book of the *Poetics*, the study of ancient comedy and the concept of catharsis. Its very existence has been questioned, but there are sufficient proofs to the contrary. The three catalogs of Aristotle's works prepared in antiquity include it. Eustracius, in 1100, says in his *Commentaries on the Nicomachean Ethics* that Aristotle mentions Homer's *Margites* in the first book of the *Poetics*, which implies a continuation. This we also see in William of Moerbeke, who used an illustrative title in his Latin translation of the *Poetics: Primus Aristotelis de Arte Poetica Liber Explicit.* That "primus" has made dozens of philosophy professors tremble.

There are several theories about why the text disappeared. Here are a few of the more intriguing.

- Umberto Eco, in his novel *The Name of the Rose* (1980), proposed that a monk destroyed it to contain the influence of humor on moral philosophy.

- Ingram Bywater suggests that the second book was lost at a time when Aristotle's works were on separate rolls of papyrus. For that reason they were not transferred to codices.
- Valentín García Yerba, in his prologue to the Spanish translation of the *Poetics*, says the second book disappeared during a time when there was no interest in comedy. The proliferation of superficial epitomes, or summaries, caused a lack of copies of the original.
- The Hellenist Richard Janko has another idea: the *Poetics* was the last book in the edited works of Aristotle, and that, coupled with a lack of interest, may have stopped its reproduction. The result was the disappearance of the text, except for a Byzantine epitome, the *Tractatus Coislinianus*, which he says is a summary of the second book.

I agree with Janko. A lack of interest was the true cause of the disappearance of the fabled second book. It was then that the book acquired a secret life that began with epitomes used to summarize its content. One of them is the famous *Tractatus Coislinianus*. We must also recall Galen, who said that fires and earthquakes destroyed innumerable Greek texts.

The Ark and the Destruction of the Tables of the Law

The history of Israel is the history of a people's relationship with an ambiguous god. The intermediaries in this relationship were men of anger and zeal, which may explain why the first Hebrew leader was a book destroyer. Moses, after descending from the mountain in the Sinai Desert and carrying the text Yahweh inscribed with his own finger, found the people worshipping a golden calf: "Moses' anger waxed hot, and he cast the tables out of his hands and brake them beneath the mount" (Exodus 32:19).

Then he ordered the death of his brother, a friend and associate of the guilty. By the end of the bloody day, 3,000 people died as a sacrifice to God, who pardoned the people and invited Moses to cut two tablets of stone on which he would inscribe the Ten Commandments (Exodus, 34:1).

The story grows more complicated because God ordered the construction of an ark to store the tablets. The Ark of the Covenant, fashioned by Bezalel (whose name means "in the shadow of God"), was made of black acacia wood. For centuries, the ark was a sacred talisman against enemies. It was moved around until Jeremiah hid it in a secret cave (2 Maccabees, 2:5). Nothing more is known about the tablets.

Adoration of the Hebrew Book

The book dictated by Yahweh was a sacred book, a Book of Books whose meaning enclosed all the wisdom of the world. The curious aspect of this tradition is in its consequences: since the books of the Bible are sacred, each letter came to have a magic meaning (studied in the Kabbalah) but only in its original language and in no other.

Writing was holy, and therefore to be protected at all costs. The historian Flavius Josephus records that the Jews preferred to die rather than allow the profanation of their texts. One of the reasons for the insurrection of the Maccabees was the destruction of books by the troops of Antiochus IV: "And the books of the Law that they found they tore up and threw into the fire. Anyone found with a book of the alliance in his possession and who observed the Law was condemned to death by virtue of the king's decree."

The destruction of the Temple at Jerusalem in 70 CE eliminated hundreds of texts, though the Jews did manage to hide some. Flavius Josephus himself risked his life to save volumes from the Temple. One modern hypothesis suggests that official religious texts were in the Temple; the others were copies made by competent scribes.

The Bibliophage Prophets

There are rare but famous cases in both the Old and New Testament of bibliophagy, that is, book eating. Ezekiel says God offered him a roll of papyrus and then ordered him to eat it (Ezekiel 2:8, 3). In the apocalypse of John of Patmos (Revelation 10:8), this idea of consuming a book reappears. The sweet and bitter tastes mentioned in both places refer, no doubt, to the content, beautiful on the surface and bitter within. Swallowing the book guarantees the transferral of properties, the transmitting of knowledge. Instead of reading it, the bibliophage receives teachings directly and becomes able to speak different languages or express himself more securely.

Around 130 CE, Artemidorus wrote *The Interpretation of Dreams*, in which he mentioned dreams of book eating: "To dream about eating a book is a good thing for educated people, for sophists, and for all those who earn their living discoursing about books."

Many peoples resorted to cannibalism in order to obtain supernatural powers. If we assume a book has divine properties, if we believe it to be part of God, we should not be surprised at bibliophagy. Gérard Haddad asserts: "By eating the Book of his group of origin, a person experiences a profound metamorphosis. Through one's living identification with his group, with, which that implies, being inscribed in a genealogy, he receives his future aptitude for engendering, for becoming in his turn a man and father within that group."

Chapter 6

China

In 246 BCE, at the age of thirteen, Zhao Zheng became the leader of Qin, one of many feudal baronies that made up ancient China. His youth gave encouragement to his enemies, who seriously underestimated him. Endowed with a prominent nose, large eyes, rough voice, and warlike habits, Zheng could not govern until 238 BCE, but as soon as he became king, he murdered his mother's lover Lao Ai and forced his tutor, Lu Buwei, who may have been his biological father, to flee and later to commit suicide.

He immediately embarked on a campaign against the dominant baronies and subjugated them one by one, using new fighting techniques. He believed that the cause of the interminable wars then prevalent derived from the ambitions of the feudal lords. The lords tried to assassinate him, but as always happens in such cases, they merely strengthened his resolve. In 230 BCE, he overcame the last Han prince. By 215 BCE, he was master of a true empire and ordered an inscription placed in Taishan: "I have united the entire world for the first time."

The pacification process involved murder, bribery, and destruction of all who opposed him. He confiscated estates and made himself into a rich and powerful monarch. He was nervous, egocentric, and never benevolent. One day, he decided to adopt a universal title to broadcast his majesty, and after an arduous debate, he proclaimed himself Shi

Huangdi (First Emperor). Confident of his absolute power, he now called himself Qin Shi Huang: first emperor of the state of Qin. Heeding an omen, he decided it would be proper to base his dynasty on three principles: the number six, water, and the color black.

A man of mystery, Qin Shi Huang never let himself be seen in public, and it was impossible to know in which of his 260 palaces he was staying. He wanted not only to impress his enemies but also to deprive them of opportunities. He traveled without warning to remote places, like the island of Zhifu, where he tried to find the elixir of immortality, or to other locations where he would seduce virgins and then murder them. With all the passion of a despot, he worshipped the principle of order.

Advised by his faithful minister Li Si, he imposed a legal code and uniformity on his dominions. Everything in the nation was subjected to a single model of weights and measures. He even considered the width of roads, styles of dress, opinions, ways of fighting, and language. Martial arts were eliminated and weapons confiscated. The army was centralized and economic activity controlled to benefit agriculture. Forty-one districts were governed by closely monitored administrators. The historian Arthur Cotterell notes: "In his struggle to impose uniformity, he became one of the greatest destroyers in history."

In the shadow of the emperor's absolute power stood Li Si, born in 280 BCE, one of Xun Zi's most intelligent disciples and a supporter of the Legalist school. This group had as its supreme representative the implacable Han Fei, who postulated a government capable of moderating passions, a social order based on punishments and rewards, a legal system administered exclusively by the king, and a contractual relationship between people and governors. He also opened the possibility of legal reforms if new social needs should require them.

Li Si, whose contribution to the unification of Chinese writing was enormous—he reduced the number of characters from 5,000 to 2,000—is more remembered today because, in the face of criticism of the unification process, he proposed the destruction of all books that might be conceived as critical of the emperor. Sima Qian (ca. 145–85 BCE) the great chronicler of China, preserved the report made to the monarch, which begins: "Your servant requests that the imperial historiographer burn all books, though not those of the Ts'in [Qin] dynasty."

Disdain for tradition is thus nothing new. Li Si personally believed poetry, history, and philosophy to be a potential danger.

In 213 BCE, the year when a group of men tried to gather together all books in Alexandria, Qin Shi Huang approved the burning of all books except those that dealt with agriculture, medicine, or prophecy. He hid treatises on alchemy, meditation, and shamanism. He protected the ancient divination writings, which were preserved on bones and tortoiseshells. Chinese books at that time were made of strips of bamboo or other wood. The ideograms were written vertically on those strips and ordered from right to left. They were then bound up with cord and rolled into a fascicle.

Animated by his actions against the caste of the learned, the emperor created an imperial library dedicated to the vindication of the writings of the Legalists, defenders of his regime and of the thesis that law was the principle of the state. He then ordered all other books confiscated. Functionaries went from house to house seizing books, which they then burned in a bonfire, to the joyful surprise of those who hadn't read them. More than 400 stubborn men of letters were buried alive, while their families suffered countless humiliations.

Qin Shi Huang's hatred was directed at the old schools born when the feudal baronies were still at war. He was annoyed by the Yin-Yang Jia (school), which preached the pure cosmology of the yin-yang and the five elements; he disdained the Ming Jia, or School of Names, as well as the Mo Jia, or Moism, and the Ru Jia, or Confucianism. The emperor was disgusted by the writings of Confucius because they vindicated ancestor worship. He had them burned. Perhaps he feared not only the ideas of this sage but also his historical and political knowledge.

Confucius was born in Shandong Province in the state of Lu. An orphan from childhood, he administered a grain storehouse, was a shepherd, and guarded government structures. At the age of twenty-two, he was teaching literature, history, and music. He was the justice secretary for the state of Lu, but he resigned because of an intrigue that caused him to wander the interior of China. It was there he tried to impose government reforms. In the *Shu King* he gathered up the chronicles of the ancient scribes of the feudal baronies and gave form to the *Yu Qing*, to which he added geographic and administrative descriptions. He included the penal code in the *Lu Hing*, but that did not keep him from making note of astronomical phenomena and the royal hunting parties and making the most bizarre classifications of animals. Another of Confucius's works was the *Annals of Spring and Autumn*, which covered the years between 722 and 481 BCE. His doctrines are condensed into a series of practical maxims he thought it necessary to follow to achieve good government: self-control and self-perfection; respect for the wise; love of family; consideration for ministers, the principal functionaries of the kingdom; perfect harmony with all subordinate functionaries and with magistrates; acceptance of advice and orientation from the wise and from artists; courtesy to travelers and foreigners, and honorable treatment of vassals. When Qin Shi Huang died, the servants cleaning the imperial library discovered a hidden copy of Confucian writings. It's entirely possible a librarian used that method to get around the royal decrees.

In June 2002, a group of archaeologists in Hunan unearthed almost 20,000 bamboo strips with 200,000 ideograms on them: the secret history of Qin Shi Huang. Some were only fragments, but they proved that the emperor had a mail system and that the sanctions he imposed were the most severe of all time.

Chinese Biblioclasty

In 206 BCE, there was a civil war to overthrow the weak heirs of Qin Shi Huang—the man who destroyed so many books. During the war, Qin Shi Huang's own imperial library was burned to the ground.

Only during the Han dynasty, which began in 207 BCE, was the nation's memory restored. Many learned men had memorized entire works. The Han era was a cultural period of great prosperity. Liu Pang, the first Han Kao Tsu (Supreme Han Ancestor) brought back learned men of Confucionist tendency and established a system whereby the most important positions were reserved for literary men. One day he asked the wise Liu Kia why he, who had conquered by force, should study the classics. Liu Kia answered that the classics offered the only possibility for giving form to force. Kao Tsu made Chang'an (Xian) a capital celebrated for its literary gatherings.

Around 130 BCE, during the reign of Emperor Wu, the first examinations of court functionaries took place. These tests, in question-and-answer format, were of surprising complexity. Book copying also enjoyed a renascence, and the scribes took part in it until they had "amassed mountains of books." In 124 BCE, the Poh Shih Kuan was created, an imperial institution with departments each dedicated to a single book: the *I Ching* (Book of Changes), the *Shu Ching* (Book of Documents), the *Shih Ching* (Book of Odes), the *Chun Chiu* (Annals of Spring and Autumn), the *Li Chi* (Book of Rites), the *Chou Li* (Book of Ceremonial Protocol), and the *I Li* (Book of Ceremonies). By this period, books were made of silk.

Around 99 BCE, the chronicler Sima Qian, dubbed the "Oriental Herodotus" by European sinologists, neglected to use the proper terms to describe the magnificence, power, and legitimacy of the emperor when he recounted the wars against the invading Hsiung-un. That lack of delicacy on his part, and perhaps the timidity of certain adjectives, caused him to be castrated and his writings burned. His *Shiji* exists in an incomplete version.

In 26 BCE, Liu Xiang was ordered by the emperor to catalog and edit the books in the imperial library. Some time later, he presented a curious innovation, a detailed report entitled *Bielu*, with information about its author and a historical account of all the details about each work. In studying, for example, the writings of Xunzi (Hsun-tzu), he found a surprising 322 manuscripts, which he reduced to thirty-two books and had transcribed on bamboo. His son, Liu Xin, continued his father's work and classified books in the following way: *liuyilve* or classics, *zhuzilve* or thinkers, *shifulve* or poetry, *bingshulve* or art of war, *shushulve* or numerology, divination, occultism, alchemy, and *fangjilve* or medicine. This material was revised by Emperor Ai Di in the year 6 BCE. Around the year 1 CE, the catalog of the imperial library consisted of 477 works, which still exist. Ban Gu (32–92 CE) incorporated this bibliography into his *Hanshu*, or History of the Han Dynasty, which has survived.

Around 23 CE, the degeneration of the Han and the ruin of the peasants gave birth to a conspiracy. The usurper Wang Mang attacked powerful landowners and turned himself into a patron of the educated. He made all those who had read the classics come to his court, where he gathered almost a thousand scholars. Even so, he could not maintain his power and died during a military operation. Unfortunately his extraordinary personal collection disappeared.

In 205, Cai Lun, chief eunuch, was determined to create a writing surface less expensive than the silk then in use. He experimented with mixtures of tree, cloth, and silk until he produced sheets that resembled modern paper, which resulted in an explosion of books.

Still, numerous collections perished. At the peak of its power, Luoyang became an intellectual center. In 311, it was sacked by the Huns and its libraries ruined. In 316, the pillage was repeated when the last of the Qin fell. Between 495 and 510, messengers carried decrees throughout the country in search of manuscripts in order to rebuild the imperial library. In 554, toward the close of the Liang dynasty, Emperor Yuan himself set fire to the prestigious royal library of 140,000 books when his capital Jiangling was under seige.

In 600, Niu Hung wrote a report in which he suggested it was important to keep multiple library copies in order to foil the destruction of written knowledge. Thus, the Chia-Tse Palace came to have 370,000 books. The Tang dynasty, which ruled China until 907, ordered the entire library of the previous dynasty, the Sui, to the capital in the year 621. An accident eliminated 90 percent of the books. Between 907 and 960, the destruction of libraries was frequent because of China's chaotic situation. In 975, during the time of the Tang, Li Houzhu (936–978), better known as Li Yu, asked that books be burned rather than turned over to his adversaries, the Song. In 1000, the internecine wars that raged during the time of Hsuan Tsung eliminated thousands of books. In Kaifeng, there was a library containing 73,877 books: all were burned.

Just how many books were lost in China is still unknown. What allows us to imagine a large number are the *yiwenzhi*, the catalogs of the imperial library divided according to the norms established in the *Hanshu*, such as the *Suishu*, or History of the Sui Dynasty, the *Jius Tangshu* or History of the Tang Dynasty, the *Songshi*, or History of the Song Dynasty, the *Mingshi*, or History of the Ming Dynasty, and the *Qingshi gao*, or History of the Qing Dynasty. These chronicles contained exhaustive bibliographic indexes that allow us to know precisely which works have survived and which we must mourn.

The Persecution of Buddhist Texts

The introduction of Buddhism into China was rough indeed. The neo-Confucionists rejected Buddhism as insubstantial because of its theory of renunciation and emptiness. Just as the Confucionists were persecuted by the members of the Legalist school, they fought and denigrated Buddhism. Despite such resistance, the Mahayana, or Grand Vehicle, managed to become preeminent beginning in the first century CE, following the adaptation of terms such as *sangha*, or community of monks, the revision of family relationships, and illumination. The concept that anyone might be a bodhisattva, or savior, spread among the common people. During that process, Buddhist texts were often confiscated and destroyed. Persecution of monks and destruction of Buddhist texts took place virtually from the beginning. As late as 845, Wuzong ordered 4,600 temples destroyed and dozens of texts obliterated.

In 1900, hundreds of caves were discovered along the Silk Road, in the southern section of Dunhuang, Mogao, an oasis in the heart of the Gobi Desert. The caves housed thousands of sacred Buddhist texts, many in good condition, others in fragments, written between the fifth and eleventh centuries. It seems that in 366, the monk Yuezun had a vision and began excavating the first cave; thereafter the caves began to be painted and used. Over the course of 1,500 years, from the time of the Sixteen Kingdoms until the Yuan dynasty, this spirit flourished until it produced the Cave of Buddhist Canonical Texts, a kind of library where 50,000 manuscripts and artistic works were stored. In 243 caves, there were books of sutras in eight languages: Chinese, Tibetan, Ugur, Sanskrit, Xixia, Basba, Uighur-Mongol, and Syrian. Along with other texts, there appeared a copy of the mysterious *Broken Gold* text and a few fragments of the original sutras of *Ksitigarbha*, the only copy that exists.

Chapter 7

Rome and Early Christianity

Books in Rome followed the tradition of the papyrus or vellum roll, and they were as diligently destroyed there as they had been elsewhere. The books of Numa the legislator, some dozen or so hierophantic texts and twelve philosophic books, were placed in two boxes and buried by their author. In the year 181 BCE, a flood brought the boxes to light. The praetor Quintus Petilius read them with reverential fear, then brought them to his superiors "where they were burned." Livy notes that the Senate had the right to summon magistrates so they "would gather up books to be burned," which happened around 186 BCE.

The Temple of Jupiter, built in the era of Tarquinius Superbus, last of the Etruscan kings, was the repository of the Sibylline books, studied by priests called *flamens*. Legend has it that the sibyl of Cumae brought Tarquinius nine books and demanded 300 gold pieces for them. The king laughed and roundly rejected her offer. The sibyl burned three of the books and asked him how much he would give for those that remained. Now he began to wonder if the books contained the future history of Rome. But he still refused to pay, and the sibyl burned three more. Finally the king gave her the 300 gold pieces. In 83 BCE, a fire destroyed the books, and even though some copies survived they too eventually burned (in 69 and 80). Augustus reportedly saved some of the Sibylline books and deposited them in Apollo's temple on the Palatine, where they too burned some years later. Days before his death in 408, a certain Stilicho destroyed the remaining Sibylline papyri.

Like so many bibliphiles, Augustus was a biblioclast. Pliny credited the emperor with saving the *scrinia*, the cylindrical containers that protected the manuscript, of Virgil's *Aeneid*. On Virgil's deathbed in 19 BCE, when he dictated his last will and testament, the poet ordered the burning of the *Aeneid*; his wishes were ignored, and he died believing his text was incomplete. Yet Augustus destroyed thousands of works for reasons of state. In the year 8 CE he forbade the circulation of Ovid's *Art of Love* (it was burned in Florence by Girolamo Savonarola in 1497, and yet again in England in 1599, when the bishops of Canterbury and London ordered the burning of the translation made by the dramatist and spy Christopher Marlowe). Augustus had Timagenes of Alexandria's *Acta Caesaris Augusti* publicly burned because he concluded that the author had not written his work with enough respect for him. The same emperor burned more than 2,000 Greek and Roman works he didn't like. He was a severe critic.

But inconstant as his respect for books and learning was, Augustus was notably more respectful of the written word than his immediate successors. During the reign of his stepson, Tiberius, one anonymous poet accused another of insulting the storied Agamemnon in a poem; another poet dangerously suggested that a historian had praised Brutus and Cassius. Tiberius, in a rage, sentenced both to death along with other authors whose books he obliterated. He had perhaps forgotten that the very writers he'd sentenced had read their works to his stepfather, who had praised them.

Senator Cremutius Cordus's books were burned during the reign of Tiberius and he was ordered to commit suicide. Years later, Caligula, Tiberius's successor, recommended that Cremutius's works be taken out of circulation, proving that censorship could not fully exterminate his books. It's almost never mentioned, but Caligula's successor Claudius, who ruled Rome from 41 to 54 CE, wrote a work on the Etruscans in Greek and another on the Carthaginians. He celebrated the writing of these books by creating an annex to the Museum.

To make up for the library burnings caused by barbarian invasions in the first century CE, the emperor Domitian sent to Alexandria for copies of the classics. As a counterpoint to that effort, he publicly burned all books he suspected of offending him. Poets were beaten and publishers crucified or impaled. Domitian later was accorded a *damnatio memoriae* by his succesor, Nerva.

At least 3,000 bronze tablets burned in the fire that swept Rome during the time of Nero. These had been stored on the Capitoline Hill and "were the most beautiful and ancient register of the empire, including decrees and decisions taken by the Roman people and senate almost as far back as the founding of Rome." During the reign of Justinian, John Malalas, a chronicler from Antioch, wrote a *Chronographia*, or history of the world, in which he commented on the destruction of books in Rome: "In the month of June . . . some Greeks were dragged from house to house and their books, images, and the statues of their miserable gods burned."

A World of Lost Libraries

Despite records of early popular poetry, Latin literature really began with the third century BCE. It was then, when the book as a roll of papyrus was adopted, that Livius Andronicus, a Greek slave, translated the *Odyssey* and stimulated the representation of theatrical works, thus founding the literary tradition of what would become one of the ancient world's most important empires. Books were sold on the street to supply private collections, and the first Roman public library was planned by Julius Caesar.

Caesar, his hand in all affairs, chose Marcus Terentius Varro, a famous man of letters, as the library's director. Authors like Quintilian considered Varro "the most learned of the Romans." He wrote 74 works on 620 papyrus rolls on several subjects, but practically none have survived. His lost *On Libraries*, in which he describes the organization of a library and gives reasons for defining books as cultural artifacts, is one of the earliest discussions of the subject. Using other works by him, we can conjecture that he prepared a brief history of Greek libraries, but we have no real proof. Unfortunately, the assassination of Caesar on March 15, 44 BCE, postponed the library's debut indefinitely, and when Varro died a year later, all his books were looted and some destroyed.

It fell upon the historian Gaius Asinius Pollio (a critic of Julius Caesar) to coax a public library into existence: according to Suetonius, it was made up of both Greek and Latin works. The images of many writers were displayed in the atrium, which Pollio adorned with war booty.

The emperor Octavius Augustus created two libraries, both of which burned. One was next to the Temple of Apollo on the Palatine Hill. It was organized by Quintus Pompeius Macer (who had the dishonorable task of eliminating Ovid from the archives and determining the degree of access for certain texts by Julius Caesar) and was later in the hands of Gaius Julius Hyginus. Everything suggests that this library was made up of two chambers, with Greek texts on one side and Roman texts on the other, with niches for the bookcases and decoration enhanced by statues. This center was destroyed by fires in 64, again in 200, and finally in 363. The other library was the Portico of Octavia, which burned down during the reign of Titus. Marcus Ulpius Trajan (53–117), the first emperor of Hispanic origin, spent many years in the company of Dio Chrysostom, and out of that relationship came the emperor's desire to build a gigantic forum, where he installed the Ulpia Library in 114. This bilingual library was praised for its almost 20,000 volumes, which dispppeared after a devastating fire midway through the fifth century. The only reference we have to the Capitoline library concerns its destruction, and with regard to the Athenaeum, site of another library, we know practically nothing. The Pantheon was a stupendous public library; it was administered by Sextus Julius Africanus during the third century.

The library of the Temple of Peace, founded by Vespasian, was destroyed by fire in 191. In that incident, we lost several manuscripts by the physician Galen of Pergamum, who had deposited his works in the temple, as Heraclitus of Ephesus had earlier—he thought it the only secure place. Sheer luck allows us to read some twenty volumes by Galen. According to Constantine's detailed census, carried out in 350, there were twenty-eight public libraries in Rome: none survived.

Libraries were connected to public baths in many cities. Trajan sponsored the construction of one that was completed before 109. Caracalla ordered the creation of a bath complex capable of serving some 1,500 people. He allowed all Romans, even slaves, to use the facilities, which included hot, lukewarm, and cold water along with two gymnasiums—and a Greek and Roman library.

The most famous Roman book collector was perhaps Serenus Sammonicus, owner of a library containing 62,000 thousand books—all lost in the chaos following his assassination. Epaphroditus of Chaeronea, a slave educated by the grammarian Archias of Alexandria, accumulated a private library of 30,000 volumes he used in composing his own works. Unfortunately, it disappeared.

Many theater administrators also possessed collections of comedies and tragedies. When there was need for a new play, often the first thought was to invite a Roman author to adapt or rewrite a work by a known and respected Greek author, as Plautus did quite frequently. Nothing remains of these collections.

Sulpicius Galo, an astronomer and voracious reader, had a library of Greek epistle writers praised by Cicero, but it succumbed to an unknown fate. Villas in Dartona and Civitavecchia also had libraries. Cicero's personal library was unique in his age but lost to posterity. In his letters, there are frequent references to books and slaves who worked as copyists or librarians. We also know that Atticus, a rich, erudite Roman, was the owner of *plurimi librarii* ("many copyists") and of a respectable number of volumes which, after a few decades, were gone forever.

Libraria taberna, places where books were sold, abounded. One of the first to refer to them by name in a work—and it's perhaps to him we owe their consecration—was Aulus Gellius, who wrote "in libraria, ego et Julius Paulus poëta consederamus." It's not impossible that the influence of this author caused the word to take hold in Europe after the fifteenth century. Cultural decay and repeated crises inevitably brought these businesses to an end, and after the fall of the Roman Empire none remained.

Small, limited libraries were established in other parts of the empire, usually with one section only for Latin authors. Once Carthage was destroyed, around 146 BCE, together with its library, Augustus decided to build another city on its ruins. Naturally, it included a library. In the city of Timgad, founded by Trajan around 100 CE, there was a library, later reduced to ashes.

Inscriptions confirm the existence of a library in Como, donated by Pliny the Younger; there was another in Suesa

Aurunca in Campania, built by Matidia, a member of Hadrian's household; and there were collections in Volsini and Tíbur (now Tivoli). In Pergamum, Hadrian compensated the zone with a library, and we know that a woman named Flavia Melitine donated a library to the sanctuary of Aesclepius for the enlightenment of the ill.

Athens contains the remains of a library founded in Trajan's honor by a man named Titus Flavius Pantainus, who, according to the inscription from the year 100 CE, paid for "the peristyle, the library and its books, and all the furniture out of his own pocket." There is another inscription that states the rules of the library (perhaps the first of its kind): "No book may be taken, as we have sworn. . . . The library is open from the first hour until the sixth." The hours referred to the morning, for reasons of visual comfort. It's thought that some sculptures found nearby, the personifications of the *Iliad* and the *Odyssey*, formed part of the structure of that ancient library.

Trajan himself ordered a library built in Athens around the year 132 CE. It contained a huge rectangular pool and was destroyed in 267 CE.

An inscription written around 135 says "For Tiberius Julius Aquila Polemeanus, Consul, Proconsul of Asia, Tiberius Julius Poelemeanus, consul, his son, built the library of Celso. He paid out of his own pocket for its decoration, sanctuary, and books." That library is still there for anyone to see, in the ruins of the ancient city of Ephesus (now in Turkey). It was begun in the year 110, with an attempt to adopt the plan of the architect Vitruoya. It consisted of a monumental sarcophagus made of marble and a two-level façade decorated with columns. In the niches were statues representing Wisdom, Knowledge, Intelligence, and Excellence. The Goths destroyed it during their invasion in 263, although the façade remains intact. On that sad day, no fewer than 12,000 volumes were lost.

The fall of the western Roman Empire thwarted the patient labor of conservation. Alaric and his barbarian hordes took Rome in 410. For a week, beginning on August 24, the city was pitilessly sacked. Papyri were used to illuminate orgies. As his troops were burning libraries, one of the Gothic chieftains suggested leaving them to the enemy to distract them from military exercises. Montaigne, the source of this anecdote, recounted it as if it were something extraordinary; we know the sad pattern is repeated throughout history.

The Papyri Burned in Herculaneum

Herculaneum was a beautiful city in Campania of approximately 5,000 inhabitants. Around 62 or 63, an earthquake reduced some of its houses to rubble and killed several citizens. Unfortunately, that was the prelude: in 79, Vesuvius buried the city. In his *Epistulae*, Pliny the Younger noted that all was "covered with a thick layer of ash, like snow."

In 1752, a chance archeological excavation in a villa revealed the private library of Lucius Calpurnius Piso, a prosperous resident of the city, containing almost 1,800 burnt papyrus rolls, written in Greek. The library was a small room, roughly ten by ten feet, whose floors were covered with mosaics of intense colors. In the center of the room there was a chest containing the papyri. The dimensions of the room suggest that it was not used for reading, and that there must have been another room for that purpose.

The papyri revealed speeches thought lost by the philosopher Epicurus and texts of Philodemus of Gadara (110–35 BCE), who was a friend and mentor of the library's owner. Since Roman libraries contained both Latin and Greek texts, and only the Greek papyri have turned up, perhaps someday the missing works of Latin authors will be excavated from the villa's grounds.

Saint Paul Against the Magic Books

The Bible tells the story of Saul of Tarsus, who visited the Greek city of Ephesus in Asia Minor, where he expels demons, effects conversions, and preaches the very Christianity he'd attacked as a young man. Fearful, the magicians of Ephesus voluntarily immolated their books: "Many of those who had practiced magic brought their books and burned them in the presence of all; and when the tally of their price was made, they found that it was fifty thousand pieces of silver" (Acts 19:19). That figure has provoked an interesting polemic: some think that a page of papyrus cost the equivalent of $50 in today's money. Others believe that the magic texts were written on cheap papyri and that therefore the number of works destroyed must have been enormous.

Quite quickly, as Christianity became less of a sect of rebels and more of an organized religion, its leaders became less tolerant of divergent viewpoints. One of the first targets was Porphyry of Tyre (ca. 232–305), editor of Plotinus' works. Porphyry wrote *Against the Christians*, a treatise in fifteen books with clear analyses of the contradictory aspects of Christianity. A Neoplatonist, Porphyry objected to the cult of Christ. Some theologians, precursors of those who followed Plato and his school, strenuously objected to the work, and in 448 they burned all copies they could find. Since then, no complete version has been found.

Gnostic Texts

The disappearance of writings by the Gnostics, caused in great measure by their ferocious persecution by the Catholic Church, deserves a book in itself. The Gnostics, briefly stated, were a heterogeneous group influenced by Egyptian,

Hindu, Greek, and Babylonian religious notions. Before the Christian era, especially between the second and fifth centuries, this group dared to say that in this world dominated by evil, people could be saved by knowledge (*gnosis*) but not by faith.

The Gnostics considered the Christians demagogues for postulating the salvation of all. The supreme heaven could only be reached by elites granted powerful souls, they believed. They admitted dualism; they abominated the body; even so, some of them openly proposed the following thesis: if the body is rejected by the soul as something alien, then our carnal sins don't matter because the soul is superior. Jehovah for them was a secondary god, inferior in everything to the true Supreme God, the Total God, the Unnamable. Divided by their investigations, they've been classified according to schools: the Syrian, Alexandrine, and Dualistic schools and the Antinomians.

It is surprising how few Gnostic texts have survived. Basilides, leader of a group in Alexandria, wrote a gospel, twenty-four books as a commentary, and a series of hymns. But all we have are a few fragments. Isidore, his son, continued the tradition of his father and wrote prescriptive texts. In these cases, as in many others, the fragments were saved by those who refuted their doctrines (Epiphanius, Saint Irenaeus, Hippolytus Romanus) because it was necessary to quote the disputed passages. In this way, we've been able to salvage a few gems of ancient religious thought.

The Gnostics, fortunately, hid some manuscripts. In December 1945, two Egyptian *fellahin* were searching for natural fertilizer about 78 miles northwest of Luxor and found a vase. They thought it might contain gold, and it did, of a sort: it was a group of thirteen codices, at least fifty-two texts of a mythological, exegetical, liturgical, and gnomic nature. This little library is known as the Library of Nag Hammadi; the psychoanalyst Carl

Jung purchased one of the most significant codices for his personal collection.

The Heterodoxy of the Early Years

Aside from problems caused by the Gnostics, the church had to fight other heresies. The result was a regular series of conflagrations. The bishop of Dacia, Paulinus, for example, was expelled because he defended magic as a legitimate tool, and the intervention of Bishop Macedonius brought about the burning of his books. In 398, Arcadius rejected the works of Eunomius and ordered them destroyed. In 435 and 438, Theodosius and Valentinian directed groups who went from house to house confiscating books, especially those of the Nestorian sect, condemned by the Council of Nicea and the Fourth Ecumenical Counsel of Ephesus. The Nestorians believed in a dual God with one divine person and one human person, and they thought it absurd to call Christ's mother, Mary, the "mother of God." For them, it was a contradiction. They did not recognize the supremacy of the bishop of Rome and preached the simple life of the apostles.

The Assassination of Hypatia

This history, like all good histories, should include a dream and a murder. Hypatia was the first woman in history put to death for conducting scientific investigations. Familiarity with her life is one way to understand the decadent period in Alexandria.

Hypatia was born around 355. She was the daughter of Theon, a man known as "the wisest of philosophers," and an important member of the Museum of Alexandria.

Theon wrote treatises that have survived on astronomy, geometry, and music, and was widely recognized for his commentaries on Ptolemy's *Tables*. He taught Euclid's elements for students so well that the Byzantines used his guidelines for decades. He was also the author of works on the orphic initiation rites and of poems about cosmic chaos and the world of Ptolemy. In the texts of the *Catalogus codicum astrologorum graecorum* he is mentioned several times as the wisest astrologer and magician.

His daughter Hypatia was his collaborator and quickly surpassed him, coming to dominate the mathematics of her era. We know she wrote dense texts: a commentary on Diophantus's *Arithmetica*, a commentary on Apollonius's *Conics*, and an edition of the third book of a text in which her father explained the *Almagest*. Unfortunately, little remains of these writings, because they were destroyed or lost. One of her students and friends, Sinesius, sent her his work *On Dreams*, because only Hypatia knew the most profound mysteries related to that subject.

Hypatia was also a devoted professor. She gave classes to a group of initiates, and her Neoplatonism revived the study of geometry. Influenced by Plato and Plotinus, she was lucky enough to find an attentive public. It is said that people begged to attend her lectures, and that the high functionaries of Alexandria asked her advice. That aroused jealousy in many sectors.

During the spring of 415, a mob of devout monks, led by a certain Peter, a disciple of the venerable Cyril, bishop of Alexandria, seized Hypatia while she was in the midst of a lecture, accusing her of being a witch. She defended herself and screamed, but no one dared help her. The monks dragged her to the Cesarion church. There, with the public looking on, they brutally beat her with roof tiles. They pulled out her eyes and cut out her tongue. When she was dead, they carried her body to a place called Cinarus and cut it to pieces. They removed her internal organs and bones and finally burned her remains on a pyre. Their intention was simply the total annihilation of everything Hypatia symbolized as a woman.

Cyril was a nephew of Theophilus, the man who brought about the destruction of the Serapeum. He had a family precedent to live up to and certainly did so. Between 412 and 422, he ruled Alexandria's spiritual life. He could not tolerate Hypatia's wisdom because the scientific method would cast doubt on Christian doctrines. In his *Life of Isidore*, Damascius recounts: "Cirilus was so eaten up with jealousy that he plotted the murder of that woman so that it would happen as soon as possible." The city prefect, ashamed of himself, ordered an investigation of Hypatia's death and put a certain Edesius in charge. Almost immediately, Edesius received money from Cyril to "forget" things, and Hypatia's murderer remained unpunished.

In a strange way, the library at Alexandria was marked by crime. The founder, Demetrius, was killed by a mysterious asp; several librarians died in cruel fashion; Hypatia, in almost the final moments of the intellectual center's existence, was tortured and murdered. Later, the library itself disappeared without leaving a trace. Is there a greater paradox in human history?

Chapter 8

Oblivion and the Fragility of Books

Juvenal complained about the ephemeral nature of papyrus. He was ignorant of an even more fearsome and destructive danger: lack of interest. Among the Greeks, at the beginning, there were few copies of a single text, so it was natural that only a few readers could gain access to it. Homer and Hesiod were exceptions: they were extensively copied. When copies were rare, they deteriorated, and after some years, moisture or other environmental factors facilitated total destruction.

Nowadays, there are no examples of Greek papyri prior to the fourth century BCE. In fact, despite the labor of libraries and the widespread book business of the Hellenistic era, texts on papyrus not recopied or copied onto codices were lost. Archaeological discoveries show that Christian communities substituted rolls of papyrus for codices because of the low cost of vellum: many biblical texts of the second century were codices; those of the third and fourth centuries were almost all codices. The texts of the so-called pagans, on the other hand, had the bad fortune to be transcribed slowly in a process that favored very few.

The Christians' lack of interest in pagan literature caused the disappearance of many books. Around 363, Jovianus burned a gigantic library in Antioch, possibly founded by Antiochus the Great, only because his predecessor, Julian the Apostate, had favored the presence of books by Greek and Roman authors. Thousands of Greek comedies vanished because ecclesiastical authorities damned them as frivolous and immoral. Theatrical productions were attacked, which meant that actors' copies of plays also suffered. This brought about a period of darkness when thousands of comedies had to be hidden on library shelves, becoming archaeological curiosities. In 691, the canons of the Council of Trullo included Canon LXII, which forbade the representation of comedies.

An Alexandrian tendency that occurred throughout the ancient world contributed to the loss of works: the anthologizing of books by one or more classic authors and epitomes of long books. The idea was that certain works of certain writers should be read but not others. Philo of Byblos, for example, proposed a list of recommended texts in his specialized treatise *On the Acquisition and Selection of Books*, which itself ran to twelve rolls of papyrus. Telephos of Pergamum did the same in his three-roll text *Book Expertise*.

During the Hellenistic period, it was absolutely necessary to read Sophocles' seven consecrated texts, but not the hundred or so other works by him, which were retained in official copies that ultimately disappeared from the libraries of Athens and Alexandria. The Alexandrian librarians, perhaps following Plato's advice, would make "Selections," but these did not constitute "canonical selections." The word "canon" was used by the Greeks to refer to ethics, in the way we use the term "model" for all those acts that should be committed for their virtues. The first person to apply the term "canon" to Alexandrian selections was David Ruhken, who followed the ecclesiastical term as applied to the Bible—the books deemed authentic.

In Alexandria, because of the influence of Aristophanes of Byzantium, authors like Homer or Hesiod topped the list of epic poets; Archilochus led the selections of iambic poets. There were nine lyric poets: Pindar, Bacchylides,

Sappho, Anacreon, Stesichoros, Simonides, Ibicus, Alceus, and Alcman (Corinna may have replaced Alcman from time to time or became an exceptional addition). There can be no doubt that this attitude spurred the forgetting and, of course, the disappearance of hundreds of books by authors considered minor by the demanding librarians. L. Bieler reaches this conclusion: "One of the causes of book disappearance, especially of longer works, was the practice of making epitomes, very popular after the third century CE. These were the precursors of our *Reader's Digest* abbreviated editions." With time, the epitomes became absolutely necessary because they alluded to books that no longer existed.

Language and Domination

The imposition of Latin was slow but ultimately definitive, and it was certainly a contributing factor to the loss of Greek texts. While this was not the case in cities like Byzantium, it was true generally in Europe. Christianity, in principle subservient to Greek as a language for propagating the gospel, abandoned Hebrew and other languages and moved to Latin for social reasons. There were, nevertheless, some initial hesitations until the consolidation of the long process was a fact; after that we see disdain for Greek classics. Irenaeus of Lyon, who prayed and spoke in Latin (or ancient Celtic), curiously wrote his attacks on heretics in Greek. Tatianus wrote in Rome, but, like Hippolytus, he did so in Greek.

No matter. Texts and documents during the third century CE began to be written in Latin, as we see in an ancient document dated January 20, 250. Novatianus was, perhaps, the first Christian to use Latin to propagate his doctrines in Rome. The Council of Elvira (300 CE) left its testimony only in Latin. The consequences of this change were obvious: Greek, the language of philosophers and poets, was repudiated, with some exceptions, by all those church fathers who detected in literature and philosophy the source of numerous heresies. Tertullian went so far as to claim that "all heresies are instigated by philosophy." Then came the transition from papyrus to vellum, together with the practice of selecting useful, famous, and, of course, orthodox books, itself linked to a desire for control. We can never even begin to quantify the losses that took place between the second and sixth centuries CE.

Part Two

From Byzantium to the Nineteenth Century

Chapter 9

Constantinople

"New Rome" was founded by Constantine I in 330. It had a forum, a senate, and the royal palace, a hippodrome, theaters, baths, churches, reservoirs, granaries, and statues. On May 11, 330, the work was finished and the city officially inaugurated. It became the capital of the Byzantine Empire, where the traditions of Greece and Rome were maintained. In fact, the world is indebted to Constantinople for the possibility of reading authors who otherwise would be nothing more than names. Without its contribution to the transmission of ancient texts, we would probably not have the works of Plato, Aristotle, Herodotus, Thucydides, or Archimedes—to name just a few.

The changes that the learned of Byzantium introduced were considerable. Between the second and third centuries, a new book format became dominant: the codex, which allowed for writing on both sides of a page; and parchment. Both were more resistant to wear and time than papyrus. The writings that were published using the new system have survived despite the conflicts of the seventh and eighth centuries, when the library of the Royal College with its 36,500 volumes was pitilessly burned.

During the ninth century, the number of copies grew. This was the high point of Byzantine culture: the patriarch Photius (820–891) could read works we no longer possess and summarize his arguments in a monumental *Biblioteca* consisting of 280 sections filled with reviews of prose works by historians, novelists, and orators. He read speeches by the Athenian orator Lycurgus and philosophical treatises by Aenesidemus, which today do not exist. Photius read Achilles Tatius's adventure tales and, despite condemning their obscenity, he did not hesitate to praise the beauty of the heroines. He also distinguished himself by protecting copyists who saved ancient works in manuscripts they transcribed in tiny writing, which guaranteed greater space and allowed them to work more swiftly. These books replaced papyri and codices with uncial characters (a script in capital letters) and led, naturally, to the obliteration of earlier copies.

During the reign of Constantine II Porphyrogenitus, hundreds of historical, philosophical, and juridical texts were copied. The manuscript known as *Parisinus Graecus 1741* dates from that period: a didactic text that includes the first-known versions of the *Rhetoric* and *Poetics* of Aristotle, a philosopher admired at the time for his *Organon* but disdained for his harsh, labyrinthine style.

The Byzantines limited the use of papyrus to imperial books and documents (like the Saint Denis Papyrus). It's thought that the last-known example of a Byzantine document on papyrus is the *Tipkon* of Gregorios Pakourianos, dated 1083. With respect to paper, a Chinese invention, obviously it profoundly interested the copyists. The Greek manuscript on paper of greatest antiquity is Codex Vaticanus 2200, written around 800 by an Arab scribe. In Byzantium, on the other hand, paper was introduced during the ninth or tenth centuries, and the first paper found there is of the oriental type (called *bombykinon* or *bambakeron*). The fact that it was cheaper than any other material gradually gave it ascendancy, but its rapid deterioration was a matter of great concern to the monks.

Byzantine pride was present in all the empire's spiritual manifestations. Themistius praised the possibility that an imperial library might be built to stop the extinction of the classics. Like all the learned men of his age, he thought himself a promoter of the last intellectual refuge in the West. Of course the monasteries were refuges for books, but cultured, wealthy people had libraries as well: Michael Psellus, a Neoplatonic scholar, bragged about his mother's library, which contained the works of Orpheus, Zoroaster, Parmenides, Empedocles, Plato, and Aristotle.

Bibliophilia extended to all fields. John Tzetzes, who died around 1180, loathed his poverty because it didn't allow him to buy books: "As far as I'm concerned, my library is my head. Given the penury in which we live, we have no books at home. For that reason, I can't give the exact name of the author." Tzetzes knew myriad poets, playwrights, historians, orators, philosophers, geographers, and novelists. We know of a letter he wrote to the Emperor Michael I, in which he explained the nightmare he had involving a book. He dreamt that during the tumult of a battle, he saw Dexippus of Athens' *History of Scythia*, a book he'd sought all his life. The book was in flames, but it was still intact. The word, Tzetes declared, had conquered fire. In some way, that dream is symbolic of the desires of the era.

Nevertheless, the serial destruction of books continued. In 781, a fire in the palace and part of the city incinerated hundreds of texts, among them those by Saint Chrisostomos. The usurpation of Basilicas, between 802 and 807, caused a fire that destroyed more than 120,000 books.

Iconoclasm

During the iconoclast movement, between the seventh and ninth centuries, the burning of images also extended to the books of authors on one side or the other of the dispute. Iconoclasty began when Leo III proscribed images, supposedly in order to reconcile Christians, Jews, and Muslims, but an important factor in the decision was a desire to reduce the influence of the church on the state. Around 725, an edict repudiated ecclesiastical images and a statue of Christ was destroyed. Leo III's son, Constantine V, nicknamed "Copronymus" (which means, literally, "name of excrement") continued iconoclasty and augmented measures taken against those who protected images. In 754, the bishops gathered in the Council of Hieria. In what later came to be known as a *Latrocinium*, or "robber council," they heeded the emperor's expressed preferences and proclaimed:

> With the support of Scripture and the Fathers of the Church, we unanimously declare, in the name of the Holy Trinity, that all images of whatever material made by the cursed art of painters shall be rejected, cast out, and expelled with curses. Anyone in the future who dares to fabricate such a thing or venerate it or expose it in a church or private house, or possess it in secret, will be, if he is a bishop, priest, or deacon, deposed; if he is a monk or lay person, he will be anathematized; and he will fall under the blow of the laws of the secular authorities as an adversary of God and enemy of the doctrines transmitted by the Fathers.

The edict legalized an unprecedented persecution, and thousands of images were burned or covered over with stucco. The images of the Virgin disappeared. All defenders of images were tortured and assassinated and their property was confiscated. In libraries, illuminated manuscripts were ferreted out and hundreds were destroyed.

When the Byzantine church censored a work, it was almost never by a classical author. In 1117, Eustachius of Nicea analyzed scores of works in order to attack the Armenian church and discovered two or three heresies hidden in the works of the orthodox Saint Cyril. Naturally, he wrote a long report that provoked the destruction of hundreds of copies of the books in question. In 1140, the authorities ordered the works of a rebellious monk confiscated and burned three copies.

In 1204, chaos reigned. The Fourth Crusade reached Constantinople, and thousands of manuscripts were destroyed. On April 12, the crusaders sacked the city. Mobs of soldiers entered the Hagia Sofia, and a prostitute was seated on the throne of the patriarch. The attack was savage: women were raped and the church tapestries were stolen, along with works of art and candelabra. The priests themselves stole all the relics they could find and promised absolution to the mob. Theft was so general that almost all the churches of Europe came to have treasure or relics from Constantinople. According to the historian Steven Runciman, "The sack of Constantinople has no parallel in history. . . . There was never a greater crime against humanity than the Fourth Crusade."

That same disastrous year, one of the best texts by Callimachus of Cyrene, the *Hecale*, cited and read with a pleasure that today fills us with envy by Michael Choniates, also disappeared. Copies of Sappho and other classics were also destroyed. Even so, the Byzantines reestablished the stability of their city and continued their philological labor. From 1261 until midway into the fourteenth century, manuscripts proliferated and all classes honored the teachers. The Codex Ambrosianus C222 declared that the entire work of Aristotle should be read carefully.

Barlaam of Calabria (ca. 1290–1348), an Aristotelian, was a great friend of Andronicus III in Constantinople, but his criticism and polemics made him unpopular, and the city council condemned him in 1341, with the express condition that all his writings be burned. He fled to Avignon, where he taught ancient Greek to Francesco Petrarca—Petrarch, one of the great lights of the early Renaissance.

In 1453, Constantinople fell after a ferocious siege by Turkish troops commanded by Sultan Mahomet. The Turks sacked the city for three days, following an established routine. Neighborhood by neighborhood, they butchered women and children. They mercilessly destroyed icons, churches, and manuscripts. In the imperial palace at Blachernas, they exterminated the Venetian garrison and burned everything they could. They eliminated every book they found, first prying off any jewels set into their covers. There is proof that they sacked the churches of Saint Sophia, Saint John of Paras, Chora, and Saint Theodosia, as well as the triple church of the Pantocrator. Many religious centers were made into mosques. According to Edward Gibbon, 120,000 manuscripts unacceptable to the faith of Muhammad were piled up and tossed into the sea. Constantine Lascaris, in a quotation saved by Migne in his *Patrologia Latina*, declares that the Turks destroyed a complete copy of Diodorus Siculus's *Bibliotheca historica*. In any case, "most of the books were burned."

News of the fall of Constantinople spread all over Europe. The empire was definitively extinguished.

Chapter 10

Between Monks and Barbarians

There came a moment when not a single library existed in Europe. Amianus Marcelinus, around the fourth century CE, was the privileged witness who wrote: "The libraries are locked up like tombs, in perpetuity."

Copying and reading were rare activities between the fifth and sixth centuries, almost always carried out by nobles or clerics. Gaius Sollius Modestus Apollinaris Sidonius, in Gaul, had a monk chased down and captured when he found out that the monk was carrying a rare manuscript to Brittany. He forced the monk to dictate the manuscript to his secretaries because he feared he'd never see the text again.

An exceptional passage in the *Institutiones* of Cassiodorus, a politician and later a monk, gives us an idea of the fear people had of the barbarians. Cassiodorus, who himself served the Ostrogoths, speaks of a treatise on music by a certain Albinus and notes there is a copy in a Roman library: "If that copy has disappeared because of the barbarian invasions, you will find in its place here a copy of Gaudentius." In 540, Cassiodorus established the Vivarium, a monastery on his family estate on the Ionian Sea, where he established a modest school of copyists and a library dedicated to preserving ancient texts. We don't know if the so-called pagan classics were copied there, but it is likely, given Cassiodorus's encyclopedic culture. In fact, he was

in Constantinople between 550 and 554, where he could
have acquired Greek and Latin books.

The Manuscripts of Ireland

Greek classics survived in Byzantium; Latin and Celtic classics
were saved in great measure by the monks of Ireland.

In 432, Pope Celestine I sent Saint Patrick to Ireland to
preach the gospel on that remote island where he had lived as
a slave. There he founded monasteries, abbeys, and bishoprics
adapted to the idiosyncracies of the natives. These religious
centers conserved both the faith of Christ and ancient Latin
manuscripts. The monks, who knew Greek and Latin, used
the ancient Irish alphabets of Ogham, and, after creating a
sublime and artistic calligraphy, copied hundreds of works.
They also saved Celtic literature—the myths of Ulster, Tain,
and Finn—in places like Aran, Glendaloch, Armagh, Clonard,
Bangor, Lismore, and Clonmacnois.

A Celtic poem, dated by the German scholar Kuno Meyer
to the sixth century, inaugurated Irish literature with a
celebrated testament in which Dallan Forgaill thanked
Columcille for his defense of the *filid*, an order of poets
accused of exaggerating their political authority in an assembly during the year 575. Heirs of the Druids, the Irish poets
could not call themselves *filid* without first achieving the
status of masters, or *ollam*. This took twelve years of study
that was divided into grades. The lowest grade, *oblaire*,
comprised knowledge of seven stories; the highest grade,
ollam, meant knowing hundreds of stories as well as grammar, mythology, topography, and laws. There were annual
examinations, and the candidate had to stay in a dark cell
while he managed to versify what he'd learned in such a way
that his work was equal to or better than what the tradition
already offered. These poets narrated tales with spontaneous

and marvelous concepts of the world. *The Story of Tuan Mac Cairill* tells how a man metamorphoses successively into a deer, a wild pig, an eagle, and finally a salmon. The salmon is caught by a man and eaten by a woman. In the woman's womb, he turns into a man, is born a prophet, and writes the poem admired today.

The Book of Kells (Codex Cenannensis), kept today in the library of Trinity College, Dublin, demonstrates that the art of copying was not limited to the text but also preserved visual works capable of arousing mystical sentiments. The Book of Kells, Giraldus Cambrensis said, was made by an angel and not by a man. Each work has the form of a codex, easier to read and more durable, made of dry goatskin. The monks prepared the book by cutting the skin, folding it, and sewing it until it made up a volume. They then began the transcription and decoration of the texts. Thomas Cahill theorizes that the strokes of Irish writing obeyed a prehistoric mathematics oscillating between equilibrium and imbalance, a harmony without manifest center. The illuminations of Irish books often eschewed human figures, emphasizing obsessive geocentric ornamentation: diverging spirals, zigzags, and zoological elements.

Columcille ("Dove of the Church"), known as Saint Columba, was destined for leadership in part because he was a descendant of the Irish high king Niall of the Nine Hostages. Columba founded his first monastery at Derry; he followed that with forty more, where dozens of books were copied. Around 563, accompanied by twelve disciples, he went to the island of Iona, near Scotland, and established a monastery to create incredible editions of sacred books. It is said that he died after writing a strange sentence from Psalm 34. His most devoted biographer, Adamnan, states that he never let a day pass without setting aside time for study or for spreading knowledge.

This magic phase of Irish history, which quickly extended to Europe, ended with the Viking invasions. Around the ninth century, the Vikings, who knew of Irish riches, destroyed the monasteries and their books. The kings of Ireland and their puny armies could not stop the Vikings, whose attacks destroyed centuries of masterpieces and ended the region's stability. On the prowl for gold and precious stones, the Vikings tore the covers off books and tossed the rest into the sea.

The raiders did not confine their attacks to Ireland; they ranged throughout the North Sea. One of the great monastaries so attacked was Lindisfarne, in Northumberland, founded by a monk from Iona around 635, which produced codices for the entire world. The Vikings knew of its wealth and repeatedly attacked it. The Anglo-Saxon Chronicle, when it refers to the year 793, notes that the looting and outrages perpetrated by the pagans caused the destruction of the church of God in Lindisfarne. In 801, Vikings again burned the buildings; in 806, they murdered monks and burned buildings; in 867, they destroyed everything utterly. They destroyed other monasteries: Glendalough was burned at least nine times; Clonfert, Clonmacnois, Inismurray, Bangor, Kildare, and Moville simply disappeared. In Ireland and England, libraries were left in ruins. The library of ancient York, for instance, completely disappeared. The Peterborough collection ended up in the hands of the same Danes who burned down the Crowland monastery in 860. In 1091, a fire took away all that had been reconstructed in Crowland, initiating the place's decline.

Monasteries

History declares Charlemagne (742–814), king of the Franks, grandson of Charles Martel, to be the founder of modern Europe. Blessed with an international vision, he stimulated the bishops to found schools and libraries. He convinced the clergy and persuaded the learned Alcuin to leave the city of York, where he'd founded a library, and take up residence in Aachen in order to foment new programs of study. Alcuin's program involved the seven liberal arts, and when he wearied of Aachen, he retired to the Abbey of Saint Martin of Tours, where he created a school of copyists distinguished for a handwriting style later called Carolingian minuscule.

Several important libraries flourished during the Carolingian era, but their fate was horrible. Fulda, the best library in Germany, survived only to suffer during the Thirty Years War. Monte Cassino in Italy was destroyed several times in its long history. Its stupendous collection of books was diminished by various circumstances and reduced to debris. Around 585, the Lombards captured the monastery and destroyed some rare books. In the ninth century, the Saracens burned the library. Giovanni Boccaccio, who visited the library, sadly noted dozens of books littering the floor. Most recently, in World War II, the Allies bombed the monastery to rubble, although its library had been removed to the Vatican, reportedly by Nazi officers.

Palimpsests and Other Paradoxes

For 200 years, between 550 and 750, Europe endured one of its grimmest periods. Not only were classical books not copied but they were used to make palimpsests: the original text was actually erased and a new text was transcribed in its place, usually more widely read works that brought higher prices. Works by Plautus, Cicero, Livy, Pliny the Elder, Virgil, Lucan, Juvenal, and Fronto were sacrificed so sermons and theological treatises could be published.

In Bobbio, the monks erased Cicero's *De republica* in the seventh century in order to transcribe a study of the psalms by Saint Augustine. Ironically, the fragments of that work by Cicero, on a manuscript called Vat. Lat. 5757, were recovered by a chemical process. In today's world, Saint Augustine's treatise is of little importance, but thousands of philologists and readers want to understand Cicero's magnificent work, which, according to some sources, is itself a copy of a lost work by Aristotle, possibly a dialogue.

Defenders of Books

During the early years of the Middle Ages, a Spanish deacon from Zaragoza, a certain Vicente, stood up to a judge who intended to burn the books of his sect. After a useless struggle, he shouted: "The fire with which you threaten sacred letters will burn you in an act of justice!"

A similar story takes place in the monastery of Saint Gall, Switzerland, attacked in 926. Huns attempted to slaughter the monks and set fire to the monastery, which would have meant the end of thousands of carefully preserved works. The Swabian woman in charge of the library, Wiborada, had a vision. What she saw we don't know, but the afternoon of the day before the attack, which began at dawn on May 1, she buried the books. According to the chronicle, the besieged overcame their attackers. However, the fire consumed the monastery and Wiborada's library. Mutilated, she was lying on top of a mound of earth where the books were later discovered intact. Her act won her sainthood; she is the patron saint of all bibliophiles and the first woman formally canonized by the church.

Chapter 11

The Islamic World

Islam transformed much of the world with a message as alive today as it was then: "There is no God but Allah, and Muhammad is his prophet." Over the course of twenty-three years, the angel Gabriel revealed to Muhammad a series of norms, which would become the Koran. The Koran consists of 114 suras or chapters, composed of 6,236 verses. Over the years, the Koran—the word alludes to recitation—would itself become sacred, and followers of Islam think of it in different ways. But as a matter of principle it is impossible to recite the text without purifying oneself. The book is carefully wrapped in silk or other adorned cloth and placed in an elevated position. For the faithful, the greatest glory is to memorize it. Those who do so earn the title *hafiz*. It is believed that if the Koran is recited a certain way, it produces miracles. The perfection of the calligraphy in which it is written is taken as a pious act. Before being transcribed by Zaid ibn Thabit, it had been written down on palm leaves, the flat bones of camels, pieces of wood, or parchment.

The unity surrounding the Koran stimulated the Ommiad dynasty to expand between 661 and 750. Using Damascus as their capital, the caliphs spread the doctrine of the Koran, founding numerous libraries. The historian Ibn al-Nadim has found a curious testimony, where it is said that "Ibn Isha, who was dedicated to revealing the ancient contribution of chemists, says that Yazid bin

Muawiya, polemicist, poet, thoughtful man, was the first to gather together books about medicine, astrology, and chemistry so they could be translated. A generous man. It's said that when asked why he spent time on the practice of chemistry, he answered that he wanted to make his colleagues and brothers wealthy." Unfortunately, the conquests that brought about the fall of the Ommiads saw the destruction of their libraries. Not a few alchemical works were burned.

Gundeshapur, in southeast Persia, was a refuge for the Nestorians of Edesa and the Neoplatonic philosophers of Athens. The first hospital in the world was created there, and medical research made Harith bin Kalada the most important physician in the region. Around 638, the troops of Omar I arrived, and the importance of the schools of medicine became international, to the point that Razi, perhaps the greatest physician anywhere of the period, always acknowledged that part of his education derived from the knowledge accumulated in that small Persian city. Later conquests left it in ruins.

The Abbasid caliph al-Mamun (786–833), son of Harun al-Rashid, was one of the greatest patrons of arts and letters. According to some chronicles, he once dreamed of a venerable figure with a well-cared-for beard who approached him from a doorway and explained the value of philosophy. The figure spoke a strange, anachronistic language, but without knowing how, al-Mamun could understand him and discuss faith, goodness, the meaning of a botanical etymology, the value of the classics, the desert. . . . At a certain moment, he realized the sage was Aristotle, who asked him to have all his works translated in order to preserve them. When he woke up, the caliph summoned magicians, learned men, and astrologers and ordered them to construct a building for knowledge whose name would be Dar al-Hikma ("house of wisdom"). Sahl bin Harun and Saeed bin Harun were put in charge of the library.

A few months later, all the learned men left for Byzantium and other capitals in search of the Greek manuscripts of Aristotle. They transported them on camels, fearful of bandits, and began their labor of translation and commentary. Ptolemy's *Almagest* was translated into Arabic by Hajjaj Ibn Mater (827–28) and Humayun Ibn Ishaq. The founder of the first public library in Baghdad was Sabur bin Ardeshair, a minister of Bahal al-Daulah. The library contained 10,000 volumes and was constructed in 991. At a certain point, there were thirty-six libraries in Baghdad. The poet al-Mutanabbi, born in Kufa in 915, said a man's best friend is a book.

When the Fatimids conquered Egypt in 969, they founded the city of al-Qahirah ("Victorious") where one of the greatest libraries in Islam was erected. It contained thousands of books from all known peoples. The Turkish invasion of 1068 destroyed everything.

In Damascus, the Zahiriya library was created, where numerous Greek classics that later went to Europe were copied. In 1108, the crusaders destroyed that center of learning and annihilated more than three million books. In July of 1109, after a fierce siege, they entered the city of Tripoli. Enraged over the years they'd spent fighting and the losses they'd sustained, the Christian soldiers burned 100,000 volumes from the famous Islamic Library, where there were 50,000 copies of the Koran and 50,000 commentaries.

In Iran, during the Islamic era, the first libraries were created between the eighth and ninth centuries. The royal library in Bokhara, now part of Uzbekistan, was famous. Avicenna, one of the great philosophers of the era and the author of over 400 books, was given permission to study in that library because he saved the life of the emir.

This library was as important as those in Shiraz, Isfahan, or Rainy. The emir enriched the library with gifts of rare texts brought from Baghdad and China.

The library of Sayvan ul Hikme in Isfahan was also important. In 1029, when Sultan Massud, son of Mahmd el Gaznawi, invaded and looted the city of Isfahan, the works in the royal library of the Buyes princes were transported to Gazna. Some were burned during the invasion of the city by Alá el din Ghurí in 1151. Among the works lost was Avicenna's *Al-hikmat al-mashriqiyya* (Oriental Philosophy).

The Mongols Versus Islam

Having conquered Mongolia, the bloody Timujin (ca. 1167–1227), better known as Genghis Khan, set about conquering China. In 1219, he sent his nomad army west and seized what is today Iraq, Iran, and part of Turkestan. In 1220, he reached Bokhara, chasing the sultan, who had already fled. Chronicles of the attack on the Bokhara mosque tell how books were confiscated and burned. After Bokhara, Genghis Khan attacked Samarkand, where, in 751, the secret for papermaking had been revealed to the Arab world by two Chinese travelers. The Mongol troops continued on to Nisapur, a city famous for its libraries, and then to the ancient metropolis of Merv: now forgotten, but in the eleventh century one of the world's largest cities.

In his history of Baghdad, Ahmad Ibn Tahir Taifyr tells that when King Yazdegerd III (632–665) took refuge in Merv, he brought with him an extensive collection of manuscripts and books. The learned Abu Said Abdulkerim ibn Muhammad as-Samani, author of a vanished history of Merv, created two libraries there; in 1218 an Arab traveler to Merv found no fewer than ten public libraries, one of them, the Damiriya, with 12,000 volumes. The geographer Yaqut ibn-Abdullah al-Hamawi (1179–1229) borrowed about 200 volumes and then left, astounded at the area's intellectual activity. If someone wanted to study, he could do it in those libraries, and it was possible to borrow a book for a full day.

The destruction of Merv's entire culture could stand as an example for all nations, but the Mongols were not yet done; they were determined to add to their infamous record.

Hashshashin

The Hashshashin, a sect of assassins, had its seat high in the mountains in Alamut (south of the Caspian Sea), where along with dining halls and training installations, the faithful had an extraordinary library. According to the most widely accepted etymology, the word "assassin" derives from the name given to the members of a sect that consumed hashish, a hallucinogen obtained from female plants of the hemp plant *Cannabis indica*. But another convincing etymology suggests that the word derives from "followers of Hassan." Arkon Daraul suggests that the Arabic word means something like "guardian." In that case, an assassin is the guardian of esoteric doctrines.

The leader of the sect of assassins was a Persian born around 1054, al-Hassan ibn-al-Sabbah, called "The Old Man of the Mountain," a friend of the poet Omar Khayyám, author of the *Rubaiyat*. Hassan had been initiated into the Ismaili doctrine, and in 1090 conquered the Alamut region in Iran. There he created a complex order with a hierarchy of nine levels, including apprentices (*lassik*), the sacred (*fedawi*), and comrades (*refik*). The *fedawi* engaged in suicide missions: when they were given instructions to murder someone, they did it no matter what sacrifices were entailed. Hassan would order a death by telling his disciples that if they fulfilled a mission his angels would carry them to paradise.

In December of 1256, the Alamut library fell, along with the fortress. Despite heroic resistance, the members of the sect succumbed to the Mongols. An anecdote relates that a Mongol examined the books in the library, where to his surprise he found, along with religious texts, a huge number of poetry anthologies and treatises on astronomy. Some he loaded onto his horse. The chronicle of Arif Tamir notes that after that examination, "The Mongols destroyed the Ismailite library, which contained one and a half million books." Other sources say there were no more than 200,000 books in Alamut, but no matter how many there were, they were all destroyed.

Steven Runciman notes: "In Alamut, the assassins had a great library filled with philosophical texts and studies of the occult. Hulagu sent his Muslim chamberlain, Ata al-Mulk Juveni, to inspect it. He separated some examples of editions of the Koran along with other books of scientific and historical value. All heretical works were burned. By a strange coincidence, at the same time there was a huge fire in the city of Medina, and its library, which had the greatest collection of orthodox Muslim philosophy, was totally destroyed."

Hulagu and the Destruction of the Books of Baghdad

After Alamut, the Mongols moved on to Baghdad, which, at this time, held the most important schools of law, mathematics, and literature. The earlier displacement from Damascus to Baghdad by the Abassids gave the city untold bibliographic wealth. The Abassid caliph Abu Ahmad Abd Allah idn al-Mustasim, known as Al-Mustasim

Billah, brought books to the capital from throughout Persia. Today we know that Yahya Barmeki had a gigantic collection of theological texts and that Fateh bin Khaka possessed another great library of astronomical treatises. Abdul Malik Ziyat, minister of Caliph Wasiq Billah, also had another great collection, as did Alama al-Waquidi, of whose collection it was said "it couldn't be transported by six hundred camels."

Hulagu Khan, grandson of Genghis Khan, repeated his predecessor's cruelty in Baghdad, which he reached in 1257. Following his usual method, he began with diplomacy, sending a messenger with an ultimatum (unconditional surrender) to Al-Mustasim. Hours later, the astrologer Husim al-Din, seriously upset, recommended the siege of Baghdad be abandoned because signs and planets were unfavorable: "If the king does not listen and abandons his plan, six demons will appear to him: first, all his horses will die and his soldiers will become sick; second, the sun will not reappear; third, it will not rain; fourth, there will be storms and the world will be devastated by an earthquake; fifth, grass will not grow on earth, and sixth, the Great King will die this very year."

Caught in this dilemma, Hulagu summoned Nasir al-Din al-Tusi, chronicler and mathematician (he invented trigonometry). Hulagu had incorporated him into his retinue after the capture and destruction of Alamut and the Hashshashin, of which he was a member. After listening to all the advisers, Nasir declared: "The calculations are false. Nothing will happen if you attack Baghdad." Those words decided the matter for Hulagu, who immediately ordered his troops to cross the Tigris. After destroying the villages around the city, he besieged Baghdad on November 15, 1257. The caliph counterattacked on January 17 and attacked the Mongols in Bashira. Four hours of fighting left 12,000 soldiers dead. On February 4, Hulagu received word that his troops had entered Baghdad, where fierce fighting continued for a week.

Al-Mustasim surrendered, but the bloodbath continued. There were more than 500,000 bodies on the streets, houses were sacked, and only Christians were allowed to live because Hulagu's wife was a Nestorian. The caliph was captured and entered the palace along with Hulagu. There the royal family was assembled and (except for one son, sent back as a prisoner) murdered. The Mongols wrapped the caliph in a rug and beat him to death, because it had been prophesied that if his blood reached the ground, the Mongols would suffer.

The manuscripts in the library were carried to the banks of the Tigris and then thrown in so the ink mixed with the blood. This was a premeditated act of destruction directed at the intellectual prestige of the people of Baghdad.

Another descendant of Genghis Khan, Tamerlane, attacked Baghdad in 1393 and reduced everything he found to rubble. His soldiers advanced into Syria and eliminated every book their enemies possessed.

Chapter 12

Misplaced Medieval Fervor

In Spain during the caliphate, Al-Hakam II tried to distinguish himself from his predecessors. He was cautious, pious, and stubborn—virtues that helped his kingdom stay at peace. He took it upon himself to found, in Córdoba, the most important library in medieval Europe, at a time when there were said to be only sixty libraries in all Spain. Within a few years, Al-Hakam had acquired many rare texts, and he sent messengers to spread the word that he wanted copies of the best books in the world. His advisors chose 400,000 volumes dealing with all aspects of human knowledge. The catalog of the library was over 2,000 pages. What is surprising is that Al-Hakam said he'd read all the books, and one of his habits was to place at the start or ending of a book all the details available about the author. His acquisition system was so efficient it was said he read books published in Baghdad or Syria before the inhabitants of those places.

Upon his death, his son Hisham II al-Mu'ayyad became king. Unfortunately, he was still a minor and unable to restrain the ambition of his father's friend and intendant, Muhammad ibn Abu Amir al-Mansur, known as Almanzor (938–1002), and lost power. In 981, Almanzor took on the title al-Mansur bi-Allah ("unique victor for Allah"); in 994, he adopted the title al-Malik al-Karim. Since he was a frustrated writer, he protected theologians, but in a moment of inexplicable fervor, he allowed his advisers to burn all books not held to be sacred by Muslims in the royal library. The works were piled up and burned for several days. Almanzor, conscious of his act, wrote out the entire Koran and became fanatically devoted to the book. Today, only one book from Hakam's library, dated 970, survives.

The Forbidden Verses of Ibn Hazm

Ibn Hazm (994–1063), author of *Tawq al-hamanma* (The Dove's Neck Ring), one of the best treatises on love, was persecuted for his desire to dedicate himself to the *zahiri* rites instead of the *malequi* ritual of al-Andalus (the Muslim part of Spain). Known in Spain as Ben Hazam, he explored amorous sentiments with a skill yet to be equaled.

The king of Seville, al-Mutadid, protector of poets, husband of a poet, father of poets, decided to burn all of Ibn Hazm's works. He did not eliminate all of them, but he certainly succeeded in terrifying Ibn Hazm. Historians have noted that al-Mutadid lost power and was deported to Morocco, where he suffered from hunger and wrote hundreds of verses in which he imitated with genuine fidelity the metaphors of the man he'd humiliated in his distant and unforgettable Seville.

Abelard's Forbidden Books

Great thinkers live dangerously. Socrates had to drink hemlock; Protagoras watched as his book was burned in Athens; Democritus tore his eyes out like Oedipus just to be able to think; Plato was almost assassinated; Aristotle fled to Chalchis because he was accused of impiety. Peter Abelard did not escape the curse and suffered castration for improperly loving a young woman who, it seems, was not as beautiful as she was sweet: Héloïse.

As if love weren't enough to condemn him, in 1120, he published his *Introductio ad Theologiam*, an attack on heretical propositions. An orthodox synod promptly condemned it for deviations from the true faith. They also sought to have the book burned and its author confined to the Convent of Saint Medardo. Twenty years later, all of his works were condemned by the Council of Sens, and around 1141, Pope Innocent III, worried about Abelard's sophisms, had his works burned, terming the author "an infernal dragon who is the precursor to the Anti-Christ." As late as 1930, a U.S. court prohibited the circulation of Abelard's love letters to Héloïse because they discuss traditionally repressed feelings and constitute a "respectable," intellectual introduction to sex.

Erigena the Rebel

An heir to Irish rebelliousness, the mysterious Johannes Scotus Erigena, John the Scot (ca. 815–877 CE) was one of the most original philosophers of the Middle Ages. He had a perfect knowledge of Greek and translated Dionysius the Aeropagite for Charles II the Bald between 860 and 862. We owe the existence of Giordano Bruno and Spinoza to his most celebrated book, *De Divisione Naturae*—no small debt.

A fearful Pope Honorius III exhorted faithful Catholics to seek out the text and burn it. Borges comments on that burning: "*De Divisione Naturae, Libri V*, the controversial work that preached [John the Scot's] doctrine, burned in a public bonfire. A proper measure that aroused the fervor of bibliophiles and caused Erigena's book to reach our hands." In combating the heresy of the theologian Gottschalk, who held that God had condemned almost all men to hell, Erigena fell into another negation when he wrote, in *De*

Praedestinatione, that no one is condemned to hell because God is omnipotent and no being is alien to him. On a curious (and almost certainly false) note, William of Malmesbury claimed that Erigena was stabbed to death by the boys in the abbey where he taught. They were fed up, he claimed, with being mistreated by the philosopher.

The Talmud and Other Hebrew Books

The Talmud, a compilation of rabbinic commentaries on the Bible and Jewish history, has been one of the most persecuted books in history. In Egypt, in 1190, someone ordered the elimination of several copies in order to comply with the noble truth of the Gospels. Gregory IX, in 1239, called upon his censors to find copies of the Talmud. They did, and he had the books burned. In Paris, in 1244, priests eliminated hundreds of copies. Between 1247 and 1248, Louis IX of France had copies located and then incinerated. In 1319, in Perpignan and Toulouse, the church burned scores of copies. In 1322, the good-natured Pope John XXII had it burned in public. In 1490, in Salamanca, an auto-da-fé included the Talmud and dozens of other Hebrew books.

In the spring of 1559, 12,000 books written in Hebrew were burned in Cremona, Italy, where there was a press for printing Hebrew characters. Among the destroyed books was one by the kabbalist Menahem Zioni, known as Ziyyuni, whose thousand copies completely disappeared. On September 9, 1553, a group of priests in Rome sequestered copies of the Talmud and burned them in the Campo dei Fiori.

A famous polemic brought the sixteenth-century humanist Johannes Reuchlin into confrontation with the Catholic theologian Johann Pfefferkorn, a converted Jew. In 1509, the emperor, supported by the pious fanaticism of Pfefferkorn, ordered the destruction of all copies of the Talmud in his realm. Reuchlin opposed the decision and defended the use of the Talmud, the Zohar, and studies by Rashi, Ibn Ezra, Gersonides, and Nahmanides for theological purposes. At the same time, he did reject other texts, the Toledot Yeshu for example, where the figure of Jesus is denigrated. For reasons best known to himself, the emperor revoked his edict on May 23, 1510. But in 1514, the citizens of Cologne witnessed the burning of Reuchlin's books.

In Warsaw, in 1635, the Jesuits burned the traveler Gershom ben Eliezer Ha-Levi's *Gelilot Erez Yisrael*, probably published in Lublin, Poland, in 1635. In 1757, authorities in Kamenets-Podolski seized a thousand copies of the Talmud and publicly destroyed them. Naturally, the Nazis, of whom we shall speak later, annihilated the Talmud in Germany.

A keter is a manuscript, usually elaborately decorated, of the Hebrew Bible, accompanied by commentaries. The keter of Aleppo, Syria, was written in the tenth century C.E. and was at one time the oldest complete manuscript of the Hebrew scriptures in existence; it was reportedly consulted by scholars throughout the Middle Ages, among them Maimonides. In 1947, following the partition of Palestine, rioters set fire to the Aleppo synagogue, heavily damaging the Aleppo Keter: tiny pieces of the manuscript were painstakingly salvaged from the wreckage and enclosed in lockets that to this day are worn around the necks of Aleppo Jews. Two hundred ninety-five of the original Four hundred eighty-seven pages were eventually smuggled into Turkey and from there into Israel. What is left of the manuscript now resides in Israel's Shrine of the Book, in Jerusalem.

Censorship Against Maimonides

The life of Moses ben Maimon, one of the most influential Jewish thinkers of all times, was marked by paradox.

He was born in 1135 in Córdoba, Spain, then under Muslim domination. His parents practiced Judaism in secret. Without knowing it, he was a Jewish Arab Spaniard. At the age of twenty-three, he began a treatise on the *Mishneh Torah*, or Second Law, which he completed ten years later. That work won him the respect of both Jews and Muslims. In 1176, he began, in Arabic, the book that would make him world famous: the *Guide for the Perplexed*, a contradictory study whose logic vindicates allegory and repudiates materialism.

He also composed medical texts and didactic epistles—the *Epistle to Yemen*, the *Epistle on Apostasy*, and the prophetic astrological study, the *Epistle to the Community of Marseilles*. On his deathbed, he had visions about Aristotle's works and tried to correct some paragraphs in his own work, but to no avail: he died in 1204. Many years later, when his works were read by everyone, they were also burned: in 1232, in Marseilles; a year later, in Montpelier. The Dominicans could not tolerate his vision of God and destroyed his books.

Heresies

Canonical law defines heresy as "a religious error in which a person persists by his own free will and for a considerable time, against the truth proclaimed by the Church." Heresy required the creation of a means to combat it, both in theory and in practice. There was no lack of justification for persecution directed against members of any sect unwilling to accept the authority of the church. The principal problem of the Middle Ages was the diversity of movements, which made it virtually impossible to know the true motives of each group considered heretical. In 1259, the Flagellants appeared: they promised salvation to all those who whipped themselves for thirty-three days.

In the same year the Adamites proclaimed a return to original nudity; the Bogomili exalted free love; the Cathars proposed a return to Manichaeism and denied the sacraments; the Städinger, or sect of the Catini, defended total sexual freedom; and the Euchites refused to reject the devil because he was God's son. Pope Innocent III authorized crusades against the Cathars. In addition to killing them, the soldiers burned their writing. According to Caesarius of Heisterbach, it was decided in Paris to prohibit even the reading of books on physics and copies of the works of David de Dinant and the so-called Gallic books were burned.

The sermons of the preacher Arnaud de Bresse burned in 1155. The works of Amaury de Chartres, founder of the Almaricians, who maintained that God and the creatures were merely a strategy of providence where God was all and all was God, were burned in 1215 after being condemned by Pope Innocent III. *L'évangile éternel*, a text attributed to Joachim of Flora and his disciples, was eliminated around 1256. Marguerite Porete was sentenced to death on May 31, 1310, for, among other reasons, refusing to accept her position as a woman. The next day she was burned at the stake along with her books on mystic love. One, especially, was the cause of discord: *The Mirror of Annihilated Souls*. In 1318, Dante Alighieri's treatise *De Monarchia*, in which he proves royal power is not legitimized by the pope but by God, was burned in Lombardy. In 1322, Lolar Walter was burned along with his own books.

In the case of the Waldensians, historians have pointed out that the absence of documents derives from their systematic destruction. Originally known as the Poor Men of Lyons, the Waldensians were inspired by an ascetic preacher named Peter Waldo (d. 1217) to confront Catholic hypocrisy and return to the poverty of the primitive church. Starting in

1160, the Waldensians questioned the authority of the church and dedicated themselves to the open teaching of the Bible. They wrote in Provençal and evolved new interpretations of the psalms and both testaments of the Bible. They were excommunicated and savagely persecuted between the thirteenth and sixteenth centuries. Their resistance was exemplary, but it ended in massacre. On June 5, 1561, in San Sixto, a village of 6,000 was attacked and its writings burned. The prisoners were impaled on stakes and burned like torches.

Heresy wasn't always religious; it could be political or even fictitious. In 1328, for example, John XXII ordered a book burned because it cast doubt on his omnipotence with regard to ecclesiastical property: "At that time, two men were condemned by the pope for having composed a tome full of errors in eight books. They tried to prove that the emperor could correct, place, and dispose of, as he saw fit, and that the books of the church were at the mercy of the emperor."

There is a chronicle left by Gabriel Peignot, bearing the date August 16, 1463, which describes the burning of a book on magic. After reviewing its content in Dijon, Jehan Bonvarlet, accompanied by priests and local figures, made an irrevocable decision, preserved in the chronicle: "and this book was condemned to the fire." The same author, in fear and reverence, and not without irony, pointed out that burning the book provoked great confusion among those present.

Around May 23, 1473, a jail was erected outside the entry to the Church of Saint Mary in Alcalá de Henares, Spain. Almost immediately, Pedro Martínez de Osma's *De Confessione* was cremated there. He was a professor of theology at the University of Salamanca, but his book was paraded through town, spat upon, and then burned; he was excommunicated.

The Destruction of the Koran in Spain of the Reconquista

A rumor is usually an exaggerated truth. At least this is what the Moorish inhabitants of the exuberant city of Granada discovered one day in early 1500. It all began with the screams of old men and women, and finally a mob gathered in the streets. An austere priest named Francisco Jiménez de Cisneros had given an order that would, in radical fashion, bring about the integration of a new culture and the elimination of another.

Going house to house, priests and soldiers confiscated books and put the populace on notice that the time had come for burning an ancient sacred book, the Koran. The reaction of the Muslim faithful was not long in coming, though the disturbances were controlled by the Spanish troops who had taken the city in 1492 after ten long years of siege. Some Muslims buried their Korans, but the search was painstaking and brought in more than 5,000 books. King Ferdinand V and Queen Isabella I, now called the Catholic monarchs, the victors, the great heroes of the reconquest of the kingdom of Spain, authorized the burning because they knew they were living through decisive years. Cisneros, the astute confessor of the queen, had pointed out that tolerance in a city where Muslim texts were read in secret might be dangerous. It was not enough merely to proclaim the unity of a people; it was not enough merely to conquer the Moors; it was not enough to impose a new faith. It was necessary to erase a different faith, a concept of the world summarized in a book with the power to galvanize the enemy at any moment.

Cisneros could never be bribed. Born in a Castilian village in 1436, he came from a poor family and overcame his origins by studying at Salamanca and Rome. His ecclesiastical career began in an abnormal place: jail. Pope Paul II sent a letter recommending Cisneros for a "benefice," a gift of land, but the archbishop of Toledo refused to accept the pope's suggestion. In the face of Cisneros's ill-mannered insistence, the archbishop had him jailed. He spent six years locked up, forgotten, devoted to reading the Bible, and became a Franciscan. Finally, he was released and granted his benefice after all. In 1495, on the recommendation of a friend, Isabella named him archbishop of Toledo and made him her confessor. Anyone who knows the life of Isabella can immediately understand how Cisneros acquired absolute power over her. It also explains his attitude toward the Koran. He wanted to strike fear in all Muslims, whether they lived in Granada, North Africa, or anywhere else. As a friend of Cisneros noted: "He ordered the learned Muslims to take all their Korans and other private books, more than four or five thousand volumes, make great fires, and burn them all."

One of Cisneros's disciples was Alvar Gómez de Castro, who wrote his master's authorized biography in Latin. What is surprising is the way in which the burning and the religious purge are confirmed: "Joyful over the success and thinking he should take advantage of such a favorable opportunity to extirpate from their souls in a radical way all the Islamic error, he was not restrained by the opinion of those who judged it more prudent to wean them from inveterate custom little by little." Thus Cisneros carried out Catholicism's first auto-da-fé in Europe. Experts insist that the destruction was not limited to the Koran but included religious treatises and Sufi poetry as well. Their poems, which constituted a separate chapter in Arab literature, were destroyed. At least half of Sufi literature was devastated by the Christians. Even so, the monarchs thought their order had not been carried out thoroughly enough. An ambiguous document of 1511 proves that King Ferdinand himself was dissatisfied because "books of medicine and philosophy and chronicles" were saved. And his disappointment favored the continued destruction of Arab culture in Spain.

Cisneros achieved unprecedented prestige, especially as a biblioclast. But he distinguished himself in other tasks, which also won him the fear and the uncritical admiration of those around him. He imposed clerical celibacy, advised the monarchs to expel all Jews, and tortured thousands to convince them to convert to the faith of Christ. In 1507, he was named cardinal and grand inquisitor for all of Spain. Some say it was he who appointed an obscure monk named Torquemada to the post of chief of the Inquisition. In 1508, he witnessed the realization of an old dream, the foundation of the University of Alcalá de Henares (where he stored the Arabic manuscripts on medicine and science). The Complutensian Polyglot Bible, in Greek, Hebrew, and Chaldean with a Latin translation, was created there because he ordered it.

In 1517, with Isabella and Ferdinand both dead, he was informed he should meet the new king, Charles I. He was eighty-one years old, and while he was visiting the town of Roa, in Burgos, where he had family, he died. Some say he was poisoned; others say he died because his health was bad.

Reconstruction of the Library of Alexandria (H. Goll, *Die Weisen and Gelehrten des Alterthums*, Lepizig, 1876).

ARISTOTLE's
COMPLEAT
MASTER PIECE.

In Three Parts:

*Displaying the Secrets of Nature
in the Generation of Man.*

Regularly digested into Chapters and
Sections, rendering it far more useful
and easy than any yet extant.

To which is added,

A Treasure of HEALTH;

OR, THE

FAMILY PHYSICIAN;

Being Choice and Approved Remedies for
all the several Distempers incident to Human Bodies.

The Twenty-fifth Edition.

Printed and Sold by the Booksellers, 1753.

Aristotle's first dialogues, letters, and poems have all disappeared
(courtesy of Fernando Báez).

Qin Shi Huang and the Burnings of the Year 213 BCE. (copyright
Bibliothèque Nationale de Paris).

Suns and book burning, image from Hartmann Schedel's Nuremberg Chronicle, 1493.

Priest burning Aztec books in Tlaxcala Codex (copyright Glasgow University Library).

Priest Juan de Zumárraga (courtesy of Fernando Báez).

Detail from "The Burning of the books," by Pedro Berruguete, c. 1500, showing the destruction of heretical works of the Albigensians.

Poster condemning Nazi book burning (courtesy of Fernando Báez).

A 1933 cover of the AIZ (Arbeiter-Illustrierte-Zeitung—the "Illustrated Daily Worker") by John Heartfield: "Through Light to Darkness." (courtesy of Fernando Báez.)

Nazis burning books in Berlin, 1933 (copyright Corbis).

The Holland House Library in London, after a German air raid, 1940 (copyright Hutton-Deutsch Collection/Corbis).

Burning books in Argentina, 1980 (photo by Gustavo Garias; copyright Judith Gociol).

Burned book from the Anna Amalia Library (courtesy of Fernando Báez).

National Library in Baghdad, 2003 (courtesy of Fernando Báez).

U.S. soldier reading rescued books in Baghdad, 2003 (courtesy of Fernando Báez).

Chapter 13

The Destruction of Pre-Hispanic Culture in the Americas

In the second half of 2004, I traveled from Caracas to Mexico City. I spent a long week there that was, in all senses, one of the strangest in my life. During my first outing, on a dark and languid September afternoon, I reached the robust and ancient Metropolitan Cathedral in the city's main square, the Zócalo. I was shocked to see that the entire building was slowly sinking.

I learned that beneath my feet there had existed in earlier centuries another city, Tenochtitlán. Mexico City had initially been founded on a lake in 1325 by the Aztecs. Using *huejote* pilings, volcanic rock, and *tezontle*, the Aztecs created new land. Their city, with a quarter million inhabitants, had a great temple. It grew until it contained seventy-eight buildings, with a gigantic commercial center in Tlatelolco, itself divided into four important neighborhoods. No one imagines that a Christian cathedral could be built on top of the pyramids of Egypt or the Sphinx, but that is exactly what happened in Mexico during the sixteenth century. European architecture was superimposed on pre-Hispanic architecture in an act that masked history. And so, without anyone having to tell me it was there, simply by walking the streets of Mexico City, I discovered for myself the repressed past could reappear centuries later, as if it were a palimpsest.

When Spain reached the New World in 1492, the auto-da-fé was already a part of its repertoire for governing. The Inquisition had been created in 1478, and Spain was a distinctly warlike society: it had suffered seven centuries of war, beginning in the year 718, when Pelagius (also known as Pelayo) rebelled against the Muslims.

But by the late fifteenth century, the religious and political unity achieved by force was in danger because most of the peasants had been ruined and the financial resources of crown and church had been depleted by war. A miracle was necessary. A solution came from a part of the planet geographers—and even more so philosophers and theologians—did not know existed.

Christopher Columbus, a character of murky background, probably from Genoa, an assiduous reader of Marco Polo, convinced Ferdinand and Isabella to finance an unusual project he'd already presented, with no luck, in Portugal. He wanted to discover a new route to the Indies and was given money and permission to make the voyage from the port of Palos on August 3, 1492, the same day the Alhambra Decree was promulgated, informing practicing Jews they had to abandon Spain. Columbus, an obsessive seeker of the fabled island of Cipango, or El Dorado, crossed the Atlantic and, on October 12, discovered a new world that became the salvation of imperial Spain.

The invasion of America saved Spain from chaos; hence, everything was allowed: genocide of the native population, slavery, and open theft. Columbus, fearful he would not be believed on his return, kidnapped seven Taino Indians and pointed out to the Court what would be the most tragic reality of the coming years: "With fifty men, we can dominate all of them."

The invaders realized it would be impossible to subjugate the inhabitants of the new lands without imposing imperial Spanish culture. Antonio de Nebrija published the first grammar of the Castilian tongue in 1492 with this pronouncement: "Language was always the partner of empire." With this apologia in mind, historical accounts of the obliteration of native culture, which first inspired admiration among the visitors, take on new meaning.

The contrast between the vision of the Spaniards and the peoples they conquered is notable. Bernal Díaz del Castillo on Mexico City:

> We were astonished and said that it looked like the magic things in the book of Amadís of Gaul . . . and no one should be surprised that I write here in this way because there is much to be pondered in the affair that I have no idea how to tell: seeing things never before heard of, never before seen.

On the opposite side, the natives denounced the conquest of Tenochtitlán:

> And when they reached the house of treasure, called Teucalco, then they brought out all the artifacts made of woven feathers, quilts made of quetzal feathers, fine shields, golden disks, necklaces of the gods, nose jewelry made of gold, armor made of gold, bracelets of gold, diadems of gold. The gold was immediately removed from the shields as well as from other insignia. And then they made a great ball of gold and burned everything else, including everything that remained, no matter how valuable: everything burned.

How could reverence turn so suddenly into theft? There is much to say on this, but all we have to do is point out that the attack on Tenochtitlán was the greatest cultural sacking in Latin America. From 1492 to the present day, the process has continued: more than five hundred years of plunder. The same mind-set that melted down golden works of art in the sixteenth century continues today with the illicit trade in art. The quantities have changed but not the procedure.

The incredible, unacceptable fact is that the Spanish attack reduced powerful cultures to ashes. In the Nahuatl language, still spoken today by over a million Aztec descendants, the word for truth is *neltilztli*, derived from "foundation," and if we look carefully we see that what the conquistadors sought to annihilate were historical foundations. The Spaniards deliberately eliminated the paintings prepared by the *tlamatinime*, or wise men, on astronomy, history, religion, and literature. In the *calméac*, or higher-education centers, the so-called codices were chanted: "They were taught to speak well, they were taught the canticles." Another poem reflects this idea.

> I sing the paintings in the book,
> I unfold it,
> I'm like a florid parrot,
> I make the codices speak,
> Inside the house of paintings.

In Nahuatl literature, poetry was called *cuícatl*—meaning "song" or "hymn"—while prose was called *tlahtolli*, or "language." An important Aztec tradition was *itoloca*, best translated as "what is said about someone or something." According to Diego Durán, a sixteenth-century Dominican friar, the Aztecs documented all "their memorable deeds, their wars and victories . . . they had everything written . . . with accounts of years, months, and days when the events took place." Their writing was an autonomously created system based on glyphs or pictograms that could represent ideas such as *Teotl*, or God. There were three categories of writing: numbers, dates, and everything else. Codices were called *amaxtli*. Paper, *amatl*, was made from the bark of the *amacuahuitl*, or fig tree, though texts have been found on deerskin (or parchment) reproducing drawings. These were prepared by scribes, or *tlacuilos*, and kept in depositories called *amoxcalli*. Bernal Díaz del Castillo notes: "We found the houses of idols and sacrifices . . . and many books made of their paper, which we seized by fraud." Most of these codices disappeared.

The Spaniards built the new Mexico City on top of Tenochtitlán. The monks ordered the temples buried or destroyed, and the Spaniards exiled the natives from their own city, consigning them to miserable huts on the outskirts. Meanwhile, the wealth obtained from the conquest over the next two centuries allowed the construction of a great city that incorpored the most opulent baroque architecture, synthesizing the European ideal of the Catholic Counter-Reformation. Churches took the place of Aztec temples, monasteries took the place of the houses of wisdom, and mansions displaced the ancient palaces. In 1604, the Spanish poet Bernardo de Balbuena could sing "of famous Mexico the seat / origin and grandeur of buildings / horses, streets, manners, compliments, / letters, virtues."

The ancient Aztec buildings were abandoned and left to be plundered, but the literary tradition acquired new dimensions when a nostalgic literature arose that attempted the rewriting of lost texts. It's worth noting that most of the Aztec codices that have survived, and which allow us to reconstruct their past, are of colonial origin. Between 1524 and 1530, the learned used the Latin alphabet to write down the most remote chronologies, like the Tlatelolco Annals transported to the National Library in Paris.

A census of the codices of this culture would indicate that pillage and destruction could not keep writings of great importance from being preserved. Among the most outstanding are the Cocatzin Codex, which recounts the events that took place between 1439 and 1572 involving the *tenochas* and *tlatelocas*; the Durán Codex, which narrates the history of the *mexicas*, or Aztecs, from their departure from

Aztlán until the fall of Tenochtitlán; the Magliabecchiano Codex, in the Central National Library of Florence; the Matritensen Codices, written by the indigenous collaborators of Sahagún; the Mendocino Codex, produced around 1541 or 1542 and kept in the Bodleian Library of Oxford University; the Mexicanus Codex, in Paris; the Osuna Codex, which recounts the suffering of the Indians; the Tlotzin Map, which tells the story of the *acolhuas* from their earliest days until the reign of Nezahualpilli; and the Tudela Codex, in Madrid's Museo de América. The list is not very long, but the irony is that the most important codices are now housed in Europe.

The fate of Aztec art was and continues to be tragic. Gold objects were either melted down or turned into trophies for European collectors. The headdress of the emperor Moctezuma Xocoyotizin (1466–1520), made by the *amantecas*, or feather artisans, of quetzal feathers set in gold and precious stones, endured several indignities until it reached the place where it is today: the Museum of Ethnology in Vienna. The government of Mexico has made hundreds of requests to have it repatriated, with no luck.

The first bishop of Mexico, Juan de Zumárraga, was born in 1468 in the Basque town of Durango in Spain. One of his first tasks as a Franciscan monk was to review the most famous cases of witchcraft in his region, and he became well-versed in exorcism. A friend's recommendation brought him into Emperor Charles V's circle, and on December 20, 1527, Charles decreed that Zumárraga should be sent to Mexico. In 1530, in Texcoco, Zumárraga made a bonfire of all the writings and idols of the Aztecs. His act of destruction had enormous repercussions: all witnesses understood that his intention was to erase the past and open the way for a new era. Juan Bautista Pomar recounts that among the greatest losses were Mayan paintings "in which they had their histories, because at the time the Marquis del Valle

[Hernándo Cortez] first entered Texcoco, they were burned in the royal houses of Nezahualpiltzintli, in a large depositary which was the general archive of their papers."

The passionate Mexican patriot Servando Teresa de Mier wrote: "The first bishop of Mexico concluded that all the symbolic manuscripts of the Indians were magic figures, charms, and demons, and he made it a religious obligation to exterminate them himself and by means of the missionaries, throwing into the flames all the libraries of the Aztecs. Just the one in Texcoco, which was their Athens, contained a mountain of books when Zumárraga gave the order to burn them." Catholic tradition has tried to salvage the image of this ecclesiastic. Today, it is a commonplace in all histories of printing to attribute to him the introduction of printing into Mexico, because in 1533 he brought over the first experts in that art from Spain. Another paradox: Zumárraga was the creator of the first public library. At his request, Juan Cromberger opened a branch of his printing house in Mexico, and to that end sent Giovanni Paoli, a native of Brescia, Italy, who began his labors in 1539 by publishing the *Breve y más compendiosa doctrina christiana en lengua mexicana y castellana* ("The Brief and Most Compendious Christian Doctrine in Mexican and Castilian"), the first book published in the New World. Ironically, no copy of the first edition survives. When Zumárraga died in 1548, the faithful wept.

The Maya dominated the vast area that covers the modern-day Mexican states of Yucatán, Quintana Roo, Campeche, Chiapas, and Tabasco as well as the Central American countries of Guatemala, El Salvador, Honduras, and Belize. Their writing system consisted of glyphs, and they had two calendars: a solar calendar of 365 days and a ritual calendar of 260 days. They calculated that the cycle of Venus was 584 days, and their art, at least during their classical period, achieved perfection in jade carving. When the Spaniards arrived in the sixteenth century, the Maya were already in decline, but this did not keep the conquerors from destroying their art and burning their writing. What remains of Palenque, Yaxchilán, Tikal, and Copán we know because the wise men who remained were zealous in their preservation through oral recitation of the lost texts.

Diego de Landa continued Zumárraga's policies with the Maya. He too was a Franciscan, and had been educated in the monastery of San Juan de Los Reyes in Toledo, where he learned of another celebrated student, Cardinal Francisco Jiménez de Cisneros, who had burned all the Islamic manuscripts in Spain. It would seem that both absorbed a radical form of theology, because their actions were equally drastic. Landa spent months revising Mayan writing and left a treatise describing his philological experience. He did so not out of historical interest but in order to understand the personality of the Indians better and thus have more success at indoctrinating them. In 1562, in Maní, in the Yucatán, he burned 5,000 idols and twenty-seven codices of the ancients.

Father José de Acosta described that event in his *Natural and Moral History of the Indies.* Since his text is rarely cited, we should remember it:

> In the province of Yucatán . . . there were books of pages bound in their style or folded, in which the wise Indians had the distribution of their seasons and their knowledge of plants and animals and other natural things, and their ancient past; a thing of great curiosity and great care. It seemed to one missionary that all that had to be charms and magic art, and demanded they be burned. So those books were burned, which was regretted not only by the Indians but also by curious Spaniards, who wanted to know the secrets of that land. The same thing has happened in other cases, since Spaniards thought that everything is

superstition. We've lost many memories of ancient and secret things, that could have been of great utility. This derives from a foolish zeal, which without knowing or even wanting to know the things of the Indians simply say that they're all magic charms.

This action ended in a conflict that caused the death of hundreds of Indians. Landa is considered personally responsible for the torture of more than 4,000 Indians. An investigation manipulated by Landa exonerated him, and he was later named second bishop of Yucatán. The chronicles have exalted and vindicated him as author of one of the greatest studies of the Maya, *Yucatán Before and After the Conquest* (1566). This of course is not surprising, but a reader might justifiably be astonished at the condemnation of these same events by the notorious inquisitor Torquemada, who burned hundreds of books in Spain.

The monks also prohibited Mayan theatrical performances. For example, in Chichén Itzá, at the temple of Kukulcán, there were two theaters opposite the northern stairway, with their own stairways and beautifully worked tiles. Landa himself described the performances he managed to see:

The Indians have very charming, principally farcical theatricals they put on with much style . . . they have small cymbals they play with their hands and another made of hollow wood, of heavy and sad sound; that one they play with a stick capped with sap from a certain tree; and they have long, thin trumpets of hollow wood, and also some long, twisted calabashes; and they have another instrument made from a turtle, with its shells but with the flesh removed; they beat it with the palm of their hands, and it is a lugubrious, sad sound. They have whistles made of deer bones and big conch shells and flutes made from bamboo;

and with those instruments they accompany the dancers, and they have two dances anyone would like to see.

Just three pre-Hispanic Mayan codices survived that fury. One of them is the Dresden Codex, in the state archives of the Landesbibliothek of Dresden. The second is the Peresianus Codex, in the Bibliothèque Nationale in Paris. The third is the Madrid Codex preserved in Madrid's Museo de América. None are in Mexico. Over the past few years, there has been a debate about a fourth codex, the Grolier, but there are many doubts about its authenticity. Aside from these documents, the Maya wrote down their vision during the colonial period in texts that they attempted to keep secret. This we see in the case of the *Popol vuh*, the books of the people, where their cosmological and religious ideas were condensed. In a confession that recalls Ray Bradbury's novel *Farenheit 451*, the historian Francisco Ximénez wrote that the *Popul vuh* "was conserved among them in such secrecy that there was no memory of it among the ancient ministers of such matters, and when I inquired about this point, in the church of Santo Tomás Chichicastenango, I found that it was the doctrine they absorbed as babies that all of them had memorized it, and I discovered that those books resembled one another." Without the zeal for total secrecy the Indians maintained about their traditions, it's likely that none would have survived until today.

Book Destruction by Native Americans

The Indians also destroyed numerous works. For example, Itzcóatl (1427–1440), the fourth king of the Aztecs, ordered the past erased, so many texts were burned. A chronicle of the event states that the king gathered his advisers to resolve an acute crisis and was given this advice: "Burn the texts. It is not convenient that the world know the black ink, the colors." Some experts doubt this was an isolated event. A case in point is that recounted by Diego Durán, in his *History of the Indies of New Spain*.

An old Indian told me that passing through Ocuituco he'd left there a large book, four fingers thick, with certain characters thereon, and I, moved by a desire to have that book, went to Ocuituco and asked the Indians with all the humility in the world to show it to me. They swore that six years before they'd burned it because they could not read the writing, saying it was not like ours, and that fearing it might cause them some harm, they burned it. This grieved me, because perhaps it would have satisfied our doubt that it might be the holy gospel in Hebrew. I severely reproached those who ordered the book burned.

Chimalpahin Cuauhtlehuanitzin mentions one of the books of his Eighth Account, destroyed because it had been left on a terrace, where it rotted.

Chapter 14

The Renaissance

The alchemist, astrologer, and poet Enrique de Villena was born around 1384 and died in 1434. Like so many bastards, he descended from royalty, or so he claimed: he was the illegitimate grandson of Enrique II of Castile. He was a mythographer, wrote a notorious book on the evil eye, and published a treatise on the art of using a knife at table, in which he explained proper posture and positioning while dining.

Villena was the first to translate all of Virgil's *Aeneid* into a vernacular language, and he also made the first translation of Dante's *Divine Comedy*. The *Arte de trovar*, published around 1420, a history of the Castilian language and of the poetic techniques of the troubadours, is attributed to him. He wrote a letter about esoteric love, the *Epístola a Suero de Quiñones* (1428). However, his prestige did not protect him from misfortune in his later years. The church incessantly persecuted him, and, in 1414, caused him to lose the right to be in the Order of Calatrava.

On the very day of his death, his books were confiscated after being examined by the Dominican Lope de Barrientos, tutor to Prince Henry. Many were destroyed because of their pagan topics.

The Disappearance of Matthew Corvinus's Library

Suleiman I, known as the Magnificent, reached Mohács, Hungary, with his Turkish army on August 29, 1526. Soon after, his troops faced the Hungarians under King Louis II (1506–1526), an expert on hawking and herbal medicine. In a few hours, 20,000 European soldiers were dead, among them the Hungarian king. The carnage wrought by the Turks culminated in the slaughter and torture of 2,000 prisoners. Thus was avenged the Turkish defeat in 1456 at Nándorfehérvár (Belgrade), where János Hunyadi had humiliated the Ottomans and, for a few years, halted their expansion.

Suleiman followed the Danube and marched on the city of Buda. Villages along the way were mercilessly sacked, despite the monarch's good intentions. According to his diary, in Buda he encountered a submissive populace, but he could not prevent a terrible fire that devastated the city. Years before, he'd toured the palace of Matthew Hunyadi (1443–1490), called Corvinus, king of Hungary between 1458 and 1490. While there, Suleiman had been astounded by the gigantic library, founded in 1476.

At the time, the Corvinus Library was one of the most important in the world, second only to the Vatican's. It contained many notable illuminated manuscripts and texts in Greek, Latin, and Hebrew. At least four assistants worked copying books on geography, medicine, and architecture. According to some sources, there were between two and three thousand volumes in the library.

Suleiman confiscated the library and shipped it down the Danube. That was the last time the collection was complete. Today, we know of 216 Corvinus books, either copies of books in the library or originals from the collection. Some 53 are still in Hungarian libraries; 39 are in the Austrian National Library. The rest are scattered over France, Germany, England, Turkey, and the United States.

Savonarola

A few names in history will forever be associated with the worst excesses of biblioclasty. One name on that list is that of an Italian Dominican friar named Girolamo Savonarola. In August 1490, Savonarola began his sermons with a new interpretation of the apocalypse; after seven years, his followers looked for sources of evil in their immediate neighborhood. On February 7, 1497, Savonarola replaced the Carnival of Florence with a feast of penitence. At Florence's Piazza della Signoria they built a great pyramid (a "bonfire of the vanities") into which were thrown cosmetics, statuettes of nude women, jewels, musical instruments, and "dirty" books by writers such as Dante, while astonished artists like Botticelli watched their "heathen" works go up in smoke.

One year later, in the same square where the Dominican had destroyed so many books and works of art, the church tortured Savonarola and burnt his body, along with all his writings.

The Library of Pico della Mirandola

Ironically enough, it was at the invitation of a singularly bookish man that Savonarola had come to Florence: Giovanni Pico della Mirandola (1463–1494), one of the strangest notables of the Renaissance. A precocious reader and linguist, possessed of a phenomenal memory, he studied theology in Paris. Back in Italy, Lorenzo de' Medici saved him from being sent to jail because of his amorous adventures, but Pico della Mirandola was already a marked man: in December 1486, when he was barely twenty-three, he sent out a circular inviting the major theologians of Rome to argue 900 theses on topics that included "Dialectical, moral, physical, mathematical, theological, magical, and cabalistic propositions related to Chaldean, Arab, Hebrew, Greek, Egyptian, and Latin wisdom." In March 1487, a commission convened by Pope Innocent VIII rejected his propositions and labeled them alien to the true spirit of the church. Pico was condemned as a heretic.

Pico della Mirandola defended himself in *Apologia* (1487), but he could not stop the church's attack. He wrote other books—a commentary on Genesis, an attempt to reconcile the epistemology of Plato with that of Aristotle, and *Disputationes Adversus Astrologiam Divinatricem*, a condemnation of astrology, published in 1496, two years after his death.

Pico's sudden death at the age of thirty-one has long been a historical mystery, and the 2008 exhumation of his remains led scientists to conclude he had died of arsenic poisoning—perhaps at the hands of the Medici, who may have had enough of his meddling in affairs of state.

Pico Della Mirandola's wealth had allowed him to accumulate an immense library of over 1,000 volumes on magic, philosophy, the kabbalah, history, and mathematics in Latin, Greek, Hebrew, Chaldean, and Arabic. Each of these books contained manuscript notes by its extravagant owner, who was never a passive reader. Two years after Pico's death, Cardinal Domenico Grimani bought the books. The Venetian wanted to have in his hands the works of Homer, Plato, Euclid, Aristotle, Sextus Empiricus, Averroës, Raymond Lull, and Leonardo de Pisa. In 1523, on his deathbed, the cardinal bequeathed the books to the monastery of Saint Anthony in Venice. There they remained until 1687, when a fire reduced them to ashes.

Steganography

Johannes Tritheim (1462–1516), formerly Johannes Heidenberg, is one of the most complex figures in the history of European culture. He was, insofar as we can judge, a member of a secret society, the Celtic Brotherhood, which

studied astrology, magic, kabbalah, mathematics, and literature. A will to survive, stimulated by his poverty, drew him
to religion, and he became abbot of Sponheim, in western
Germany. There, he created a monastic library. Years later,
he was abbot of Saint-Jacques in Warburg, where he died.

His writings reveal his interest in magic and history, but
what interests us here is his study of the kabbalah, summarized in the eight volumes of his *Steganography*, a manuscript
dictated in the aftermath of a dream. The work describes
methods of secret writing, telepathy, and telekinesis. King
Philip II of Spain, following the advice of counselors who
did not know the work, had it burned out of fear its content
might become known. After 1609, the work figured on the
indexes of forbidden books published by the church and
was regularly burned. Even today, it is extremely difficult
to find a copy.

The Heretic Michael Servetus

At twelve noon on October 27, 1553, a procession of magistrates and clergy brought a prisoner to the Champel field in
Geneva. On his head was a traditional green cap with drops
of sulfur; his clothing was filthy and torn from beatings. At
his feet, someone placed a copy of his book *Christianismi
Restitutio* (The Restoration of Christianity), rejected by
both orthodox Catholics and reformers.

The heretic was Michael Servetus, a proud Spaniard who
had annoyed Catholic authorities in the past. Through his
theological defense of a Christocentric Catholicism, he
also aroused the wrath of the reformers. He was arrested
on August 13, and his trial lasted until October 26, when
he was sentenced to death by the syndics of Geneva. The
wood had already been piled up—dampened, to prolong
the act. A manuscript and a "thick octavo printed book"

were tied around his waist. Farel, one of John Calvin's ministers, said a few words to the assembled officials, and for a moment his speech mixed with the victim's screams. Two hours later, the ashes and burned remains were tossed into the nearby lake. Not content with this, an ecclesiastical tribunal made up exclusively of Servetus's former friends declared on December 23 in Vienna: "We decree that each and every one of the books composed by the so-called Villeneuve, besides those already burned, be consigned to the flames."

Servetus was a well-known polymath: a geographer, mathematician, philosopher, expert on Greek and Latin classics, grammarian, theologian, and astronomer. Though the facts of his life remain hard to discern, we know he was born in 1511, in Aragon. In 1528, he moved to Toulouse to study law. He admired Erasmus of Rotterdam and sought him out, but instead found the reformer Johannes Oecolampadius in Basel, in whose house he lived for ten months. In 1531, he published *De Trinitatis Erroribus*, wherein he violently attacked the idea of the Holy Trinity.

Naturally he provoked Oecolampadius, Zwingli, and others. Even so, he persisted in his ideas and in 1532 published *Dialogorum de Trinitate*. The translation of this book into the vulgate caused the Council of the Inquisition to put him on trial, and he fled to Lyon. With his friend and colleague Andreas Vesalius, he studied anatomy. In his astronomy classes, he correctly predicted that on February 13, 1538, Mars would be eclipsed by the moon. A skilled swordsman, he fought a duel in France, leaving his adversary badly wounded.

Saddled with debts and hounded for his religious beliefs, Servetus practiced medicine in Vienne, near Lyon. In 1545, he brought out an edition of the Bible in seven illustrated volumes. In 1552, Servetus finished the work he considered his great legacy, *Christianismi Restitutio*. Among other things, it included a precise description of the circulation of the blood and postulated pan-Christism. Servetus tried to have the book published in Basel, but printers there were too fearful. Even so, convinced of the value of his text, he persisted, and arranged to have the book printed secretly. On January 3, 1553, 800 copies were released to the world; its author went unheralded, although the last page contained the initials M.S.V.

Despite Servetus's precautions, the inquisitors set about finding almost every copy of the book, which they destroyed. Today there remain only three copies, one somewhat charred. It was not reprinted until 1790, in Nuremberg.

The Anabaptists of Münster

During the years of Luther's reform movement, the Anabaptists chose a radical path to Christian salvation. Because of the persecution directed against them, we have very few documents relevant to their origin in Zurich, but we do know their extreme propositions. They believed in the separation of church and state; they rejected the baptism of children and baptism as a means of salvation for adults; they believed in freedom of conscience; they rejected industrial labor and the paying of taxes; and they held the Bible to be literally true. Like many today, they believed in the imminent end of the world. Anabaptist prophets tried to convince the people to expiate their sins and redeem themselves.

Their great opportunity came in 1534, with the fall of the city of Münster, in Westphalia. Led initially by Jakob Hutter and, after his death, by Jan Matthys, they created a community based on their religious beliefs. On the day they finally took the city—which was the seat of a bishopric—they burned and destroyed the books in the library, especially theological works: "The Anabaptists boasted of their innocence of book-learning and declared that it was the unlearned who had been chosen by God to redeem the world." Private book collections were piled onto a public bonfire that burned an entire night. The intention of the leaders was clear: to abolish the past and give the Anabaptists absolute control over the interpretation of the Bible. Matthys anounced that he was God's chosen. Accordingly, he faced the forces of the attacking bishop of Münster with only thirty followers. The "battle" refuted his divinity, and he died a horrible death.

The first German edition of a 1559 book by the Anabaptist heretic David Joris, a fascinating character who publicly preached the most controversial theses against the Roman Catholic Church, was prohibited in Holland. Copies were confiscated and burned. Shortly thereafter, Joris took up residence in the city of Basel and adopted the name Jan van Brugge, which allowed him to die in peace. A chance discovery by a commission from the University of Basel revealed his true identity, and the church ordered his remains exhumed and burned publicly, along with all his books and all pamphlets related to him, on May 13, 1559.

The Forbidden Book of Nostradamus

The physician Michel de Notredame (1503–1566), better-known as Nostradamus, is the most celebrated prophet in the Western world. We know little about his life. His most important work—one cited more with each year that passes—is the *Centuries*, a book of 100 verses, first published in 1555 in Lyon by Macé Bonhomme. Its original title was *Les Prophéties* ("The Prophecies"); it consisted of the first three "centuries" and fifty-three verses for the fourth.

This first edition is a rarity because the book was systematically destroyed. In the nineteenth century there was a copy in the Bibliothèque de la Ville de Paris, but the destruction of the building obliterated it. There was another copy in the Mazarine Library, but it was sold for 12,310 francs to the Hôtel Drouot on June 17, 1931. There are two copies known to exist today: one in the Vienna Library, the other in the Rochegude Library in the Tarn region. There were, however, numerous reprintings of the first edition.

Pinelli's Library

One of the greatest book collections of all times was that of Gian Vincenzo Pinelli (1535–1601). His prestige stimulated other humanists of the period to ask him for copies of his prize books, and some, like Scaliger, got them. According to one historian, the collection was sent to Naples on three ships, but when they were between Venice and Ancona, Turkish pirates, thinking the ships carried gold or precious stones, captured them, sinking at least one ship with thirty-three boxes of ancient books, including the original of an Arabic manuscript by Leo Africanus, aboard.

The heirs stored the rest of the books in an attic and then sold the lot to Cardinal Federico Borromeo, who was consolidating the Ambrosian Library in 1609, though some manuscripts found their way to the Vatican Library and the Bibliothèque Nationale in Paris.

The Holy Office and the Censoring of Books

The Inquisition was of course one of the most severe religious institutions ever created to fight dissidence and heterodoxy. It oversaw and made possible a terrible period of censorship, persecution, torture, and destruction, both of human lives and books, that coexisted alongside the immense intellectual richness of the Renaissance.

Dogma requires protective mechanisms and intimidation, and in that sense the Inquisition faithfully served the political consolidation of the Roman Catholic Church. Myriad religious movements had sprung up in Europe at the moment when the power and authority of the church became established. The church therefore found it necessary to dissuade people from straying by excommunication, torture, pitiless ordeals ("proof of God"), immolation, and attacks on entire populations. These techniques gradually became institutionalized, especially after the Reformation was inaugurated by Martin Luther, the most dangerous challenge to official Catholicism.

In 1520, Pope Leo X excommunicated Martin Luther and publicly prohibited the dissemination, reading, or quotation of any of his writings. In the streets, the general populace burned his books and his effigy. Luther, in turn, burned Leo's bull in a bonfire. The emperor, Charles V, concerned about the spread of Luther's doctrine, ordered all his books destroyed. The failure of that measure had consequences: on October 14, 1529, publishing any book not authorized by a clerical body was forbidden. Later, the emperor reiterated his order and in another ordinance sentenced to death all authors and publishers of heretical books.

What alarmed the Roman Catholic Church was not Protestantism's teachings but its success. In 1542, Pope Paul III created the Sacred Congregation of the Roman Inquisition of the Holy Office. The medieval inquisition was ruthless with regard to all heresies that might cause political problems, while the Holy Office focused on theologians and priests, tracking down any suspect idea through a network of spies and mercenaries. Pope Paul IV, a fanatic who suffered enormous emotional problems, ordered the Holy Office to make a list of the books most dangerous to the faith, and in 1559, the fearsome *Index Librorum Prohibiturum*, or Index of Prohibited Books, was first published. Actually, there already existed indexes of this kind—at the Sorbonne (1544, 1547) and the University of Louvaine (1546, 1550) and in Lucca (1545), Sienna (1548), and Venice, where, in 1543, the *Index Generalis Scriptorum Interdictorum* was first published.

The Spanish Inquisition

In Spain, the Inquisition acquired a local flavor. In 1478, King Ferdinand and Queen Isabella petitioned the pope to allow them to create a chapter of the Inquisition in Spanish territory to persecute Arabs and Jews. Those who did not convert were executed. When Philip II became king, he installed a genuine apparatus of Catholic censorship. The Duke of Alba, who put that system into practice, hanged authors and publishers and called into service the deacon of the Faculty of Theology at Louvaine, Arias Montano, to establish an official catalog, which appeared in 1570 under the title *Index Librorum Prohibitorum*. An edict conferred legal status on the catalog and brought about the confiscation and destruction of thousands of works all across Europe.

The Spanish Inquisition was composed of an inquisitor general who led the Supreme Council of the Holy Inquisition, which had seven members, as well as a treasurer, three secretaries, a sergeant, three interviewers, graders, and consultants. In Spain, there were fourteen such tribunals; in Portugal, three; and in the New World another three (in Mexico City, Lima, and Cartagena de Indias).

Audacious thinking meant Luis de León endured two trials: the first, in 1572, for having rejected the Vulgate, the Latin translation of the Bible; the second for translating

Solomon's Song of Songs from the Hebrew. From March 1572 until 1576, Brother Luis was held in one of the Inquisition's jails in Valladolid. Years later, in 1582, he was again involved in an inquisitorial trial, this time for defending the Jesuit Prudencio de Montemayor.

The royal decree of the Regent Juana expressly prohibited the importation of books and obliged printers to request clearance for their work from the Council of Castile. The Index forbade all Bibles in the vernacular. Works by Luther, Calvin, and Zwingli, the Talmud, the Koran, and books about divination, superstition, sexuality, or necromancy were likewise not allowed to circulate.

The Inquisition in the New World

From the moment of their arrival in the New World, the Spaniards' greatest concern was religion. Their monarchs ceded huge powers to the church in order to indoctrinate Native Americans. As for the Spanish populace in the New World, the Holy Office thought it essential to establish three centers of power in the newly conquered lands.

The Inquisiton in Lima, like that in Mexico City, was created by royal decree in 1569, and organized twenty-seven autos-da-fé. The first was on November 15, 1573, when a man named Mateo Salado was burned at the stake for being a Lutheran. Heretics were burned at El Pedregal, near Cerro San Cristóbal. By the nineteenth century, a change in attitude resulted in a gradual reduction in the number of inquisitorial trials, and in 1813 the court of Cádiz suspended them.

In Mexico, between 1522 and 1532, sanctioned by papal bulls, monks assumed the role of inquisitors. The Indians, castigated during the early phase of the conquest for their religious practices, were no longer covered by inquisitorial trials after 1571.

The inquisitors busied themselves with port inspections, looking for books listed on the indexes—Bibles in the vernacular, chivalric novels, and compromising scientific or political works. Publishing houses were constantly examined, booksellers could sell nothing until their stock had been registered, and private libraries were subjected to exhaustive examinations. The Second Provincial Council of 1565 restricted the circulation of Bibles and forbade Indians from possessing them. The Third Provincial Council of 1565 threatened anyone possessing forbidden books with excommunication.

Chapter 15

England

One of the earliest defenders of books against their destruction was Richard de Bury (1281–1345), also known as Richard Aungerville, author of the *Philobiblon*. He owned one of the largest libraries of his era, and an essay survives by him consisting of a series of personal reflections intended as rules for the library of Durham College, Oxford. De Bury wrote that wars are the principal destroyers of books. He defended books as repositories of wisdom and said that taking care of them is a way of serving God, and he apparently believed that only a person possessed by hatred of wisdom could destroy books. The first edition of his book appeared in Cologne in 1473 and Paris in 1500. It came out in England between 1598 and 1599.

The Crimes of Orthodoxy

Despite a few enlightened voices such as de Bury's, almost as soon as books began to circulate in the land of Shakespeare, they were tracked down and destroyed. In the 1520s, about 6,000 copies of the New Testament, translated by William Tyndale and smuggled into England, disappeared when a group of priests, scandalized by the appearance of scripture in a vernacular tongue, burned every one.

The purge of books perpetrated by Henry VIII in England between 1536 and 1540 was religious in nature. In 1550, minions of Edward VI burned and stole the books in the Oxford library: "The works of scholars such as Peter Lombard, Thomas Aquinas, Duns Scotus and . . . papist scholia were expelled from all the libraries of the university and private studies." During the time of Elizabeth I, Thomas Bodley restored the lost fame of that library, which over time became so closely linked to him that we know it today as the Bodleian Library.

John Dee's Secret Library

One of Elizabeth's favorites was the astrologer, mathematician, spy, magus, and writer John Dee, born in England in 1527. Dee was irascible, impulsive, and sharp and lost no opportunity to curry the favor of royalty. He convinced both Mary Tudor and Elizabeth I that he had supernatural powers. Elizabeth never left her palace without reviewing the indecipherable horoscope he contrived for her.

A devotee of Abbot Tritheim's *Steganography*, Dee traveled throughout Europe and studied the most arcane alchemical lore. In 1581, he met Edward Kelley (1555–1597), a fraud also known as Edward Talbot, and impressed him when he demonstrated his abilities for speaking with the dead. Kelley spread the rumor that he and Dee could transform lead into gold, and both were received in royal courts. The partners remained on good terms for years, but one day Dee heard Kelley say he'd had a dream in which a superior being told him that Dee should share his wife with his friend. Dee's philanthropic good nature abruptly soured. When Dee abandoned Kelley, he wasn't sure if Kelley had in fact seduced his wife, but he did learn that he'd been severely discredited because of Kelley's lies.

Elizabeth I admired Dee and not only pardoned him but also entrusted him with missions not even her closest advisers knew about. Among other things, Dee brought to England Mercator's first globes, contributed to the first translation of Euclid's *Elements*, and wrote a mysterious book called *The Hieroglyphic Monad*. But while he was traveling, his house in Mortlake was attacked by a superstitious mob, and when he returned in 1589, he discovered that his library, one of the most complete with regard to esoteric texts, had been pillaged.

There are several theories about the size of that library, which included mathematical instruments—a quadrant made by Richard Chancellor, Mercator globes, compasses, a clock made by Dibbley, magnets, and maps. The most widely accepted estimate states: "Based on the principal sources, particularly the catalogue of 1583, we know that Dee's shelves held between three and four thousand titles and included virtually all aspects of classical, medieval, and renaissance learning." While most of his books disappeared, stray volumes materialized in various English libraries. It is thought that many of Dee's books burned, along with the rest of the city of London, in 1666.

The Censor Censored

William Prynne, a famous English theologian and radical legislator, savagely attacked the bawdiness of actors, and more than once invited his friends to condemn the excesses of theatrical works. In 1633, he published *Histriomastix: The Player's Scourge, or Actor's Tragedy*, in which he formalized his denunciations. As it happened, he was unlucky, because an innocent work of his in the pastoral mode, authorized and highly thought of by some clerics, provoked the inexplicable rage of the court. Lord Cottington refused to explain what repelled him about the work, but he advised the queen to publicly burn all copies. Thus the censor was the victim of his own ideas. He was jailed and beaten, and even had his ears chopped off. Nevertheless, he had the courage to defend himself in a pamphlet called *A New Discovery of the Prelates' Tyranny* (1641), which caused some of the charges against him to be annulled.

English Religious Struggles

During the sixteenth century, hundreds of thousands of manuscripts disappeared in England. A short text with a long title, *The Discovery of a Gaping Gulf Where into England Is Likely to Be Swallowed by Another French Marriage* (1579) was burned in the kitchen of Stationer's Hall. Its author, John Stubbs, lost his right hand for opposing the marriage between Queen Elizabeth and the Duke of Anjou. Stubbs maintained his loyalty to the crown and proved it before witnesses when, immediately after the amputation, he removed his hat with his left hand as he shouted, "God save the Queen!"—and then fainted.

On June 27, 1659, the brief treatise *Iconoclasta*, an attack by John Milton on religious hypocrisy, was burned; a year later another book of his, *Pro Populo Anglicano Defensio* (1652), was also destroyed.

Puritans, themselves persecuted, had little tolerance for others. In 1664, Benjamin Keach, a Baptist pastor, published 500 copies of *The Child Instructor*. It was an innocent manual devoid of theology that alarmed the dour Thomas Disney, who ordered the author pilloried at Aylesbury, "with a sign on his head saying: For writing, printing, and publishing a schismatic book." Disney also burned the entire edition. In some measure, he need not have bothered, for in two years the entire city of London went up in flames.

The Great London Fire

The mysterious London fire of 1666 devastated about a quarter of the city. More than 13,000 houses and about ninety churches were reduced to ashes. The number of fatalities was not huge, but thousands of books were destroyed.

One was the *Ars Signorum, Vulgo Character Universalis et Lingua Philosophica* (1661) by George Dalgarno, though a later account asserts that it was John Wilkins (1614–1672) who burned the work, taking advantage of the fire to avoid accusations of plagiarism. Whatever the truth may be, the first version of Wilkins's *Essay Towards a Real Character, and a Philosophical Language* burned in 1666, obliging its author to rewrite his project to construct a universally understandable language.

In 1683, some Oxford scholars, unhappy with Thomas Hobbes's ideas about the state, condemned two of his books: *De Cive* and *Leviathan*. *Leviathan* was dedicated to the principle that religion should be a means for maintaining peace. It was said it deserved to be burned. Some fanatics in fact did burn it in a small public bonfire.

Prudes in power sought to eliminate the entire edition of John Cleland's 1748 novel *Memoirs of a Woman of Pleasure*, the sexual experiences of Fanny Hill, an English prostitute. At the time, Cleland was in debtors' prison. Often considered the English languages' first erotic novel—that is, a book written expressly to titillate the reader—the work was prohibited the very year it was published. As late as the 1960s, moral action groups burned copies both in England and Japan.

Self-censorship

Self-censorship abounded as well: John Donne wrote *Biathanatos* to study suicide, though he was not entirely sure of its worth. Jorge Luis Borges observes that Donne left the manuscript to Sir Robert Carr with no injunction other than that he should either have it published or burn it. Donne died in 1631; it was not until 1644 that it appeared in print, when Donne's eldest son printed the old manuscript "to defend it from fire."

John Flamsteed

John Flamsteed, the royal astronomer at Greenwich, was moved to destroy his own work because of the machinations of one of the most brilliant scientists of the Enlightenment, Sir Isaac Newton. Newton, also notorious for his efforts to blackball Leibniz, his rival for the discovery of calculus, first rejected Flamsteed's work and then appropriated his ideas about the stars. In 1712, without Flamsteed's permission and without crediting him, Newton and Edmond Halley arranged for publication of Flamsteed's unfinished *Historia Coelestis Britannica*. The coronation of a new king gave Flamsteed the opportunity to petition for the confiscation of 300 copies of his own book, and it was burned. Only after his death was Flamsteed's *Historia* published, in 1725. Newton took revenge by removing all references to Flamsteed from his principal work, *Philosophiae Naturalis Principia Mathematica*.

Newton himself suffered the destruction of his work: his dog knocked over a candle and his papers caught fire. Among other losses were his manuscripts on optics and religion.

Certain of his fame and uncomfortable with the possibility that some of his badly written manuscripts might be read after his death, Adam Smith, author of *The Wealth of Nations* (1776), had numerous texts destroyed, among which must have been those related to rhetoric—probably his readings in Edinburgh and his lectures on natural theology and jurisprudence given in Glasgow.

Out of shame, Isaac D'Israeli burned his pamphlet *A Defence of Poetry* (1790), though a few copies survived. A forgotten poet, Robert Tannahill, author of *The Soldier's Return: A Scottish Interlude in Two Acts, with Other Poems and Songs* (1807) and *Poems and Songs* (1815), burned almost all his papers because no one would publish him after his first book appeared in 1807.

James Thomson, author of *The City of Dreadful Night* (1880), describes in his diary the sorrow he felt when he burned his manuscripts: "I've burned all my old papers, manuscripts, and letters, except the manuscript of the book mostly printed now. It took me five hours to do it, because I was careful not to set the chimney on fire and because I had to watch over the burning. I felt sad and stupid; I barely leafed through the papers: if I'd begun to read them I perhaps would not have been capable of burning them." After his death in 1890, the explorer and ethnologist Sir Richard Francis Burton was censored by his own family, in this case his wife. Isabel Burton, also a talented writer, decided to burn her husband's diaries, letters, and private papers, reportedly after receiving express orders to do so from Burton's ghost. Before she did so, she examined the irreverent chapters of *The Scented Garden*, a new translation of *The Perfumed Garden*, an erotic work of Arab origin, in which the sexual faculties are analyzed and remedies offered for impotence and nymphomania. The widow had received two offers for the manuscript: one for 3,000 pounds and later a second for twice that sum. These huge amounts aroused her curiosity. After reading it, she elected to destroy the manuscript despite the amount offered. A friend of the family, Grenville Baker, told a journalist that *The Scented Garden* was a masterpiece, with hundreds of notes, superior to those in *The Perfumed Garden*.

A Defender of the Book

During the nineteenth century, the bibliography on the destruction of libraries and books expanded. In 1880, Cornelius Walford published a small pamphlet on the subject: *The Destruction of Libraries by Fire Considered Practically and Historically*. In his preface, he observes: "The destruction of libraries, be they large or small, public or private, is always an event to be deplored; not only with regard to the intrinsic value of the objects consumed but because, quite often, those treasures cannot be replaced by pecuniary outlay alone, and frequently in no manner." About William Blades, the great initiator of the English tradition of studies on the subject, we know little. He was born in Clapham, London, on December 5, 1824. He grew up amid books and printing devices in the printing house East & Blades, his father's property. Enamored of the typography of William Caxton, he studied hundreds of books composed by that master, the result of which was his first great book, *Life and Typography of William Caxton* (1861). This exhaustive study transformed Blades into a bibliomaniac.

In 1881, he wrote *Enemies of Books*. The relevance of that rare text resides, perhaps, on the fact that it was the first systematic study of book and library destruction. He divides the causes into sections—fire, water, gas, heat, dust, negligence, ignorance, malice, collectors, booksellers, bookworms, insects, children, and servants. When he placed fire at the head of the list he was certainly correct.

He seems to have been fond of paradoxes, as we see in his denunciation of John Bagford, founder of the Antiquarian

Society, for practicing biblioclasty: this obscure personage had the perverse habit of tearing the covers off old books to collect them. He would often toss the book itself into the garbage. Blades died in Sutton (Surrey) on April 27, 1890.

Chapter 16

Revolutions in France, Spain, and Latin America

France was both the cradle of European liberty and the cradle of censorship. In 1657, Pascal's *Provincial Letters*, written to reveal certain moral distractions on the part of the Jesuits, was burned. King Louis XVI would not sanction the content of the letters. Pascal, for his part, had already noted that "men never do evil in such a perfect and acclaimed way as when they do it moved by religious conviction."

Voltaire's *Philosophical Letters* (1734) aroused the ire of the church. The author was arrested and a parliamentary decree authorized the hangman to tear apart and burn the letters because they "inspire the most dangerous licentiousness, dangerous for religion and for the social order." In one of his personal letters to the Count of Rochefort, dated November 2, 1768, Voltaire says with all his irony: "The best thing would be to celebrate a new Saint Bartholomew's Night with all the philosophers and to slit the throat of anyone who has Locke, Montaigne, and Bayle in their libraries. I would like all books burned, except the *Ecclesiastical Gazette* and the *Christian News*." Voltaire expresses the same cynicism in a letter of September 29, 1764, written to a certain Damilaville: "I have thrown this misguided *Portable* [he refers to the *Philosophic Dictionary*] I just bought into the fire along with Pierre's tragedy, and all my papers; I've decided to dedicate the rest of my life to agriculture."

In 1750, the publication of the first volume of the *Encyclopédie* caused such scandal that the authorities suspended the printing of 1759 and confiscated numerous copies, which were later destroyed. The printer himself, Le Breton, destroyed numerous copies.

No sooner did Denis Diderot's *Pensées philosophiques* (1746) appear than it was burned by order of the Paris parliament because, among other things, of its atheism. The book was banned all over France. Montesquieu's *Spirit of the Laws* (1748) was another persecuted book. In 1790, the church included it on its Index of Forbidden Books, and the Spanish crown kept it out of the New World colonies. Copies found on ships were confiscated and destroyed.

Claude-Adrien Helvetius's *De l'esprit* provoked the outrage of the Sorbonne, the Paris parliament, the pope, the bishop of Paris, and all the priests of France: It was publicly burned. The same Paris parliament rejected the theses in Jean-Jacques Rousseau's *Émile*: The book was burned, and Rousseau had to seek asylum in the lands of Frederick the Great of Prussia. Rousseau commented: "Individuals in the parliament said openly that it was useless to burn books and necessary to burn their authors." He added, "They burned my book and condemned me to prison on the 18th, that is, nine days after it happened in Paris." In yet another passage, he notes that the scandal aroused by his *Letters from the Mountain* in 1765 "began the whispering, and my book was burned somewhere or other."

Fear generated violent reactions by monarchs and members of the French nobility. In 1768, the Paris parliament had J.-B. Jossevand, Jean Lécuyer, and Marie Suisse arrested for selling forbidden books by Baron d'Holbach, Voltaire, and Dubois Fontanelle. The books, of course, were burned by order of a bureaucrat named Saint-Fargeau. The intimate scandal caused by *Portefeuille d'un talon rouge*, which recounted the most incredible sexual excesses of Marie Antoinette's circle, was confiscated and burned in April 1783. Two years later, Louis XVI forbade the circulation of Beaumarchais's *Le mariage de Figaro* and jailed the author. The edition was often confiscated and destroyed.

Book Destruction During the French Revolution

The revolution that began in 1789 destroyed the monarchy and the feudal order, but it brought with it riots, looting, murders, and attacks on the property of anyone defined as an enemy of liberty. On October 10, 1792, the National Convention had announced that France would be revolutionary only until peace was established, but of course that took more than ten years. An attempt to assassinate Robespierre brought on the Reign of Terror, which sent thousands to the guillotine. But Saint-Juste remained unsatisfied, demanding the death of Louis XVI, who was executed on January 21, 1793.

During that violence, libraries, too, were attacked. In Paris alone, more than 8,000 books were destroyed; elsewhere, more than 4 million, of which 26,000 were ancient manuscripts. Many books were used to make munitions. A little-known and little-read text by the Jesuit Jean-Joseph Rossignol, *Traité sur l'usure,* was almost wiped out by the fearsome sans-culottes. Fires annihilated thousand of books, and even the *Conciliorum Galliae* (1789) was reduced to ashes. In the archives, a fire eliminated the *Recueil des édits, déclarations, lettres patentes et arrets du conseil enregistré au parlement de Metz* (five volumes, 1774–1788).

The revolutionaries did not respect the *Réflexions édifiantes* (two volumes, 1791) of J. A. Brohon, hardly an orthodox woman. A magnificent edition of *Sancti Gregorii Nazianzeni Opera Omnia* (1788) was interdicted and all copies destroyed. A study of the juridic norms in the French provinces, *Costumes et status de la ville de Bergerac* (1779), simply a translation of a Latin text, was cremated in 1792. On June 19 of the same year, hundreds of books and pamphlets burned at the Place Vendôme, and in 1794, the Abbey of Saint-German-des-Près burned. Little was saved of its 49,387 published works and 7,072 manuscripts.

It was a bad time for books. When wasn't it?

Honoré de Balzac's books were persecuted from the start of the novelist's career, but there are accounts reporting that *Le vicaire des Ardennes* was burned in France in 1822 because of its content. *Monuments de la vie privée des douze césars* (1780) by Pierre François Hugues d'Hancarville was ordered burned, along with its erotic illustrations, by the court of Paris in May 1815 and again in September 1826.

One of the most interesting events in French nineteenth-century politics was the Paris Commune, considered by Karl Marx to be the first great proletarian revolution of the modern age. It included not only workers but writers, artisans, and small-business people. The Commune began on March 18, 1871, and ended ten days later. During the terrible Bloody Week between May 21 and 28, more than 20,000 French citizens died at the hands of the army, while the Communards assassinated the archbishop of Paris and destroyed property.

It was impossible to stop the burning of libraries and books. The Tuileries fire in 1871 destroyed hundreds of books and the building along with them. One of the texts lost, fairly rare, was the *Chronique de la pucelle d'Orléans* (1512). On the night of May 23, scores of manuscripts disappeared in the fire that consumed the Louvre library. The loss of these manuscripts was more than a loss to France; it was a blow to the whole world. To give an idea of the scale of the disaster, consider that the catalog of materials was nine volumes long, the alphabetical catalog twenty-two volumes, the catalog of anonymous texts filled six volumes, and the manuscript catalog was one volume. Numerous manuscripts by the poet Guillaume Colletet were lost, along with his *Vies des poètes français par ordre chronologique, depuis 1200 jusqu'au 1647*, more than 459 biographies. Neither the original nor a legible copy survived.

The manuscript of *Heures de Charlemagne* did not survive, nor did the bull on papyrus of Pope Agapet from the year 951. *Huit herbiers* by Madame de Genlis and Alexandre Lenoir vanished, as did *Documents sur la Picardie*, by M. H. Cocheris. Nicolas-Philibert Hémey d'Auberive's *Bibliotheca Magica* was also lost.

On May 23, the Palais Royal, which housed the Conseil d'État, caught fire and many works were lost. Émile Zola, in a panic, wrote: "The immense fire, the most enormous, the most horrible, the gigantic cube of stone, the two floors of porticos, vomited flames."

Similarly, the fire devastated the archives of the police prefecture and destroyed all copies of the *Rapport général sur les travaux du conseil d'hygiène publique et de salubrité du département de la Seine* (1861) by Adolphe Trébuchet. The Library of Sainte-Geneviève, already attacked by the Prussians, suffered irreparable damage in the geography section when the troops occupied Paris. Volumes of a collection in twelvemo format (a sheet folded to form twelve leaves, or twenty-four pages), the *Histoire des voyages*, were burned as well.

In October 1873, the young poet Arthur Rimbaud went to Brussels to get copies of his recently published book *Une saison en enfer* (fifty-three pages). His publisher, the owner of Jacques Poot et Cie., gave him ten or twenty copies. Rimbaud gave one to the jailer at the prison where his lover Verlaine was held and others to friends and admirers. For years, a legend persisted that he then burned all copies of the edition at his family's home in Charleville, a myth that perpetuated the poet's image as the quintessential rebel. In fact, the rest of the edition remained in the publisher's warehouse until 1901, when a bibliophile stumbled across a "filthy bundle" containing the books and recognized their value.

Friends of authors often destroy their works. We have only to think of Gustave Flaubert. In September 1849, he invited his best friends, Maxime du Camp and Louis Bouilhet, to his house in Croisset, outside of Rouen. He read to them, over the course of four days, his *Temptation of Saint Anthony*, inspired by one of Brueghel's paintings. The verdict of the friends was negative: "You should burn this and never speak of it."

Étienne Gabriel Peignot (1767–1849) was one of the first Frenchmen to produce reliable studies on the subject of book destruction. Perhaps the greatest of these was *Essai historique sur la liberté d'écrire chez les anciens et au moyen age* (1832), extremely interesting because it contains historical information about book destruction, which the author links to attempts to silence the press and publishing throughout the world. Peignot left other writings on the subject: *Dictionnaire critique littéraire et bibliographique des principaux livres condamnés au feu, supprimés ou censurés* (1806) and *De Pierre Aretin* (1836).

Presaging the marvelous fiction of Chilean exile Roberto Bolaño, Charles Nodier noted that it was strange that no one ever thought to write bibliographies of lost books: this absence was as regrettable as the absence of studies on imaginary books and libraries. Two men who were inspired by Nodier's suggestion dedicated their lives to the subject and opened a new path for French bibliophiles: Gustave Brunet and Paul Lacroix.

Brunet (1807–1896), known as Philomneste Junior, was a recognized and prolific French bibliophile who wrote, among other essays, *Essai sur les bibliothèques imaginaires*

(1862) and a monograph on Chapter 7 of the second part of *Gargantua* by François Rabelais: *Catalogue de la bibliothèque de l'abbay de Saint-Victor au seizième siècle* (1862). His volume *Fantasies bibliographiques: Un catalogue de livres singuliers que jamais nul bibliophile ne verra* (1864) and his *Imprimeurs imaginaires et libraires supposés* (1866) are genuine curiosities. He published hundreds of pamphlets about curious works, some of which are practically extinct, and was among the first to catalog destroyed books. He did so in various texts, most notably in *Dictionnaire de bibliographie catholique* (1858) and *Dictionnaire de bibliologie catholique* (1860). He also compiled a surprising text, *Livres perdus et exemplaires uniques* (1872).

Like Brunet, with whom he collaborated, Paul Lacroix (1806–1884) could not resist the temptation to imagine lost libraries and books. He published many classics of French literature and, following the custom of the time, used a pseudonym, Bibliophile Jacob. Among his other books, he compiled a *Catalogue de curiosités bibliographiques, recueillis par le bibliophile voyageur. Dixième année.* (1847). His passion for the bordellos of Paris produced a detailed *Histoire de la prostitution chez tous les peuples du monde* (1851).

In 1880, Lacroix published his *Essai d'une bibliographie des livres français perdus ou peu connus.* He included 115 books and considered the first fifty-two totally lost, either destroyed or untraceable. Lacroix made no attempt to explain why the books were lost but simply addressed the task, not always pleasant, of documenting the problem with the intent of arousing interest in the situation of certain books. His catalog contains some genuinely attractive titles: item 11, for instance, is *Le débat de deux gentilshommes espaignols sur le faict d'amour* (Paris, Jean Longis, 1541, in octavo); item 42 is *Silene insensé, ou l'estrange metamorphose des amans fidèles* (Paris, 1613, in octavo).

The influence of Nodier, Brunet, and Lacroix on Fernand Drujon (b. 1845) is undeniable, and he synthesizes the ambitions of all his precursors. His still unrecognized achievement is simply magnificent. One of his first great volumes on the destruction of books is *Catalogue des ouvrages, écrits et dessins de toute nature poursuivis, supprimés ou condamnés depuis le 21 Octobre 1814 jusqu'au 31 Juillet 1877* (1879). This 430-page catalog, with detailed notes, lists all the books, manuscripts, and publications legally eliminated or proscribed in France over a period of sixty-three years. The book begins with an extensive catalog, then continues with a description of the censored texts. Page 29 offers a list of obscene photographs, themselves interesting examples of early photography.

Some years later, Drujon published *Essai bibliographique sur la destruction volontaire des livres ou bibliolytie* (Paris, 1889). Revising and augmenting this volume led Drujon to produce his best work, *Destructarum Editionum Centuria* (1893), whose objective he states at the outset: "I have proposed to describe a certain number of works whose editions have been destroyed, either totally or in part, by disasters, catastrophes such as fire, shipwreck, revolution." He lists them in alphabetical order and includes historical notes. Silently, Fernand Drujon transformed his tradition, though he had no followers in the twentieth century.

During the twentieth century, other theories about book destruction appeared. The first was that of Jacques Bergier, who suggested that there is a secret society that conspires to eliminate any book that may contribute to "a too rapid and too extensive diffusion of knowledge." This conjecture has been supported by an entire generation of readers accustomed to secret brotherhoods, secret societies, and the spies that populate the novels of John Le Carré. According to Bergier, "for a long time now, there has been a systematic destruction of books or documents about dangerous discoveries either before or at the very moment of their publication." From the books of Thoth to the case of James D. Watson's *Double Helix*, Bergier lists the reasons behind this persecution, which has been going on for centuries. In doing so, he has infected his followers with a more or less intense case of conspiracy paranoia.

It was not until the 1990s that the psychoanalyst Gérard Haddad, author of *Manger le livre* (1984) and *Les biblioclastes* (1993) brought out the first scientific studies on the subject. He sees in the book "the materialization of the symbolic Freudian father cannibalistically devoured." With this premise—a work is the father of a given people—he assumes two positions to explain book destruction. If someone eats a book, he does so to receive its generative gift, its power to engender. If on the other hand someone burns a book, he does so to negate its paternity, reject its function of being a father: "The auto-da-fé acts out in veiled but extreme form the hatred and rejection of the father."

Book hatred, says Haddad, often leads to racism, since racism negates another culture's color, understood as the other culture's act of generation. Also, Haddad deciphers millennial movements, identifying them "with a cult whose central sacrifice will be the holocaust of the book." In Christian millennial thought, notes Haddad, there are diverse modes of rejecting the book, and one consists in the will to erase all traces of the metaphor of the father. Another of his related ideas is that defamation is a tool to annihilate the value of a text.

Independence and Revolution in Spain and Latin America

The wars of independence that finally separated Spain from its New World colonies lasted from 1808 to 1814, when Fernando VII once again became king of Spain after the defeat of Napoleon. The Napoleonic era in Spain was marked by cruelty, vividly depicted by Goya in his etchings on the horrors of war. Napoleon's troops used hundreds of books as munitions paper.

The Abbey of Montserrat contained one of the most extraordinary libraries in Spain, and perhaps in all of Europe, with a complete archive. French troops totally destroyed the abbey to keep it from being used as a fortress: the library and archive were simply burned. A few works were saved because they were on loan at the moment. A good part of the abbey's own publications—it had had a press since 1499—disappeared. The archive of the oldest music school in Europe—the Escolanía de Montserrat—which had supplied important musicians from the sixteenth to the eighteenth century and which housed abundant examples of medieval music, disappeared forever.

The Montserrat episode produced a loss that continues to pain bibliophiles. In 1495, Francesch Vicent published in Catalan a book with one hundred chess problems, *Libre dels jochs partits dels schacs en nombre de 100*. No one knows if the incunabulum was destroyed or simply lost during the looting. Mariano Aguiló Fuster explains: "No copy of this extremely rare book is known, and it is assumed to be totally lost because the only copy ever noted disappeared in the sacking the French carried out at the monastery of Montserrat during the war of independence."

The looting of palaces, libraries, and monasteries became so extreme that José Bonaparte, brother of Napoleon and for a time king of Spain, prohibited his generals from seizing Spanish goods and carrying them off to France. Some of those treasures were returned to Spain, but much remained in France because of the treaty of the Peace of Vienna (1825). Of course, what the French left, the English—including the Duke of Wellington, who fought against the French in Spain—took away.

Around 1868, Spain's continued political decomposition produced a crisis that culminated in the September Revolution, the establishment of a provisional government and, a year later, a constitution. Amid all that confusion, the ambitious Manuel Ruiz Zorilla, minister of public works, published a decree on January 26, 1869, that shows the extent of the deterioration of books in nineteenth-century Spain:

> Documents exist in the Ministry of Public Works that show these and other scandalous facts: for the sum of one thousand reales, several bundles of extremely rich parchments from the Ecclesiastical Libraries and Archives of Aragon were saved from being used for fuel in a factory; the codices Cisneros used for the Polyglot Bible were used to make firecrackers and skyrockets for a fireworks show; an employee of the libraries rescued from a cardboard factory and donated to the state a good part of the papers of the Valencia Inquisition; a silver watch and shotgun were exchanged for a book bought a short time later by the British Museum for forty-five thousand reales; the National Library has spent some thousands in buying manuscripts fraudulently removed from the Libraries of the Military Orders. Finally, a German scholar has published a catalog in which he gives detailed information about bundles of Spanish codices and documents bought abroad. His precision shames all those who love Spain.

> The documents to which this decree refers belong to no person or corporation: They belong to the people, they belong to the Nation, they belong to everyone, because they are national glories or monuments in which the history of our country must be studied and the truth of past events verified. The ministry that emits this decree can only censure, as any enlightened person would, the criminal egoism of religious corporations which have

hidden, by bricking closed a room, rich codices whose discovery is owned to the tireless research of the Academy of History.

For these reasons, exercising the powers allotted to me as member of the Provisional Government and the Ministry of Public Works, I decree:

Article 1. The State, and in its name the Minister of Public Works, will seize all archives, libraries, private collections, and other collections of scientific objects, art, or literature that under whatever name are today under the care of cathedrals, town councils, monasteries, or military orders.

Article 2. This wealth will be considered national patrimony and placed at public service after classification in national libraries, archives, and museums.

Article 3. The libraries of seminaries will remain under the control of the clergy.

Latin America

Latin American emancipation, begun under the influence of the French Revolution and the U.S. Declaration of Independence, was an explosive response to the corruption of the Spanish colonial administration and its abuse of power. By 1825, the entire region, except Cuba and Puerto Rico, had acquired relative independence in the political and economic dimension, but years of constant war produced myriad episodes in which cities, historical monuments, archives, libraries, books, and valuable works of art were destroyed.

In Venezuela, the retreat caused by Simón Bolívar's defeat at La Puerta caused all the books he had accumulated in 1814 for a public library to fall into Spanish hands. Manuel Pérez Vila, a historian, summarizes the consequences: "In March of 1817, the representative of the Holy Office ordered 691 books burned, miscellaneous works that were supposed to be the nucleus of a public library in Caracas, this during a war to the death."

Over the course of the nineteenth century, the losses were extreme, but among many disasters, the loss caused by the sacking of libraries and convents in Mexico stands out. In 1861, monks and nuns fled in horror at the decree of expropriation of ecclesiastical property in Mexico, refusing to negotiate on the subject. As the historian Fernando Benítez puts it: "Abandoned: the ivories, the relics, the Chinese porcelain, the Infant Jesus, the saints, the paintings, the furniture, and the libraries with their marvelous shelves, their lecterns, their tables, their thousands of books and manuscripts bound in parchment or engraved and gilded skins."

There was no way to keep the masses from entering the religious centers and carting away everything they could. But even earlier, the cloister of San Francisco was destroyed and hundreds of figures of Christ, the Virgin Mary, and other saints disappeared. The sculptures were used as firewood and jewels were scattered far and wide. Another denuded convent was that of San Agustín, which had survived a terrible fire in 1676. Its principal retable, carved by Tomás Xuárez, was destroyed and the library burned, though almost all the books were stolen first.

In 1861, Benito Juárez named a commission to save all the books in the country, but a lack of funding kept bibliophiles from carrying out their mission. While the books passed from the convents to the city, thousands were left on the road, where they were used as bedding or kindling. The process went on until 1884, when the number of lost books reached 100,000. José María de Agreda y Sánchez relates that he once picked out of the trash of the Palafox Library the imperial documents of Charles V and that on another occasion he bought from an old lady a series of thick volumes she was using to make a fire.

In a note on February 10, 1861, the newspaper *El Siglo XIX* made a plea about libraries:

> We have been informed that some depopulated convents have been entirely abandoned. Their doors, like the convents themselves, are wide open, and the books and manuscripts left to the mercy of anyone who wants to carry them off. One of our collaborators, who just yesterday was in the convent of San Agustín, has seen that its library is in this condition, a multitude of books destroyed, scattered throughout the cloisters and cells, others thrown on the floor of the library in the most complete disorder. Everything in a state that clearly shows the place is subject to looting. What are the commissioners doing to protect these libraries? Why are the authorities not doing anything to remedy such scandalous disorder? Have we returned to the times of barbarism, to a time when these rich treasures of knowledge are left to the rapacity of those who wish to steal or destroy them?

The books scavenged from the convents were devoured by water, neglect, and casual or premeditated theft. There was a plan to transport the books to the university with the goal of establishing a national library, but thousands of books never reached their destination.

Chapter 17

Fires, Wars, Mistakes, and Messiahs

From the eleventh century to the present, accidental fires have destroyed countless public and private libraries. Earthquakes and floods contribute their part to this annihilation; as a result, the history of the book is a story of not only persecution by Philistines but also relentless attacks by nature itself, which constantly puts the survival of human memory to the test. I've discovered that the inventory of disasters affecting libraries, book collections, and publishing houses is impossible to document precisely, but this summary of diverse moments of ruin in the history of culture will suffice.

I'll begin this arbitrary list with library fires. Today, we can say that no ancient library was exempt from fire. In Canterbury, for example, in 1067 a fire reached the original monastic buildings and reduced hundreds of books to ashes. Around 1184, an intense fire in the library of Glastonbury Abbey, where the Holy Grail was supposedly hidden, burned scores of books. This tragedy was repeated everywhere: in 1318, the library of the All Saints Church was destroyed. In 1440, the entire library of the monastery of Megapisleon burned, and in 1660, rebuilt, it burned again. According to legend, the fire spontaneously leapt out of a book. Unsurprisingly, one of the worst library fires by any standard occurred in one of the greatest libraries of all time, at the building complex known as El Escorial.

The Escorial and the Burning of Ancient Manuscripts

King Philip II of Spain (1527–1598) is known principally for his defeats, but for our purposes it is more important to recall him as the man behind one of the greatest monuments in the history of Europe, the eighth wonder of the world, the royal monastery of San Lorenzo de El Escorial. According to the royal "Statement Concerning the Foundation and Endowment," dated April 22, 1567, the structure's reason for being derives from the triumph at Saint Quentin on August 10, 1557, when the forces of France were defeated by a small Spanish army. Even so, it seems obvious that Philip II, like the Ptolemies or the Medici, wanted to express his power through a unique work; it is rare that military triumphs engender libraries.

The first man in charge of the building was the architect Juan Bautista de Toledo. After his death in 1567, Juan de Herrera, a cosmographer and mathematician, took over. Ultimately there were three libraries: a main library opposite the Patio of the Monarchs, another containing manuscripts, and finally a library for choral and liturgical works. There was also an archive, where letters, foundation statements, apostolic bulls, privileges, and royal decrees were all stored in chests open to very few. The organization of the library is owed to the humanist Benito Arias Montano, Philip II's chaplain and also his adviser on secret matters related to Flanders and Portugal.

Philip wanted his library to be the world's best. To that end, he donated his own books and provided unlimited resources for acquiring texts. The closest collaborators received instructions to buy rare books and manuscripts in Paris, Rome, and Venice. A letter of May 28, 1567, to his ambassador in France says:

It would give me great pleasure that the rarest and most exquisite books available be taken from there, because this is one of the principal memories that can be left, both for the particular benefit of the clergy who will live in this house and for the public benefit of all men of letters who would like to come here to read them.

Conscious of the importance of this project, some courtiers bequeathed their libraries to the crown. Don Diego Hurtado de Mendoza added his collection of 2,000 volumes, mostly Italian, and many other nobles followed suit. At the third battle of Lepanto (1571), the Spaniards obtained twenty Arabic, Persian, and Turkish codices, among which the Koran of Lepanto is outstanding.

In 1573, Philip II contracted with the copyist Nicolas Turrianos (also known as Nicolas de la Torre), a native of Crete. He spent thirty years copying at least forty Greek codices. The collection—2,000 manuscripts and 2,500 printed texts—grew with the addition of travel diaries, maps, musical scores, and scientific objects: armillary spheres, astrolabes, and globes. There was a special section of forbidden books made up of volumes sewn shut so no one could read them.

In 1612, the flotilla of Luis Gajardo captured a ship carrying the library of Muley Zidán, the sultan of Morroco—4,000 volumes, all of which came to the Escorial.

The chronicles list small fires at the Escorial, but on Sunday, June 7, 1671, at two o'clock in the afternoon, a genuine catastrophe transpired: "The entire building burned in a grand and terrible fire, which reduced the rooms of Philip II, the library, and the basilica to somber stains." The fire spread rapidly because of the winds blowing from the Guadarrama and in about eight hours the monument was almost entirely reduced to ashes. Later it was determined that it began in a chimney in the college, in the northern section, and spread violently to the manuscript section. At least three manuscripts with the writings of the skeptic philosopher Sextus Empiricus were lost forever, and the same fate befell other Greek codices: "Paintings, tables, works of art, scientific instruments, and many extremely rare Greek codices perished . . . some six thousand in all languages and disciplines were burned and quite a few of those that survived show the ravages and the danger they suffered."

The losses were enormous. Among others, a codex of the Visigothic councils, texts by Dioscorides, and the *Natural History of the Indies*—nineteen volumes written by Francisco Hernández, a scholar from Toledo who studied the botany, zoology, and customs of Mexico. Under orders from Philip himself, Hernández went to the New World between 1571 and 1577 in search of scientific information. He described 3,000 species of plants unknown in Europe, 400 animals, and fourteen new minerals. The particularly tragic aspect of this is that when the work burned, the plates painted by Native Americans burned with it. Ultimately, some 4,500 codices were saved, and for more than fifty years remained stored in the upper hall of the monastery.

In the Library of Printed Works, where the archive of dangerous books was stored, rapid action saved the books. Many were simply tossed out of windows. The Chorus Library was saved.

The Library of Anders Spole

In the history of science, the personal library of the Swedish astronomer Anders Spole deserves special mention because it was the most complete science library of its time. Spole, a reserved and somewhat distracted man, was the first royal astronomer at the University of Uppsala and counted among his friends astronomers and mathematicians such as Christiaan Huygens, Jean-Dominique Cassini, and Nicholas Mercator. Over decades, he managed to accumulate hundreds of scientific works, but the fire that ravaged Uppsala in May 1702 eradicated his collection along with his instruments. Among the books lost were *Atland eller Manheim, Atlantica sive Manheim* (1675–1689), *Campi Elysii Liber Primus* (1701), and *Nora Samolad sive Laponia Illustrata* (1701) by Olof Rudbeck.

The Library of Árni Magnússon

Árni Magnússon is considered among the most important book collectors ever. He was also a hero in Iceland, where he was born in 1663. The son of a priest, he moved to Copenhagen to study at age nineteen. Through diligence, he became the assistant to Thomas Bartholin, the royal antiquarian, in 1684.

At the age of thirty-eight, Magnússon assumed the chair of history at the University of Copenhagen. His bibliophilia led him to seek out texts from around the world about Icelandic culture. He was interested in medieval manuscripts, many of which had belonged to the powerful families of his country. By 1690, Magnússon owned excellent copies of the main Icelandic sagas. Six years later, he declared he was the owner of the best collection of sagas in the world. After a two-year residence in Germany, he returned to Copenhagen in 1697, where he was named secretary of the Royal Danish Archives.

He learned from precursors like Brynjólfur Sveinsson, the bishop of Skálholt, where works were to be found. In 1656, Sveinsson presented the king of Denmark with a plan to transcribe the texts of the *Flateyarbók*, the *Grágás*, and

Volsunga. Later, he collected the Edda poems and an early version of *Njál's Saga*. Thanks to his zeal, Sveinsson was able to have these works copied, a task he assigned to Jón Erlendsson of Vilingaholt. The result of these labors was the diffusion of medieval Icelandic literature and a renewed interest in the sagas.

Magnússon's collection eventually held 2,500 objects, including whole manuscripts and fragments. He had documents, letters, about 200 sagas, and about 16,000 diplomas and copied manuscripts. But on the afternoon of October 20, 1728, Copenhagen was destroyed by fire. Over the course of three days, it burned neighborhood after neighborhood until it finally reached Magnússon's collection. He managed to save many manuscripts but not his printed books, notes, and personal papers. One of the books lost was the *Breviarium Nidarosiense*, the first book printed in Hoolum, a city in Iceland, during the sixteenth century.

The library at the university also burned, and Magnússon, in a gesture that is still moving 280 years later, bequeathed everything he saved to that institution. He died on January 7, 1730.

The Cotton Collection

On the night of October 23, 1731, a fire broke out in Ashburnham House, in Westminster, London. The horror of the spectacle increased when it became known that the manuscripts in Sir Robert Bruce Cotton's collection were burning inside the building. Cotton, a friend of Francis Bacon, was an eccentric bibliophile who arranged his books beneath busts of the Roman emperors and catalogued them accordingly.

When the theologian and classicist Dr. Richard Bentley learned of the fire, he recalled the curse put on the library

by the Duke of Buckingham. He was sure the books had
caused the death of their owner, but he ran to the blaze
and plunged into the library. Bentley sprang out carrying
the Codex Alexandrinus under his arm. When he tried to
go back in, he was restrained.

The next day, the manuscripts that were saved were brought
to a room in Westminster School. A year later, a report about
the damage was completed. It stated that of 958 manuscripts
in the Cotton library, 114 were burned and 98 were damaged.
Actually, only thirteen manuscripts completely disappeared,
though a good number were reduced to cinders.

Jacob Frank

The life of Yakov ben Judah Leib Frankovich was that of any
fanatic: unsettled, no security, immodest. From his father
he inherited, along with debts and pride, an unusual fervor
for the Judaic messianic movement of Sabbatai Zevi. Zevi
was a seventeenth-century Jewish mystic who said he could
have sexual relations with virgins "without deflowering
them." The movement had disciples in different corners
of Europe and Africa, from Yemen to Amsterdam, among
both Ashkenazi and Sephardic Jews. It was an expected
phenomenon where entire multitudes awaited the imminent return of the miracles of the Messiah and the Old
Testament prophets.

Yakov convinced himself that he was the reincarnation
of Sabbatai Zevi and Barujia Russo, another messiah, and
in 1751, after a visit to Turkey, changed his name to Jacob
Frank. For obscure reasons, he hated certain Judaic etymolo-
gies, and for doctrinal reasons, he hated books. In 1755,
he found some disciples whom he called "Frankists" and
forced them to burn books. In 1756, he was condemned
as a heretic, but that did not lessen his zeal.

Around 1757, after besting some rabbis in debate in Kamianets-Podilskyi, the Ukraine, he went from house to house gathering hundreds of copies of the Talmud—the collection of rabbinic discussions on Jewish law and history—and burned them in a public square. For that, his sect became known as the "anti-Talmudists." He regularly reminded his followers of his divinity. "I am the word, I am the son, I am," he would say. He invented a trinity where there was a true God, alien to everything, an incarnate God, and a Woman. He considered himself that incarnate God. Speculating about the law exalted him, and in his dreams he thought he'd discovered the signs of the new principles of a mixture of Christianity and Judaism.

At a certain point, he ordered his followers to wear sandals made from rolls of parchment bearing texts from the Torah. He created an order with twelve apostles and twelve concubines, all saints, pious and implacable, and at once defenders of the most intense sexual activity. In 1760, he was arrested and jailed in Warsaw and later expelled. Legend has it he died in Offenbach. On his deathbed he requested the destruction of all books. "Burn it all," he begged. "The truth dies with me." A curious note: He said God's face had acquired his features.

The Library of the College Seminary of Mérida

Between the seventeenth and nineteenth centuries, there existed an extraordinary library in the College Seminary of the city of Mérida, Venezuela. It was made up of the books of the Jesuits and the Augustinians and the books of Bishop Juan Ramos de Lora and his successor, Bishop Torrijos, who augmented the number of works in an unusual way. Torrijos, it seems, was an impressive bibliophile: he ordered a mule train to carry

3,000 volumes to Mérida, including literary classics and theological works.

This library, unusual for its time, was destroyed by an earthquake that leveled Mérida in March 1812. The building collapsed, and the books, which included incunabula and unique editions, were scattered far and wide. Francisco Javier Irastoza, in an 1815 report, noted that the year before, Spanish troops under Sebastián de la Calzada reached Mérida and destroyed or sold scores of incunabula. The civil wars of the nineteenth century finished the work of destruction. Juan de Dios Picón has corroborated all this information: "The earthquake, the assault of the enemies of independence, the abandon into which the library fell, and the looting it was subjected to, have left it virtually stripped." By sheer good luck, an *editio princeps* of Galileo and another of Baldassare Castiglione were preserved.

The Burning of the Library of Congress

In 1812, the Library of Congress announced its first catalog, compiled under the direction of an ill-tempered and devoutly religious man named Patrick Magruder. It was a simple, austere list and classified books by genre, number of copies available, and even price. There were about 3,076 volumes and fifty-three maps.

The same year, Congress authorized President James Madison to invade Canada. On April 27, 1813, after their victory at the Battle of York, American soldiers advanced on what is present-day Toronto and there burned the Parliament and the legislative library. The English responded rapidly, and reached Chesapeake Bay in August of 1814. Library director Magruder had left the capital for "reasons of health," and named one J. T. Frost, forty-five years old and thus too old to be called up for military duty, to take his place. One of the few government employees to remain at his post as the British inexorably advanced on the city, Frost busied himself evacuating hundreds of books and documents. He saved what he could, and finally left just hours ahead of the invading forces.

Madison, bereft of munitions and defenses, fled Washington. The British general Robert Ross ordered that everything representing the enemy's culture be destroyed—the White House, the Treasury, and the Capital. The new Library of Congress was torched on August 24.

When he learned the news, Thomas Jefferson wrote a famous letter to Samuel H. Smith, dated September 21, 1814, expressing his profound disgust with the destruction of the library: "Dear Sir, I have learned from the newspapers that the vandalism of our enemy has triumphed in Washington over science and art thanks to the destruction of the public library and the noble building in which it resided." A State Department report gave a clear account of the destruction of the library, though its main purpose was to detail the thousands of books and documents lost as a result of the attacks.

Once the war was over, everything had to be rebuilt. There would be a new director and a new collection. Not all had been lost, but at least 2,600 books burned. Jefferson, in an act of cynical philanthropy, suggested that the government purchase his own collection of 6,487 volumes. In 1815, he was given $23,950, which annoyed his political enemies. The catalog created for the occasion was not alphabetical but divided by subject.

By Christmas 1851, the collection boasted 55,000 volumes, but a fire incinerated 35,000, including some of the Jefferson collection. The library has grown over the 150 years since to the point where it is one of the most renowned on the planet. It contains 29 million books in 470 languages, 56 million manuscripts, 500,000 microfilm documents, 4.8 million maps, and 2.7 million recordings.

The Anna Amalia Library

The history of so many German libraries is disastrous, but none more so than that of the legendary Anna Amalia Library in Weimar. Founded in 1691 by the Duchess Anna Amalia of Saxony-Weimar, the library was, in its day, one of the most important in the world. The library became a symbol because it housed the best Faust collection in the world (13,000 copies), but it also had first editions of Shakespeare, 500 incunabula, and 2,000 manuscripts. In addition, it possessed an admirable Bible collection, including a 1534 copy owned by Martin Luther. By the end of the twentieth century, the collection consisted of a million items.

Between the 2nd and 3rd of September, 2004, an electrical problem unleashed a ferocious fire in the Rococo Room. It quickly spread throughout the building, which UNESCO had designated "Cultural Patrimony of Humanity." Fifty thousand books, almost all from the seventeenth and eighteenth centuries, disappeared; music books and scores were water-damaged. More than 28,000 burned, and almost 34,000 fell victim to the firemen. A human chain of more than 500 people braved the fire and saved thousands of books. "We were on the point of losing the cradle of our classical national culture in a single night," said Helmut Seemann, president of the Weimar Classical Foundation. The library itself reopened in October 2007, but many of its books are lost for all time.

Los Angeles, 1986

"Nothing like this has ever happened in the history of U.S. libraries," a preacher lamented in the streets of Los Angeles, as he watched the smoke pour out of the imposing Central

Library building on April 29, 1986. "The fragility of things was never so clear to me," he said. "We are smoke, and we are dust." It was the single worst library fire to take place in a nation where the most modern mechanisms for the protection of libraries exist.

It was six days after the world celebration of the Day of the Book. Despite the efforts of sixty fire companies, the fire burned for seven hours. At least 400,000 thousand books burned, and 400,000 more were damaged. The special collection dedicated to American inventions, science, and technology completely disappeared. The next day, all was ruins and desolation. Starting at four in the afternoon, some 1,500 volunteers carried the books, in 100,000 boxes, to a salvage depot. The wet books had to be dried and cleaned. The losses exceeded 20 million dollars. The fire had been deliberately set.

A Sampling of Other Mishaps

The General Central Archive of Spain at Alcalá de Henares survived censorship, war, oblivion, lack of funding and negligence. But a child playing with matches on August 11, 1939 burned a mile and a half of its stacks. Much of the documentation of nineteenth-century Spain was lost, as was an 8,000-volume history-of-law collection.

Only desperate measures on the part of Italian librarians saved thousands of works when the Arno flooded Florence in 1966. At the Central National Library, 1.2 million books, 100,000 manuscripts, 50,000 folios, and 400,000 volumes of newspaper compilations were submerged.

At the end of the twentieth century, the library of the Monastery of Dabra Damo in Ethiopia, north of the Adwa highway, was destroyed by fire. Founded at the outset of the sixth century CE by one of the so-called nine saints, Abuna

Za-Mika'el Aragawi, it once held more than 1,000 volumes. When Dr. Otto Jaeger visited in 1965, he found about fifty invaluable manuscripts. All burned.

On December 21, 1996, the personal library of the poet Octavio Paz in Mexico City burned. Paz remarked, "Books pass away like friends." First editions of authors like Rubén Darío, Manuel Díaz Othón, along with the books of the poet's grandfather Ireneo, were all lost.

The Real "Printers's Devils": Flames

Printers are prone to fiery disaster. One of the first and most famous such fires happened in Gravenstraat, at the offices of the seventeenth-century Dutch cartographer Joan Blaeu—artisan, mathematician, artist, and philosopher. Blaeu had reached perfection in the composition of atlases, and his works covered global, national, and regional maps. His importance and excellence perhaps resided in his typographical art and printing skill, both in harmony with the cultural transformations taking place in Amsterdam.

Blaeu's workplace was devastated by flames. According to the chronicle of Alphonse Willems, "Blaeu went into a deep depression. On February 22, 1672, his printing house, acknowledged as the most prestigious in Europe, fell victim to the flames . . . and the damage ran to 355,000 florins." There are good reasons to view this event with sadness, because the fire consumed *Le grand atlas* (1663), the most expensive book of the seventeenth century, prepared by Blaeu himself in twelve volumes.

This terrible event also eliminated the editions of extraordinary works such as *Casparis Barlei Renom per Octennium in Brasilia et Alibi Gestarum*, the *Flandria Illustrata* by Antonio Sandero, and the *Genealogiae Franciscae Plenior Assertio*.

William Bowyer, one of the most innovative printers in England, lost most of his work when his plant burned in 1712. Among the many books destroyed was the outstanding *The Ancient and Present State of Gloucestershire* by Roger Atkyns. Oddly enough, the second edition of that work (1768) also burned in a library fire.

On January 8, 1770, John Payne and his partner Joseph Johnson lost their shop on London's Paternoster Row, a street that came to be known as "the home of fire." (Repeatedly burned, it was completely obliterated during the Blitz.) The notoriety forced Payne to move to Marsham Street in Westminster, where he became an indefatigable worker. Joseph Johnson moved to St. Paul's Churchyard after the fire, and he too refused to give up. He was the first English publisher to bring out William Beckford's *Vathek* in 1787. He published Priestley, Horne Tooke, Mary Wollstonecraft, and Thomas Paine until he was sent to jail in 1797 for selling a pamphlet by Gilbert Wakefield. Troubled by nightmares, it was said he died dreaming of a burned book.

Thomas Cadell, bookseller and publisher, almost lost his business when his shop burned on March 2, 1776. He was a friend of Samuel Johnson and David Hume, and published Edward Gibbon's *Decline and Fall of the Roman Empire* between 1776 and 1788. He also published Adam Smith's *Wealth of Nations* (1776) and Dr. Johnson's *Lives of the English Poets*.

One of the most devastating fires in the history of the English book business destroyed the warehouses of John Nichols. He suffered his first fire on May 7, 1786 and his second, perhaps the worst of the two, when his office, warehouse, and shop burned on February 8, 1808. Nichols writes in the prologue to the second edition of his memoirs: "In May of 1802, I began to print again; and little by little, I managed to reach the halfway point in the edition when my progress was suddenly stopped by a calamity that late one night discouraged me from ever taking up the task of publishing or printing again."

One of the rare-book dealer Samuel Bagster's great achievements was the preparation of the English version of the Polyglot Bible. Each volume included text in English, Hebrew, Latin, and Greek on one page and German, French, Italian, and Spanish on the other. At the end came a Syriac version. This magnificent work appeared between 1817 and 1828 in four volumes, titled *Biblia Sacra Polyglotta Bagsteriana*. It was almost totally consumed, along with the printer's workshop, in a fire in March 1822.

Publishers Destroyed

The list of publishers ruined by fire is long as well. Just a handful of examples: in 1802, Samuel Hamilton of Falcon Court, Fleet Street, lost both his warehouse and his offices. One of the best editions of Lucretius's *De Rerum Natura Libros Sex* (three volumes, 1796–1797) was destroyed in the accident. Another book that over time would seem condemned to burn was also lost: Jean-Jacques Barthélemy's *Travels of Anacharsis the Younger in Greece* (seven volumes, second edition, 1791), published by William Beaumont. Twelve years later, this eccentric book again was incinerated when the shop of Thomas Gillet on Fleet Street burned on December 12, 1805. Unfortunately, Gillet's offices burned again on July 28, 1810. Today his books are very rare.

George Robinson II, a bookseller in Paternoster Row between 1785 and 1811, went bankrupt because a gigantic fire destroyed his print shop and hundreds of works along with it. On November 5, 1807, almost every copy of *A Complete Verbal Index to the Plays of Shakespeare* (1805), compiled by Francis Twiss, was immolated, along with the printing house itself.

Famous Shipwrecks

We will of course never be able to know how many books
have been lost at sea. Even so, here is some information.

Numerous examples of the eight-volume *Biblia Polyglotta*
(or *Biblia Regia*), edited by Arias Montano between 1569 and
1573, were lost while being shipped to Spain. According to
Benjamin Disraeli, in 1700 a storm sank a ship carrying the
Oriental manuscripts of Heer Hudde, a wealthy burgomaster
from Middleburgh.

The ingenious bookseller John Dunton describes how he
lost hundreds of books traveling by ship to Boston, where he
opened a bookstore. After its 1707 publication, the *Poema
Tograi* was almost completely lost when the ship carrying
it went down. The singular *Rituel du diocèse de Québec*
(1703) disappeared after its publication. Almost all the copies
of *Leonis Diaconi Caloensis Historia Scriptoresque Alii ad
Res Byzantina Pertinentes* (1819), en route to the famous
Count Romanoff, were lost at sea. In 1873, the impoverished Venezuelan writer and musician Felipe Larrazábal was
aboard the *Ville du Havre* correcting the manuscript of an
important compilation related to the life and work of Simón
Bolívar. He was reading some of his 3,000 documents, but
he never finished, because a storm sank the ship, and author
and texts were lost.

Some 2,227 people were aboard the *Titanic* when it sank
in the Atlantic in 1912 after colliding with an iceberg. There
were 705 survivors, but the ship's library for first- and second-
class passengers, and all privately owned texts, were lost.

Chapter 18

Books Destroyed in Fiction

By 2006, there existed several editions of this history. An anonymous reader suggested I examine the elimination of books in works of fiction. A challenging project, of course, but I realized I had in my own library almost all the books I would need, and I was overjoyed to realize that the first auto-da-fé ever presented in a novel takes place in the book that inaugurates modern European fiction, *Don Quixote*.

In Chapter Six of Part One of *Don Quixote*, a priest and a barber (the church and the censor) go into Alonso Quijano's library while he is asleep and make off with about a hundred of his books. The Inquisition is personified by these figures, who are sure the readings of romances of chivalry have driven Alonso Quijano insane. The two immediately review and select books for burning. Alonso Quijano's niece and housemaid ask that the fire be started before their master wakes up. Ultimately, the flames engulf *The Deeds of Esplandián* and all his progeny along with *Don Olivante de Laura*, *Florismarte de Hircania*, *Platir the Knight*, *The Knight of the Cross*, *Palmerín de Oliva*, *Don Belianís*, and others. Later in the book, Cervantes underlines the absurdity of inquisitorial obsession by having the priest seize two chivalric romances from a baffled innkeeper. He burns them as if they were heretics in the flesh.

The idea of books as dangerous items that threaten their owners abounds in literature. Christopher Marlowe, in

Doctor Faustus, wrote words that still surprise us: "Come not, Lucifer! I'll burn my books!" Marlowe's Faust prefers to burn his books, while Shakespeare's Prospero, in *The Tempest,* Act V, declares

> To work mine end upon their senses, that
> This airy charm is for, I'll break my staff,
> Bury it certain fathoms in the earth,
> And deeper than did ever plummet sound
> I'll drown my book.

Faust, perhaps, wants rapid salvation, while Prospero wants slow expiation.

The seventeenth-century Spanish writer Francisco de Quevedo, in his *Dream of Hell* (also called *Pluto's Pigsty*), condemns scores of wizards to burn along with their books. Some of the heretics tortured in this hell are Cornelius Agrippa, John Tritheim, Julius Caesar Scaliger, and Artifius. Baltasar Gracián, in his slow and prodigious novel *El criticón,* mentions a book burning. Referring to Juan Botero's *Reasons of State,* he says, in Part Two, Chapter Four, "he tried to buy all copies and asked how much they might want for them; and while they all believed that the question arose from his esteem for the books, which he wished to present to his prince, it was all just the reverse: in order that they might not reach the prince's hands, he ordered a great fire built to burn the copies and scatter their ashes to the winds."

Count Jan Potocki, one of the most eccentric writers in the history of literature, includes in his novel *Manuscript Found in Saragossa* (1804–1814) the chapter "Terrible History of the Pilgrim Hervas and His Father, the Impious All-Knowing Man." A scholar named Hervas writes an encyclopedia of all things in the world. After a voyage to Asturias, Hervas returns to his library only to find the labor of his entire life in ruins: "his hundred volumes destroyed, their bindings broken, and all their pages scattered and confused on the floor. . . . The cause of the disaster was this. Hervas never ate at home, and the rats, so numerous in all the houses of Madrid, refrained from visiting his, where they'd found nothing more to gnaw than a few quills. But things changed when those one hundred volumes, rich in glue, were installed in his room, a room the owner abandoned that day. Attracted by the smell and encouraged by Hervas's absence, a multitude of rats came, threw the volumes to the floor, gnawed, and devoured."

Edgar Allan Poe, in "The Premature Burial" (1844) writes: "I took vigorous exercise. I breathed the free air of Heaven. I thought upon other subjects than Death. I discarded my medical books. 'Buchan' I burned: I read no 'Night Thoughts'—no fustian about churchyards—no bugaboo tales—such as this." For Poe, book destruction was not a matter of philosophizing; he noted in the 1829 edition of *Al Aaraaf, Tamerlane and Minor Poems* that his first collection of poems, *Tamerlane and Other Poems* (1827) had been "suppressed because of private circumstances." Some think Poe could not stop publication and had to accept losing it; others think he destroyed the book in an act of self-criticism. Only twelve copies of the 1827 edition have survived.

Heinrich Heine refers to a historical book burning in *Almansor* (1821), wherein he records an inimitable dialogue between Almansor and Hassan about the burning of the Koran in Granada. Hassan concludes: "Where they burn books, they end up burning men."

Nathaniel Hawthorne, in his story "Earth's Holocaust" in *Mosses from an Old Manse* (1846), presents a recurring idea: the need to return to a tabula rasa in order to begin a new world. In this case, Americans bored with the accumulation of knowledge and things create a massive bonfire on the western prairies of the United Sates. People throw in newspapers, magazines, coats of arms, medals, liquors, arms—everything made and unmade by technology, manufacture, or ingenuity—including all books.

Robert Louis Stevenson developed the theme of book burning in *The Merry Men and Other Tales and Fables* (1887). In "The Reader," a strange conversation ends in this way: "'Who is impious now?' asked the book. And the reader threw the book into the fire." His friend Henry James, in *The Aspern Papers* (1888), wrote the devastating tale of a publisher obsessed with the manuscripts of a mysterious genius named Jeffrey Aspern. The publisher would stop at nothing to gain control of those valuable texts. As a final trick, he intended to propose marriage to a woman of oblique beauty, but unfortunately the manuscripts have already been destroyed: " 'I have done the great thing. I have destroyed the papers.' 'Destroyed them?' I faltered. 'Yes; what was I to keep them for? I burned them last night, one by one, in the kitchen.' 'One by one?' I repeated mechanically. 'It took a long time—there were so many.' "

H. G. Wells imagines a horrible future in *The Time Machine* (1895). In Chapter 11, "The Palace of Green Porcelain," the time traveler enters the ruins of a museum: "The brown and charred rags that hung from the sides of it, I presently recognized as the decaying vestiges of books. They had long since dropped to pieces, and every semblance of print had left them." These vestiges of books are all that remains of print culture in a degenerate civilization of Eloi, or imbecilic (if fairylike) beings, and Morlocks, or monstrous cannibals. Not surprisingly, the traveler brings a flower back from the future, not a decayed book.

H. P. Lovecraft, raised in a library containing more than 2,000 books, intricately imagined the existence of a perverse book, the *Necronomicon*, originally called in Arabic *Al Azif* (a name derived from the buzzing of insects), written by a seventh-century author, the "mad Arab" Abdul Alhazred. Throughout history, this imaginary book is destroyed, but reappears in some wizard's library. The surviving copy in a San Francisco library burns along with the rest of the city in 1906.

Lovecraft also wrote of destroyed books in *The Dreams of the Witch's House*, where, after an examination of the wreckage of a cursed house, "pieces of papers and books were found, and a yellow powder the result of the complete disintegration of volumes and documents." In *The Case of Charles Dexter Ward*, he describes a group of men eager to erase the memory of a wizard: they burn his library.

J. R. R. Tolkien (1892–1973) is the kind of author we regret not having read in our youth. He created the most entertaining mythological saga of the twentieth century. He is mentioned here because in *The Fellowship of the Ring*, the first volume of *The Lord of the Rings*, he talks about diverse lost writings of the history of hobbits: "The original Red Book has not been preserved, but many copies were made, especially of the first volume, for the use of the descendants of the children of Lord Samwise Gamgee."

Stephen Vincent Benét inherited military zeal from his father. It isn't strange, therefore, that what we remember of his work today—twenty-seven volumes in verse and prose—are his poems on war, death, and the exaltation of courage. In 1942, he tried to participate in public demonstrations to protest the book burning perpetrated by the Nazis on May 10, 1933, and he wrote the script of a radio play, "They Burned the Books." It includes passages in which different historical characters appear to defend books. Some of the original actors were Germans who had to flee Germany because of persecution.

In 1953, Ray Bradbury published *Farenheit 451*, whose title refers to the temperature at which paper begins to burn. François Truffaut made the novel into a memorable film in 1967. Bradbury follows a line established by George Orwell's *1984* and Aldous Huxley's *Brave New World*, a future in which books are forbidden and firemen stand ready to burn them before they disturb the vital orthodoxy of the dominant system.

In a prologue for the 1993 edition of the novel, Bradbury recognized the antecedents:

> It was inevitable I would end up hearing or reading about the three fires at the Library of Alexandria, two accidental and the other intentional. I was nine years old when I found out, and I burst into tears. I was a strange boy, already an inhabitant of the high attics and the enchanted basements of the Carnegie Library in Waukegan, Illinois.

The novel's protagonist is Montag who, when the persecution against him is over, joins the dissidents, each of whom has memorized either a complete book or a chapter of a book. They hope to join together with others like themselves to try to rewrite the great classics eradicated by official decree. In Bradbury's work, memory is a means to survive a hostile future.

Around 1950, before *Fahrenheit 451*, Bradbury wrote a short story titled "The Bonfire." The narrator recites a list of the things the protagonist hates: all are books. In 1963, he wrote "Bright Phoenix," with a radical character who burns the books in the library. But then he discovers that everyone in the town is rather odd. One is named Keats, others are Plato, Einstein, Lincoln. What the arsonist realizes is that the people in the town have a secret: they've memorized all the books in the library in order to save them. In his tale "The Exiles," included in *The Illustrated Man* (1951), all the characters in fiction flee to Mars because the works they appear in have been burned on Earth. In "Usher II" (1950), added to the second edition of *The Illustrated Man*, an avenger appears who decides to bring all the book burners to Mars so he can drown them in a lake. In *S Is for Space* (1966), he includes a tale about another dystopia, "Pillar of Fire." There, a vampire who returns to the land of the living finds himself in an ultra-hygienic society. After murdering someone, he goes to a library and finds that the works of Edgar Allan Poe, H. P. Lovecraft, August Derleth, and Ambrose Bierce no longer exist because they were destroyed in the Great Fire of 2265.

No discussion of book burning and science fiction would be complete without a reference to Walter M. Miller. In his novel *A Canticle for Leibowitz*, a religious order comes into being dedicated to copying fragments and entire texts in order to save the memories of humanity.

Like Homer, Jorge Luis Borges is the founder of a literary tradition. Among the writers of the twentieth century, he was one of those most interested in exploring the myth of the Sacred Work, and his stories, essays, and poems reproduce the horror brought about by eliminating certain texts. In "The Library of Babel," included in his 1944 *Ficciones*, he speaks of a sect dedicated to eliminating useless books: "They would invade the hexagons, exhibit credentials that were not always false, leaf in annoying fashion through a volume, and condemn whole shelves: To their hygienic, ascetic furor we owe the senseless loss of millions of books."

In "The Theologians," also in the 1944 edition of *Ficciones*, the tale begins this way:

> After the garden was leveled, the chalices and altars profaned, the Huns rode their horses into the monastery library and

destroyed the incomprehensible books and vituperated them and burned them, perhaps fearing that the letters concealed blasphemies against their god, who was an iron scimitar. They burned palimpsests and codices.

In "Three Versions of Judas" (*Ficciones*), Borges speaks about the writings of Nils Runeberg and points out that if they'd been written in the era of Basilides, "they would figure in the apocryphal *Liber adversus omnes haereses* or would have perished when the fire in a monastic library devoured the last copy of the *Syntagma*." In "The Congress," a novella included in *The Book of Sand* (1975), Borges uses one of Hawthorne's ideas. A journalist named Alejandro Ferri decides to join the Congress, a group of apolitical universalists whose members believe they represent the world and decide to incorporate representatives of all tendencies and kinds. The failure of the enterprise ends in a huge bonfire where all the books collected by the Congress (encyclopedias, atlases, Pliny's *Historia naturalis*, and others) burn. Fernández Irala, a member, comments; "Every few centuries, it's necessary to burn the Library of Alexandria."

Borges, always fascinated by the theme of the burning of the Library of Alexandria, in "Poem of the Gifts" (*El hacedor*, 1960) refers to his own blindness, which keeps him from reading the books under his supervision as director of the National Library in Buenos Aires. He alludes to the ancient Greek center, saying:

In vain the day
Rains infinite books on them
Arduous as the arduous manuscripts
That perished in Alexandria.

Years later, Borges returned to the theme of libraries in "Alexandria, 641 CE," a poem included in *History of the*

Night (1977). The text should be read along with "The Wall and the Books," an essay from *Other Inquisitions* (1954), because in some fashion it summarizes the idea that all book destruction is useless. People will again write the same works because the themes are in our souls.

> I, that Omar who subjugated the Persians
> And who imposes Islam on the earth,
> Order my soldiers to destroy
> With fire the long library,
> Which will not perish. Praised be
> God, who does not sleep, and Muhammad, his Apostle.

In "The Failed Writer," a story in the collection *El joroba-dito* (1933), the Argentine author Roberto Arlt (1900–1942) narrates in first person how a precociously famous writer becomes a cynic. Tormented and terrible, the writer at a certain moment describes the destruction of all books. One of the great stories in the Spanish language, "Nabónides," is by the Mexican Juan José Arreola (b. 1918) and included in his *Confabulario* (1952). It tells the life of a man in love with Babylonian writing and art, Nabónides, who attempts to save "the eight hundred thousand clay tablets that make up the library," and hires hundreds of scribes. He abandons military activities and dedicates himself to simplifying the alphabet, to reading and writing a history of his "hypothetical military deeds." Arreola invents a professor named Rasolom as a primary source and a monograph titled *Nabonidzylinder* (1912) by Adolf von Pinches as a secondary source. Finally, as might be expected, the tablets are destroyed, and Nabónides, in one of his possible deaths, ends his days on an island where he dreams about all the texts he recovered.

Bohumil Hrabal (1914–1997) began his literary career in 1963 in Czechoslovakia. Years later, he published a small masterpiece called *Too Loud a Solitude*, a first-person narrative in which a man describes his life in a factory dedicated to grinding up paper. His contradiction is enormous: he loves books with a passion, but by profession he destroys them.

Manuel Vázquez Montalbán, one of Spain's best writers of detective stories, has his detective, Pepe Carvalho, habitually burn books in his fireplace. In *Murder in the Central Committee* (1981), his character investigates the death of a famous politician. At a certain moment he enters a bookshop: "Sooner or later he would have to bring himself up to date in order to buy and burn books with perfect awareness of his action."

The Name of the Rose (1980) by Umberto Eco is a great mystery novel. The murders committed in the text reflect the strange zeal of a bibliophile monk who guards the only extant copy of the second book of Aristotle's *Poetics*, whose theme, according to testimonies, including the *Tractatus Coislinianus*, is a study of and apology for comedy. At the end, the labyrinthine library of the monastery burns and all that remains is a mass of fragments.

In *The Dumas Club* (1993), by the Spaniard Arturo Pérez-Reverte (b. 1951), the character Lucas Corso is "a mercenary of bibliophilia." Corso embarks on a fascinating investigation into a chapter interpolated into an edition of a book by Dumas and, at the same time, into a 1666 book called *De Umbrarum Regni Novem Portis* (The Nine Doors of the Kingdom of Shadows), published by a certain Aristide Torchia (1620–1667). It seems most copies of the book were destroyed, but a few remain in the hands of discerning collectors. In the book are nine engravings (some authentic, others false), copied or taken from the *Delomelanicon* (dictated by Lucifer), which grant unlimited power over all things. In evoking Borges, Pérez-Reverte alludes to an *Encyclopedia of Printers and Rare and Curious Books* by a certain Crozet, where the destruction of Torchia's books is mentioned.

Jan van Aken is a Dutch autodidact who has written a series of historical novels that always include book destruction. His second book was *De valse dageraad* (2000), about the loss of numerous libraries during the most obscure era in European history. Its principal characters are Otto III and Pope Sylvester II.

Since the 1990s, the theme of book destruction has seized the imagination of poets and novelists. Ross King, author of *Brunelleschi's Dome* among other books, uses the fantasy of a manuscript, lost, recovered, and finally burned, in his *Ex Libris* (1998). In Ursula K. Le Guin's *Voices* (2006), the protagonist is a young girl who studies reading in a secret library that has survived the ravages of her country's merciless occupiers, who fear nothing so much as a book. When the invaders come across a book, they commandeer one of the locals to bring it to the sea to cast it in, as even the touch of a book, any book, would defile the hands of the pure.

Part Three

From the Twentieth Century to the Present

Chapter 19

The Rise of Fascism

Some years ago, I was looking for a work by Miguel de Unamuno in an antiquarian bookshop in Madrid. The shop, dark and badly kept, was a gothic place, with rooms of different sizes, blue shelves made of metal, sterile ivory-colored walls, and windows with high arches. I recall—because I can't forget—how the owner imposed an oppressive, almost humiliating silence on the place. It was a hot afternoon, and I could barely read the almost illegible names of the authors on the spines of the books. The clerk, busy with the sports page, ignored me, so I drifted into a corner avoided by the other customers. Before my eyes, new and old books mixed: The Abad de Rute's *Didascalia multiplex* (1615) with manuscript notes, a manual of African sexual mythology (illustrated), Antonio de Torquemada's *Garden of Curious Flowers* (1570).

The book I wanted did not turn up, but by chance I picked up a volume whose binding was broken, a book being consumed by insects. It had no covers; the colophon was a stain. The long introduction had been torn out. The wormholes made a coherent reading impossible. It was a collection of poems by Federico García Lorca. Fascinated, I tried to decipher the text, but just lifting it up made pieces fall out. There was an official note by a censor: "Forbidden book. Asturias, Hell." Intrigued, I asked the price, but the implacable owner, visibly annoyed, told me to remove it from the premises. Seeing that I was upset, he said: "Take it away,

I have no idea who could have brought that Communist's book here."

His tone unleashed fears I never expected to have in a bookshop. The book's dilapidated state, the fact that it had been overlooked by the eagle-eyed owner, and then recognizing the forbidden poems of a poet who'd been murdered, alarmed me. I fled, my throat dry with nervousness. Outside, rain pelted the pavement, and when I finally found a taxi, the broken book turned up in one of my overcoat pockets.

That's how this investigation began, because of a mistake, like all things of importance. Armed with that ruined book as my only talisman, I found out that in addition to the hundreds of thousands of casualties, the Spanish Civil War, which began officially on July 18, 1936, and ended in April 1939, left behind a cultural disaster that remained hidden for decades.

Even at the start of the war, during the period of the republic, books were being destroyed. Between May 10 and 11, the libraries and archives of convents and monasteries were burned; virulent enemies of the church destroyed catechisms, books, and pamphlets related to right-wing Catholicism as they vandalized churches. Some attribute these acts to anarchist groups, but many historians see in the destruction of churches, the murder of priests, and the elimination of Catholic texts the origin of a hatred among the people that opened the way for later conflicts. This unfortunate assault on ecclesiastical texts took place against the will of republican intellectuals such as Antonio Rodríguez-Moñino (1910–1970). This bibliophile had studied with the Augustinians at El Escorial, was a member of Azaña's party, and was a spokesperson for the Appropriation Committee, which fought to stop the destruction of certain cultural properties. He was one of the few who dared to defend the numismatic collection of the Archaeological Museum, where hundreds of valuable gold coins disappeared. When the armed combat intensified, he insisted on saving archives and books.

Ironically, these attacks took place during one of the richest periods of Spanish culture: poets of the Generation of 1927 like García Lorca or Jorge Guillén were at their peak; filmmakers like Luis Buñuel were creating their first great works; artists such as Salvador Dalí (following in the wake of Picasso and Juan Gris) were changing the history of painting; and thinkers like Miguel de Unamuno and José Ortega y Gasset were infusing new vitality into the essay and Spanish philosophy.

But in October 1934, in Asturias, a popular uprising metamorphosed into a kind of Commune, unleashing a ferocious repression in which any impartial observer could detect the personality of General Francisco Franco and his followers. Police agencies destroyed the books in more than 257 libraries for the poor. The library of the University of Asturias, whose manuscript division was admired by neighboring institutions, burned on October 13, 1934. The dean of the University of Oviedo, Sabino Alvarez Gendín, along with a group of important citizens, created a Commission for the Cleansing of Libraries. Their rigor eliminated hundreds of texts until 1939. They confiscated all books defined as pornographic, revolutionary, or harmful to public morality. Some of those works were placed in a section called Hell (like the one I'd found in the shop) in the Oviedo Public Library, which did not reopen until 1974.

In November 1936, the zealous soldiers of General Franco occupied Alcorcón, Leganés, Getafe, and Cuatro Vientos. They even managed to reach the outskirts of Madrid. The fighting concentrated against the defenses of the Popular Front, a strategy that included controlling zones like that of Casa de Campo, Puente de los Franceses, University City, and Parque del Oeste. During the violence, the Parque Metropolitano, a residential area, was severely bombarded. One of the homes destroyed was located at Velintonia 3, where the poet Vicente Aleixandre, a member of the Generation of 1927 and winner of the Nobel Prize for Literature in 1927, lived. A week later, the poet, in great pain and accompanied by Miguel Hernández, returned to his home to try to rescue his belongings. Under the wreckage, he found his entire library. He wept at the sight and managed to take with him twelve dust-covered books of poetry.

That military campaign reduced many bookstores and libraries to ashes. The book collections of the poet Manuel Altolaguirre and of the painter Moreno Villa, as well as the books of the writer Emilio Prados were all lost. The war turned University City in Madrid into another combat zone, and according to the tales of the combatants, the books were right next to them: "The Moorish machine guns fire over the trenches while the young soldiers go to school." Some verses from the period reflect republican concerns about the destruction of books at the hands of the Fascists. This is from the battle song of the Mateotti Battalion.

Fascism is a vile enemy
Of peace and culture:
It suppresses books and schools
And is the graveyard of science.

In 1936, in Granada, a Francoist deputy, Ramón Ruiz Alonso, arrested Federico García Lorca, and accused him of supporting the Popular Front. But the principal reason for Lorca's arrest was his open homosexuality. It is believed he was shot on August 18 or 19.

The National Library in Madrid was bombed in 1937, and only the bravery of the librarians saved hundreds of books and manuscripts. The historical archive of the Universidad Complutense suffered numerous attacks, which meant the loss of scores of fifteenth-century books. Only through hard labor could a group of researchers manage to restore, in 2002, a book by Jiménez de Rada, the Greek Bible, the Hebrew Bible, and the Sanctorale. Taking advantage of the chaos unleashed in November 1936, the anarchist leader Juan García Oliver destroyed the principal judicial registers in Madrid, an act repeated in Barcelona and other cities.

During the occupation of Barcelona, Franco's troops confiscated the last issue of the magazine *Hora de España*. They burned all copies but one, from which a reissue was made. The high quality of the content is obvious: writings by Antonio Machado, Octavio Paz, and José Bergamín, to name just three. About what transpired in Barcelona, Hugh Thomas notes:

> Nevertheless, the principal works of art were saved, because the Generalitat mobilized its agents to save collections of art and libraries. Though many treasures of a secondary order were lost, the only act of vandalism was the burning of the ten thousand volumes in the library of the Cathedral of Cuenca, among which was the celebrated Catechism of the Indies. Also destroyed were the paintings thought to be Goya's earliest works, which were on the wooden door of a reliquary chamber in the parish church of Fuendetodos, his home town.

In addition to these disasters, the Ateneu Enciclopèdic Popular was destroyed on March 27, 1939, and at least 6,000 books were thrown out of the windows. In Barcelona, seventy-two tons of books, from bookshops, publishers, and both private and public libraries (the Can Mainadé, Esplugues de Llobregat, for example) were annihilated for their communist contents.

In Navarra, the Fascist leaders removed from schools and libraries "all antipatriotic, sectarian, immoral, heretical, and pornographic books, newspapers, and pamphlets which have brought about the state of corruption and misery in the minds of the masses." The burning of books was a frequent ritual after attacks on institutions and homes. In its first number, *Arriba España!* made it clear: "Comrade! You have the obligation to persecute Judaism, Masons, Marxism, and separatism. Destroy and burn their newspapers, books, magazines, and propaganda. Comrade! For the sake of God and the fatherland!" But even they, seeing the proliferation of bonfires, asked for calm. Censorship was fine, purging public libraries was fine, but private libraries were to be left in peace. It was now November 1936. With the left-wing libraries destroyed, an attempt was made to protect the rest.

On September 2, 1937, the Ministry of Public Education, directed by Jesús Hernánez, a Communist, ordered the Madrid archives sequestered to be used in paper factories. All Spanish archives were seriously damaged, and the nation's patrimony diminished. From the archives of the Ministry of Public Education, twenty-eight tons of paper were eliminated, with documents covering the years 1842–1914, and as if that wasn't atrocious enough, the basements were checked and a huge quantity of books (44,000 pounds) was found. They were thought to be fascistic, so they were destroyed.

The Spanish Civil War, like all civil wars, directly attacked freedom of expression. On December 23, 1936, the State Technical Committee promulgated a decree against the production and sale of pornographic literature. On May 22, the Delegation of the State for Press and Propaganda recommended that a single office take charge of the censoring of books, pamphlets, and other printed material. A 1937 order from the Office of the President of the State Technical Committee promulgated a policy of purging libraries and cultural centers. The main idea was to withdraw "any publication that, devoid of recognized artistic or archaeological value, may serve, through its reading, the propagation of ideas that may be damaging to society."

Shortly thereafter, the Ministry of the Interior limited the distribution of foreign works. It also formalized the confiscation of texts of a political and social nature. Some books were stored in warehouses, but others, for lack of space, were lost. Then came a decree imposing the norms for the purging of libraries and the creation of limited-access sections in Spanish libraries.

The juridical results were, obviously, devastating, and as Francoism triumphed, the mechanisms of censorship grew: booksellers were required to purge their stock. In 1939, the National Propaganda Service published an advisory to all booksellers, telling them that the reopening of their shops could only take place once they had personally received instructions with regard to the purging of their stock. It was under these auspices that the dictatorship of Francisco Franco began.

The Holocaust describes the systematic annihilation of millions of Jews by the Nazis during World War II. But that event was preceded by the Bibliocaust, in which millions of books were destroyed by Hitler's party. The destruction of books in 1933 was the prologue to the slaughter that followed. The bonfires of books inspired the crematory ovens.

Well before 1933, the Nazis persecuted authors. They would enter bookshops and remove the works of Erich Maria Remarque. In 1930, they interrupted a speech by Thomas Mann. They telephoned authors every day and threatened them. They painted graffiti on their houses and even attacked their homes. Among those most persecuted were Thomas Mann, Arnold Zweig, Lion Feuchtwanger, Carl von Ossietzky, and Fritz von Unruh. Authors of Jewish origin were publicly mocked. In 1932, the newspaper *Völkischer Beobachter* published a letter signed by twenty-four professors who expressed their rejection of communist writers and warned about the need to save the purity of cultural symbols in Germany.

The barbarity actually began on January 30, 1933, when Paul von Hindenberg, president of the Weimar Republic, named Adolf Hitler chancellor. Hitler wasted no time in developing a strategy to intimidate Jews, unions, and members of rival political parties. On February 4, 1933, the Law for the Protection of the German People restricted freedom of the press and announced plans to confiscate material considered dangerous. The next day, the offices of the Communist Party were savagely attacked and their libraries destroyed. On February 27, the German parliament building, the famous Reichstag, burned along with all its archives. The Communists were blamed. On February 28, a revision of the Law for the Protection of the German People imposed exceptional measures on the country. Freedom to gather, freedom of the press, and freedom of expression were all restricted. In fraudulent elections, the Nazi Party obtained a majority, and the Third Reich was born.

Germany transformed its institutions after the terrible defeat it suffered during World War I. Hitler, who was not German, was thought to be the ideal statesman to rescue collective self-esteem. His purges of the opposition transformed him into a feared leader. His efficacy was supported by several men: Hermann Göring, Alfred Rosenberg, and (perhaps the most eccentric) Joseph Goebbels. They were all fanatics, but it was Goebbels who convinced Hitler to accelerate the measures they were already executing and to name him head of a new state entity, the Reichsministerium fur Völksaufklarung und Propaganda (Minister of the Reich for Enlightening the People and for Propaganda).

Hitler gave Goebbels carte blanche. Goebbels possessed a doctoral degree in philology at Heidelberg, where Hegel once taught. He was a passionate reader of the Greek classics, and insofar as political thinking was concerned, he preferred the study of Marxist texts, along with everything else written against the bourgeoisie. He admired Friedrich Nietzsche, recited poetry from memory, and wrote dramatic texts. When he joined Hitler, he found his true vocation, and as minister, in 1933, he drafted the Law Relative to State Government, which took effect on April 7 of the same year. Now he had absolute control over education and he radically changed schools and universities.

Political police groups like the SA, the SS, and the Gestapo unleashed a campaign of intimidation that often frightened people into burning their own books. Book burnings took place all over Germany. The book dealer Wolfgang Hermann spent his days preparing a blacklist with the names of authors to be prohibited and expunged.

A kind of fervor, restrained only by international European pressure, took control of students and intellectuals. In April, the *Theses Against the Anti-Germanic Spirit* appeared. Of the twelve theses, the fourth declared: "Our most dangerous adversary is the Jew." On April 11, in Düsseldorf, books were burned. Some of the most prominent philosophers embraced Goebbels's ideas: one such was Martin Heidegger, who had recently become a member of the Community of Political-Cultural Labor for Professors at the German University, despite the fact his retired mentor, Edmund Husserl, was forbidden library access due to his Jewish heritage. In April, Heidegger was named rector of the University of Freiburg and the next month joined the Nazi Party. When Karl Jaspers excoriated Heidegger for supporting a man as poorly educated as Hitler, the author of *Being and Time* answered: "Education is irrelevant, just look at his precious hands!"

On May 2, texts in the Gewerkschaftshaus in Leipzig were destroyed, but on May 5 things really got going. The students at the University of Cologne went to the library and removed all books by Jewish authors. Hours later, delivering a message intended for the entire world to hear, they burned them. The students then went to private houses and publishers' warehouses to confiscate books. This was the case of the Schutzverband Deutscher Schriftseller, an association of 500 writers. At universities and schools, professors and teachers joined in these actions to indoctrinate new students in the frenzy of national purification.

In the morning of May 6, the youth wing of the Nazi Party, along with members of other organizations, removed half a ton of books and pamphlets from the Institut für Sexualwissenschaft (Institute for Sexual Research) in Berlin, a venerable institution founded in 1918 by Dr. Magnus Hirschfeld. Ultimately, it is thought, 10,000 books, along with letters, reports, and confidential papers, were removed. On the corner of the cathedral of Münster, tied to a tree, were "books of shame." Goebbels organized meetings every night leading up to a grand "apology to German culture."

On May 8, there were disturbances in Freiburg and book burnings in which, according to witnesses, Heidegger took part. The next day, Goebbels addressed the actors' union and warned them: "I reject the concept that says the artist can be apolitical. . . . The artist cannot lag behind and should take up the flag to lead the march." Surrounded by the most talented interpreters of the dramas of Goethe and Schiller, he invited them to purge all Jewish traits from German culture.

On May 10, the members of the Association of German Students gathered up all forbidden books. There was an unexpected, contagious euphoria. The books, together with what had been removed from centers like the Institute for Sexual Research or from captured Jewish libraries, were transported to Opernplatz. In all, over 25,000 books piled up. Soon a mob gathered around the students, who sang an anthem that made a great impression on the spectators. Each stanza began with an ideological maxim and ended with the name of an author whose works were to be burned. For example:

Against the materialist, utilitarian class.
For a community of people and an ideal form of life.
Marx, Kautsky

The bonfire burned for hours. After boisterously greeting the public, Goebbels explained the reasons for the fire and urged the students to keep at it. The Bücherverbrennung (book burning), the details of which had been kept secret until that instant, soon revealed its true dimensions: on that same day, books were burned in cities all over Germany. In Frankfurt, books were brought in on trucks, and the students made human chains to get them to the bonfire. In Munich, days before the burning, a program was distributed with a description of events: a musical prelude, a speech by Leo Ritter, the prestigious rector of the university, a speech by Kurt Ellersiek, president of the German Students Association, then more music, the overture to Beethoven's "Egmont," songs by a celebrated soprano, and finally Beethoven's "The Glory of God in Nature."

The night of the burnings, Hitler was dining with friends, and when he was informed that thousands of books were burning, he turned to his dinner partner and made a strange comment about Goebbels: "He believes in what he's doing." Indeed, he did.

The impact of the May 1933 burnings was enormous. Sigmund Freud told a journalist that book burning was an advance in human history: "In the Middle Ages, they would have burned me. Now they're happy burning my books." There were protest demonstrations by intellectuals in New York. *Newsweek* did not hesitate to call it a "book holocaust," and *Time* used the term "bibliocaust." The blind writer Helen Keller published an "Open Letter to German Students": "You may burn my books and the books of the best minds in Europe, but the ideas those books contain have passed through millions of channels and will go on." Bertolt Brecht inverted the burning in a poem "Die Bücherverbrennung," written shortly after he learned his works had been destroyed, taking the ironic role of a writer whose books had not been burned and who demanded they be incinerated.

Irony and mockery couldn't stop Goebbels. On August 14, he noted in his diary that he was thinking of convening a Reichskulturkammer, or chamber of culture for the Reich, with its various divisions: press, radio, literature, movies, theater, music, and visual arts. In September, he put the idea into practice. The purpose of this chamber was to stimulate the Aryanization of German culture and to prohibit, for example, atonal Jewish music, the blues, surrealism, cubism, and dadaism.

On April 25, 1935, Goebbels assumed complete control over censorship. This allowed him to purge all libraries in the country, public and private, with the help of the Gestapo and the Sicherheitsdienst. That same year, the Reichsschrifttumskammer prohibited the work of 524 authors. The naming of Heinrich Himmler as head of the SS on June 17, 1936, further aided Goebbels: now he had at his disposal a centralized police force that would carry out any order without hesitation.

In 1937, the Nazi regime compiled a list of artworks to be condemned. As a result, over 15,000 works of art were confiscated, and at least 650 paintings, sculptures, and books were exhibited in Munich in a show called "Degenerate Art." A year later, pieces of "Degenerate Music" were played. Siegfried Kracauer's work, "The Salaried Masses" (1930) was burned because its sociological analysis contradicted the imaginary statistics concocted by the Nazis.

Goebbels's only rival in the book-burning campaign was Alfred Rosenberg, director of the Office for General Supervision of Culture, Ideology, Education, and Instruction. Rosenberg was the author of *The Myth of the Twentieth Century* (1930), an influential book that won him Hitler's respect. But even Rosenberg, a reader of Schopenhauer and a lover of classical music, bitterly acknowledged the reason for Goebbels's triumph: "He fed the theatrical element in the führer."

Rosenberg created the Ensatzstab Reichsleiter Rosenberg (ERR), which confiscated cultural goods for the Institut zur Erforschung der Judenfrage (Institute for the Investigation of the Jewish Question). In July 1940, with the war under way, the order was given to obtain books for the grand Nazi library, the Hohe Schule, to be located in Bavaria. On March 1, a decree authorized the ERR to launch an attack against "Jews, Masons, and other ideological opponents of National Socialism." It executed its task with ruthless efficiency.

Through the Ministry of Propaganda or the ERR, the Nazis destroyed or quarantined the culture of all the nations they invaded. In 1940, Holland suffered unprecedented looting. In September 1940, the Kloss library of the Masons was confiscated along with the library of the Institute of Social History, founded in 1934, with 160,000 books. Amsterdam's Rosenthal Library, with 100,000 volumes, was seized; in 1945, when some of the Rosenthal books were recovered, it was discovered that many had been shot. The Archive of the Women's Movement was sacked, as was that of the Theosophic Society, which had works in Sanskrit.

The support of the Wehrmacht commander in Holland facilitated the massive confiscation of books. The Beth-Hamidrasch Etz Chaim library in Amsterdam, founded in 1740 and with a collection of 4,000 volumes, was ransacked. The Israel Seminary of Holland with 4,300 volumes in Hebrew and 2,000 on Jewish subjects was destroyed, as was the Jewish Literary Society, with its precious manuscript collection covering the period 1480–1560. Between 1942 and 1944, 29,000 deported Jews lost one million books.

In Belgium, the damage to the bibliographic patrimony was severe. The library of the University of Louvain was burned for the second time. On January 18, 1941, G. Utikal, operational leader of the ERR in the West, informed Rosenberg of his labors in the confiscation of libraries and his interest in the books of politicians who had fled the country: P. van Zeeland, C. Huymans, P. H. Spaak, A. Wauters, and V. de Lavaley, for example. Between October 1940 and February 1943, 800 boxes of books were sent to Berlin. It is thought 120,000 works were stolen. After June 21, 1940, the collection of the communist bookshop Obla was seized, an action followed by the search of 8,000 houses and apartments. The same thing happened to the Cosmopolis bookshop, the Instituut vor Sociale Gschiedenis, and the Jesuit House, which held 600,00 books.

France was occupied on May 2, 1940, when German tanks bypassed the Maginot Line. On June 3, Paris was bombarded. Eleven days later, the Nazi army entered the capital and marched down the Champs-Élysées. The ERR confiscated 723 libraries and 1,767,108 books. The works in the Universal Israel Alliance (40,000 books), the Rabbinical School (10,000 books), the Society of French Jews (4,000 volumes), the 20,000 texts in the Lipschutz bookshop, and David Weill's collection of 5,000 books were all sent to Frankfurt. Thousands of Jewish works were burned.

Between 1940 and 1944, the Jeu de Paume museum became a warehouse holding 22,000 works of art stolen by the Nazis. Jacques Jaujard, director of the National

Museums of France, attempted with little luck to evacuate treasures from the Louvre in order to protect them. The Sonderstab Musik unit confiscated thousands of books and musical instruments belonging to virtuosos like Wanda Landowska, Darius Milhaud, Gregor Piatigorski, and Arthur Rubinstein.

The Turgenev Library in Paris was a prestigious institution for Russian emigrés; Lenin had studied there and the papers of Ivan Bunin, the first Russian writer to win the Nobel Prize for Literature, were deposited there. The ERR seized 100,000 books and arrested the shocked director. The statues, paintings, and archives belonging to the library were also confiscated. Years later, the books were scattered, and what survived went to the Soviet Union. During the 1950s, various books were sent to the Lenin Library, but a considerable number were placed in the Legnica Officers Club. The librarian burned them.

On March 12, 1938, Austria was occupied by the Nazi army. There was no resistance, and attacks on Jews and their cultural institutions began immediately. The persecution of intellectuals was especially cruel, and many writers chose suicide. On April 24, 1939, Martin Borman signed Order 84–39, which sought to unify the work of confiscation by having all material brought intact to established centers for evaluation.

Curious excesses were committed. For example, an edition of Homer in Greek was removed from one library because agents thought it contained anti-Nazi notes in code. The books of the rabbi of Vienna, Dr. Israel Taglicht, were also confiscated. Josef Bick, director of the Vienna Library, was arrested and sent to Dachau. Many of Baron Louis de Rothschild's books were pillaged and lost forever. Some books, including the Talmud and the Torah, were thrown into the Danube.

On November 10, the Nazis destroyed 267 synagogues and their libraries. In open rivalry with the ERR, Goebbels's Ministry of Propaganda had a Department for the Evaluation of Books in Vienna, the Bücherverwertungsstelle, supported by the Gestapo and the Sicherheitsdienst, the SD. By May 25, 1939, the number of books taken from Masonic lodges in the warehouses of this department numbered 644,000, of which 410,000 were pulped.

Long before World War II, Poland's powerful Jewish community distinguished itself by creating numerous cultural centers with important libraries and archives. In Kraców, around 1837, the writer and bookseller Abraham Gumplowicz had founded the first lending library in the Kazimeirz neighborhood. It was a modest collection of a thousand books in English, German, Hebrew, and Polish. Halfway through the nineteenth century, Joanna Gumplowicz founded a lending library that came to have 6,000 books. The Ezra Library opened its doors in 1899, and became a prestigious reference center, containing rabbinical texts and newspapers.

In Warsaw, the Jewish Library of the Great Synagogue contained more than 40,000 volumes. In Vilna, the Strashun Library held a similar amount. The library of the YIVO Institute, which had been founded in 1925 by leading European intellectuals such as Albert Einstein and Sigmund Freud, possessed 100,000. The Alejchem Public Library had 41,834 books, of which 13,930 were in Yiddish. The synagogues also contained libraries for talmudic study, and some owned rare copies of incalculable value. For example, the Rema Synagogue, founded in 1553, had medieval Bibles and a copy of the *Seder haftarot* published in 1666. The Ajzyk Synagogue had books illuminated in 1646. Socialist and Zionist groups founded libraries like the Jusisze Socjalistisze Bibliotek, the I. L. Peretz Library, and the Jedno Library. In the Jewish schools there were highly respected libraries. In Kraców, for example, the library of the Association of Jewish

Students of the College of Administration and Commerce had 5,553 books.

On September 1, 1939, at 4:45 A.M., those cultural riches were ground into dust. The panzer divisions were followed by motorized infantry and supported by the Luftwaffe, which mercilessly bombed the country. Within three weeks, Polish resistance ended, and the government fled to Romania. The perverse process of cultural purification began immediately. The Brenn-Kommandos abolished Jewish synagogues and burned the Grand Talmudic Library of the Jewish Theological Seminary at Lublin. A Nazi report pointed out that it was "a source of special pride to destroy the Talmudic Academy, known as one of the largest in Poland. . . . We removed the notable talmudic library from the building, put the books in the marketplace, and set fire to them. They burned for twenty hours."

Starting in 1939, not a week went by without an attack on a Polish library or museum. The Raczynsky Library, the Library of the Scientific Society, and the Library of the Cathedral (which possessed a renowned collection of incunabula published between 1450 and 1501) suffered devastating fires. In Warsaw, the National Library was destroyed in October 1944 with savage thoroughness: 700,000 books were burned. The military library with 350,000 works was destroyed, and when the Germans retreated from Poland in 1944, they burned the archives of the public library. A similar fate destroyed the university's technological library with its 78,000 books. Some years later, bibliophiles barely managed to rescue 3,850 titles.

The mathematician Waclaw Sierpinksi (1882–1969), famous for having solved a problem created by the paradoxical Gauss and for having written unintelligible books like *The Theory of Irrational Numbers* (1910), was persecuted. In 1944, the Nazis, worried about his discoveries, sacked his library and those of his colleagues.

Kracków was bombarded for three days in 1939. The soldiers destroyed the Hilfstein Library and that of the Association of Jewish Students of the College of Administration and Commerce. School libraries, especially, were sacked and destroyed. The books in the Ceder Iwri School and the women's school were burned. By the end of the war, there were no books in Jewish schools.

On September 13, the synagogues of Kracków were closed. All copies of the Talmud and Torah were burned. German libraries, the Staatsbibliothek Krakau, created in April 1941, for instance, replaced the Jewish centers. Amid this horror, a commission coordinated by the erudite Peter Paulsen came to Kracków and ordered the confiscation of books and works of art.

Experts say some fifteen million books were lost in Poland. In 1940, the purging of bookshops and libraries was carried out by the Hauptabteilung Propaganda de Regierung des Generalgouvernements (Department of Governmental General Administration). They had the dubious honor of preparing lists of forbidden titles, which included some 3,200 works. Scores of authors were proscribed: Daniel Gross, Moses Schorr, Zofia Ameisenowa, Jakub Appenschlak, Szymon Askenazy, Maksymilian Baruch, Alexander Kraushar, Bruno Jasienski, Aleksander Alfred Konar, Januz Korczak, Adolf Rudnicki, Antoni Sonimski, Julian Tuwim, Bruno Winawer, Józef Wittlin, and many, many others.

Between 1940 and 1942, England was subjected to intense German aerial bombardment. About 100,000 books disappeared in the destruction of the Coventry library. The Central Lending Library of Liverpool and its books completely disappeared. In London, the library of the Inner Temple, restored in 1668 and augmented by valuable donations, was bombed. The tower fell on September 19, 1940, and the despairing librarians tried to put the books in boxes, but during May of 1941, the entire John Austin jurisprudence collection

(133 texts with manuscript notes) vanished. Bombs wrecked
the Grand Hall of the University of Bristol, which held 7,000
books brought from King's College. Guildhall lost more
than 25,000 works. The Minet public library lost 20,000
books. The British Museum was attacked, but the incredible
courage of the librarians kept the losses to under a quarter
of a million books and 30,000 volumes of newspapers.

In the Sudetenland, libraries were attacked, universities
closed, and, in 1942, a decree ordered the surrender of all
Czech writings in rare or first editions. Books by Czech
Jews disappeared. The library of the University of Prague
was severely damaged, with a loss of some 25,000 books.
When the occupation ended, two million books, including
the Slavic Bible and seven codices from the library of Jan
Hodejovsky, were burned.

In Russia, the destruction of memory was systematically
undertaken. In Petrovoredz there were art museums and
11,700 rare books in the palace libraries. On September 23,
1941, the Germans sacked the museums and burned any books
they considered improper. The same policy was applied in
Novgorod and Smolensk. A total of 112 libraries, four museums, and fifty-four theaters were destroyed around Moscow.
Tolstoy's House-Museum in Yasnaya Polyana was looted and
several manuscripts burned. Belorussia lost its libraries, while
the Ukraine lost 151 museums and 19,200 libraries.

Nazi policies meant millions of books and works of art
were either destroyed or moved to Germany. In many cases,
those that survived have yet to return to their place of origin.
Owners of thousands of collections have demanded their
return with no success.

According to one scholar, the works of more than 5,000
authors were destroyed. The principal works of the most
outstanding writers of early twentieth-century Germany
were continuously forbidden and mercilessly burned. The

Commission for Jewish-European Cultural Reconstruction determined in 1933 that there were 469 collections of Jewish books, more than 3,307,000 volumes in various locales. In Poland, for example, there were 251 libraries with 1,650,000 books; in Germany, fifty-five libraries with 422,000 books; in the Soviet Union, seven libraries with 332,000 books; in Holland, seventeen libraries with 74,000 books; in Romania, twenty-five libraries with 69,000 books; in Lithuania, nineteen libraries with 67,000 books; and in Czechoslovakia, eight libraries with 58,000 books. At the end of the war, not even one-quarter of those books remained.

Jewish books were considered "enemies of the people" and forbidden. Between 1941 and 1943, the owners of collections were deported and their libraries confiscated. Pulping Jewish books was a common practice. A memorandum from the ERR to the Department of Finance in the City of Mainz, August 1943, read: "Books in the Hebrew language should be sent to this office if they date from before 1800.... Books in the Hebrew language of recent date should be deposited for pulping." The Jewish collections in Poland or Vienna were burned in a fire at the offices of the Reichssicherheit-shauptamt (Central Security Office of the Reich), which occurred between November 22 and 23, 1943.

Ruins upon Ruins

Although it might not seem possible, with the collapse of the Reich, a whole new wave of cultural destruction occurred.

When the Germans retreated from France in 1944, they destroyed the municipal library in Dieppe. More than 110,000 volumes perished with the Douai library. The library of the Societé Commerciale in Le Havre, with thousands of historical and geographical works, was bombed. In the same year a German solider attempted to save his nation's honor by tossing a hand grenade into a storage chamber in Saint-Quentin. The chamber held thousands of books from the Metz library, so his heroic act destroyed the eleventh-century Reichenau Sacraments and an illuminated thirteenth-century manuscript.

In 1944, the library of the National Assembly in Paris was attacked, with a loss of 40,000 ancient books. Some 300,000 books were incinerated by German bombs in September of 1944 when the National Library and the library of the University of Strasbourg were shelled. Tours lost 200,000 works, and hundreds of incunabula and manuscripts.

On the night of March 9, 1943, half a million books on humanities and natural sciences in the Bavarian Library were incinerated, along with the greatest Bible collection in the world. In the city of Aachen, 50,000 volumes from the Technical University, along with hundreds of doctoral dissertations and newspapers, were destroyed in July, 1943.

Berlin was the scene of savage fighting. Thousands of corpses littered the streets, and the cultural losses were colossal. The Staatsbibliothek (the national library) lost two million works. Some 20,000 volumes were reduced to ashes during the attacks on the University of Berlin. Prestigious centers like the Stadtbibliothek (the city library), the Reichstag library, the library of the Deutsche Heeresbucherei did not survive.

The collection of the University of Bonn lost a quarter of its holdings. The Bremen Staatsbibliothek, famous for its rare works, ancient books, and annotated, illustrated classics were left in ruins. One hundred fifty thousand books disappeared. The Hessische Landesbibliothek in Darmstadt, with 760,000 books, 2,217 incunabula, and some 4,500 manuscripts was bombed until nothing was left but a burned-out plot of land. More fortunate, the Technical University of Darmstadt lost one third of its holdings.

About a quarter of a million books disappeared in the attacks on the Stadtbibliothek and the Landesbibliothek of Dortmund. Almost 300,000 books were incinerated when the Sächsische Landesbibliothek in Dresden was bombed several times in February and March of 1945. Dresden's Stadtbibliothek, after a surprise attack on February, 1945, no longer had a reference section; about 200,000 volumes and perhaps 12,000 books belonging to the Geographic Society, the Verein für Erdkunde, vanished. Essen's Stadtbücherei lost 130,000 volumes.

When Frankfurt was bombed, the Stadtbibliothek and the university library lost 550,000 books and 440,000 doctoral theses. More than 17,000 books and about 1,900 manuscripts by great authors disappeared in the bombing of Greifswald University. Between 1943 and 1944, at least 600,000 books were destroyed in Hamburg.

Hannover's Stadtbibliothek was twice left in ruins, first in 1943 and again in 1944: 125,000 texts disappeared. Almost 360,000 volumes were lost when the planes attacked the Badische Landesbibliothek in Karlruhe in September, 1942. The Technical University lost 63,000 books in the natural sciences.

In 1941, the Landesbibliothek in Kassel ceased to exist. The Murhardsch Bibliothek, also in Kassel, was reduced by half in 1943. The University of Kiel was attacked in April of 1942 and again in May 1944: a quarter of a million books were instantly lost. In 1944, the Schleswig-Holsteinische collection in Kiel was completely lost, while the University of Leipzig lost thousands of books and incunabula.

In Milan, bombardment eliminated 200,000 books from the public library. In Naples, the city archives, some 30,000 volumes and 50,000 documents, were moved to Montesano, south of Milan, to protect them. However, in September 1943, a German detachment examined the texts and burned them. Three hundred seventy-eight documents from the Anjou period (1265–1435), registers from Aragon, ancient manuscripts, codices, treatises from the Kingdom of Naples, archives of the Bourbon dynasty, the Farnese family, the courts, the Royal Chamber of Santa Clara, the Order of Malta, and the first notary documents were all lost.

Hitler's affection for Goebbels never waned, and he forgave him everything, even his perversions with prostitutes. On the day of his suicide in 1945, Hitler named Goebbels chancellor of the Reich, a title he held for only a few hours. When he learned that the Soviet troops demanded unconditional surrender, he refused. On May 1, Goebbels ordered a dentist to poison all his children. He watched his wife Magda swallow poison and die. Then, he shot himself. Decades later, his diary was discovered in Russia. He'd left 75,000 pages to the world to justify the Holocaust and the Bibliocaust.

Alfred Rosenberg was arrested and sentenced to death at the Nuremberg trials. He answered the hardest questions with complete calm. He hanged himself in his cell the morning of October 16, 1946.

Hitler's personal library was discovered in a salt mine near Berchtesgaden by soldiers from the 101st Division. Of a collection of more than 16,000 books, 3,000 remained. Some were stolen and others destroyed because of the information they contained. About 1,200 books were transferred to the U.S. Library of Congress in January 1952. Hitler appears to have been a voracious reader, a bibliophile fascinated by old editions, by Arthur Schopenhauer, and a total devotee of Ernst Schertel's *Magie: Geschichte, Theorie, Praxis* (1923). Hitler himself underlined this phrase: "He who does not bear within him the seeds of the demonic will never give birth to a new world." Perhaps these bizarre words explain the horrors of this chapter.

The End

At 8:15 in the morning on August 6, 1945, the "Enola Gay" dropped an atomic bomb on the Japanese city of Hiroshima. On August 9, at 11:02 A.M., another atomic bomb fell on Nagasaki. In both actions, more than one hundred thousand Japanese died. Not a single building was left standing in either city. Nagasaki's collection of classical books, a center to which Chinese books were brought in the nineteenth century, was erased. But other Japanese libraries were burned by incendiary bombs in Tokyo, Aomori, Miyagi (Sendai), Kochi, Oita, and Fukuoka.

Chapter 20

Censorship and Self-Censorship in the Modern Age

On September 21, 1915, Anthony Comstock died at the age of seventy-one. For forty long years, he had been feared as a modern inquisitor, and even today he is remembered as the man who destroyed the most books in the history of the United States.

Comstock was born on March 7, 1844, in New Canaan, Connecticut, and fought in the Civil War on the Union side. Something of what he saw must have influenced his subsequent actions. He moved to New York and, in 1872, worked in the Young Men's Christian Association. He read the Bible with a fervor that startled his friends. The devil, he thought, had taken control of many writers, and his mission on Earth was to end that atrocity. Nothing stopped him on his moral crusade.

In 1873, he founded the New York Society for the Suppression of Vice and managed to get what came to be known as the Comstock Law approved by Congress. The reverberations from this law, which made it illegal to send any text considered immoral through the mail, would be felt for almost a century in the country. (One of the more significant effects of this law occurred in 1959, when copies of D. H. Lawrence's *Lady Chatterley's Lover* were confiscated by the U.S. Post Office.) Comstock examined thousands of books and magazines and determined their moral quality with a single glance. Thanks to Comstock, about 120 tons of books, pamphlets, and magazines were publicly burned. He loathed the writings of George Bernard Shaw in particular. For his part, Shaw coined the word "comstockery," meaning "overzealous moral censorship." Comstock reputedly was proud of the number of writers whom he had driven to suicide (more than a dozen) in the course of his career.

Between 1940 and 1941, the United States confiscated and destroyed 600 tons of foreign books shipped to the West Coast. The State Department, sometimes covertly and other times openly, declared itself against certain books. In 1940, during a pre-McCarthy hunt for writers with communist sympathies, a surprise raid on a bookshop owned by one of the members of the Communist Party in Oklahoma City brought about the confiscation and burning of hundreds of works by Lenin and Marx. The shop's customers were arrested and the staff sentenced to ten years in prison.

In 1954, Wilhelm Reich's books began to be persecuted. On February 10 of that year, Civil Action No. 1056 tried to prohibit his works. On July 15, 1955, Criminal Action No. 5003 achieved the initial action's goal, and Reich's books were destroyed by the State Department.

In 1953, a blacklist was compiled of writers whose works were banned from libraries. Among the authors censored—those whose books were confiscated and either burned or pulped—were Howard Fast, Joseph Davies, Lillian Hellman, and Dashiell Hammett. The irony of all this is that no other country condemned Nazi book burning so vehemently as the United States.

From Theodore Dreiser to J. K. Rowling, with authors such as D. H. Lawrence, John Steinbeck, Mario Vargas Llosa, Jorge Amado, and Kurt Vonnegut Jr. in between, the persecution of writers' works was so common in the twentieth century that it practically became a mark of prestige to have one's work attacked. And this occurred not just under dictatorships or during wartime. James Joyce was dogged by censorship his entire life. When he published *Dubliners* (1912) in an edition of a thousand copies, the Dublin printer John Falconer burned all but one of them because he thought the book's language inappropriate. While waiting for a train, Joyce wrote "Gas from a Burner" to satirize biblioclasty, which contains these lines:

Who was it said: Resist not evil?
I'll burn that book, so help me the devil.

Dubliners was reissued in 1914. When the first installment of *Ulysses* appeared in *The Little Review*, Nora Barnacle, the author's wife, rejected it in disgust. Members of the U.S. Postal Service, heirs to the philosophy of Anthony Comstock though ignorant of the tastes of Mrs. Joyce, burned copies of the magazine to express their rage. In October 1920, the New York Society for the Suppression of Vice sued the editors of the magazine, and in 1921 Margaret Anderson and the other members of the editorial board were sentenced to pay a fine of $50. They were also prohibited from publishing any other chapters.

Lesser-known figures suffered as well. For example, in 1931 the Englishman James Hanley (1901–1984) published *Boy*, a novel about the initiation of a young sailor. A judge in Manchester fined the publisher 400 pounds and required him to withdraw the book from all shops. In 1934, the publisher released the book in a new edition. The police nabbed ninety-nine copies and immediately destroyed them. The novelist Hugh Walpole, whose works were widely read in England at the time, personally destroyed a copy in public, saying "It is so disagreeable and horrible, both in the narration and in the incidents it relates, that I am shocked the printers did not go on strike while printing it." Perhaps in recognition of his skills as a censor, Walpole was knighted in 1937.

Many better-known authors have had thousands of copies of their books destroyed. But perhaps the most egregious example is that of Salman Rushdie.

Salman Rushdie

On September 26, 1988, Viking Penguin, not without some trepidation, published *The Satanic Verses*, a satiric novel by the Anglo-Indian Salman Rushdie, who was born in Bombay on June 1, 1947. In the English-speaking world, initial criticism suggested the author did not know how to write and that when he did, he chose his themes poorly. Nonetheless, he won the Whitbread Award for the novel, a satire on Muhammad and Muslim taboos.

Islamic reaction was swift. An Indian minister, ignorant of the work's content, condemned it as blasphemous. A week later, thousands of photocopies of the most offensive passages began to circulate in Islamic centers of learning. The objective, to stir up indignation, was a complete success, because on October 8, newspapers in Saudi Arabia accused Rushdie of instigating a repudiation of Islam. In January 1989, television in Great Britain showed images of various groups of Arab intellectuals burning copies of *The Satanic Verses* in the streets of Bradford, West Yorkshire. In Islamabad, the American Cultural Center was sacked. These events were repeated around the world, and within a few weeks, the author was receiving death threats and the direct attacks of fanatics whenever he dared appear in public. In Kashmir, sixty people were wounded and one killed in a protest against the novel.

But this was just the beginning. Grand Ayatollah Sayyid Ruhollah Musawi Khomeini appeared in public on February 14, 1989, to announce that he'd decided to put an end to Rushdie's irreverence. Khomeini issued a fatwa ordering Rushdie's death. (The author V. S. Naipaul immediately commented that Khomeini's decree seemed an extreme form of literary criticism.) One million dollars was offered to the person who killed Rushdie. In 1993, the Norwegian publisher William Nygaard was attacked for publishing the work, and four years later the reward on Rushdie's head was doubled.

Worldwide burnings of Rushdie's books ensued. Some bookstores were vandalized and destroyed. And these attacks have not stopped. On February 12, 1999, a group of Muslims in India burned photographs of Rushdie along with his books. In the Jama Masjid, in Delhi, more than one hundred activists chanted against Rushdie, and some prayed for a saint would murder him. As late as 2007, when Queen Elizabeth II knighted Rushdie, there were renewed calls for his death.

Harry Potter

The crusade against Harry Potter deserves a chapter of its own, but let us content ourselves with just one example among many of the extremes of emotion aroused by the series: on Sunday, December 30, 2001, in Alamogordo, New Mexico, a religious community burned hundreds of copies of J. K. Rowling's Harry Potter books. Jack Brock, the leader of the Alamogordo Christ Community Church, explained that his intention was to point out that Harry Potter was not appropriate for youngsters because it inspired them to study witchcraft and magic. The books "are an abomination to God and to me" and likely to "destroy the lives of many young people." Of course, Brock and his flock admitted they'd never read a single Harry Potter book. But they did decide to toss a few Stephen King novels on the fire for good measure.

Proving there's more than one way to destroy a book, upon being denied a city permit to burn books, the Rev. Douglas

Taylor in Lewiston, Maine, has held several annual gatherings at which he cuts the Potter books up with scissors.

Self-Censorship

The destruction of books is no less deplorable when it is done by the proprietor of a collection, or the author him- or herself. And the burning of textbooks by students is a tradition as contemptible as it is ancient. When I finished secondary school, the first thing my classmates and I did after signing one another's shirts was to burn our textbooks. I was transfixed because I saw the teachers smiling their approval of the practice. This custom is long-lived, as we see in this description by Salvador García Jiménez:

> At one of the upper schools to which I was sent as a teacher, students burned several books at the end of the school year out on the basketball court. The faculty made itself ridiculous by standing there gaping, not knowing the key Freud gave to understanding that action with his interpretation of an episode from the childhood of Goethe. When Goethe throws the china out of the window after his brother's birth, he's carrying out a symbolic act through which he shows his desire to throw the baby out of the window because the baby has disturbed his world. For those students, the literature manual they toss on the fire represents their demanding, stupid, and pedantic schoolmarm.

In June, 2001, there was an outrageous episode on the sands of La Victoria Beach in Cadiz, Spain, where hundreds of students gathered to make a huge bonfire. Laughing and shouting, they threw all their texts, including many required readings, into the flames. An end-of-year party turned into the cremation of many classics of Spanish literature.

In 2006, in Chile, students on a protest march walked into the Humanities Section of the University of Chile and burned 1,200 books.

A common ritual at American universities (and some high schools) is for graduating students to burn the textbooks used in their final semester. One particularly ironic such burning took place in the summer of 2007, when a woman receiving her "Master of Science and Library and Information Science" from Florida State University celebrated the end of her formal scientific education by burning her books. The practice has been going on since at least the 1870s at Northwestern.

In the summer of 2007, authorities preempted students by burning more than 30,000 high school texts in West Java, Central Java, and South Sulawesi, Indonesia. The books questioned the official line on the attempted 1965 coup in Indonesia, in the aftermath of which as many as one million people were killed. For years, Communists had been blamed for the coup attempt.

"Burned without being read."

In the modern period, as in centuries past, authors often played the role of destroying angels to their creations. In his 1919 comment on *A Personal Record*, in *Notes on My Books* (1921), Joseph Conrad recalled that his father, a Polish revolutionary and a fine translator of Shakespeare and Victor Hugo, ordered his manuscripts burned. The description is still moving:

> It was done under his own superintendence. I happened to go into his room a little earlier than usual that

evening, and remaining unnoticed stayed to watch the nursing-sister feeding the blaze in the fireplace. My father sat in a deep armchair propped up with pillows. This is the last time I saw him out of bed. His aspect was to me not so much that of a man desperately ill, as mortally weary—a vanquished man. That act of destruction affected me profoundly by its air of surrender. Not before death, however. To a man of such strong faith death could not have been an enemy.

Franz Kafka asked Max Brod to burn his notebooks: "Dear Max: My last request: Everything I've left behind . . . is to be burned without being read." Brod did not do it. Kafka asked Dora Diamant to do the same thing and, faithful to Kafka, she burned the final part of his diary. Tongue in cheek, Borges suggests that anyone who wants his books burned should not leave the task to someone else.

In the mysterious blaze in June 1944 that burned down his cabin, Malcolm Lowry lost the manuscript of *In Ballast to the White Sea*. If the statement of his second wife is correct, more than two thousand pages of manuscript were lost. Some suggest Lowry set fire to his own home.

Ernst Junger, in his *Diary of the War and the Occupation*, acknowledges having burned his papers in 1945 out of fear of the Allies: "So that day I carried out the first auto-da-fè, or, to be more precise I threw a huge quantity of papers into the garbage bins out in the patio. Diaries from 1919, poetry, and letters. I did it with no sorrow; the events had a character that urged the action on. It was time to lose ballast. It even seemed agreeable."

In his *Autobiographical Essay*, Borges claimed that he would buy and burn his early works "if the price was not too high." Until the end of his life, he refused to reissue three of those books: *Inquisitions* (1925), *The Dimensions of My Hope* (1926), and *The Language of the Argentines* (1928).

Vladimir Nabokov was thwarted in destroying his manuscripts in both life and death. When he was teaching at Cornell, his wife Véra prevented him from incinerating the as-yet-unpublished manuscript of *Lolita*. After his death, he left instructions that the manuscript *The Original of Laura* should be burnt. His wife failed to do so. To date, his son Dmitri has also apparently declined to do so, and as of this book's publication, has hinted that he may release the work to the public.

When he died, the Romanian writer Emil Cioran left almost thirty-four notebooks, about a thousand pages, with one succinct instruction pertaining to them: "Destroy."

Chapter 21

China and the Soviet Union

On June 24, 1900, in Beijing, a coalition of allied Western troops faced the powerful Chinese nationalist movement. War had been declared on June 21, and some three thousand Catholics, including forty-three Italian and French sailors, took refuge in a cathedral. The Chinese set fire to the British legation; the wind spread the fire toward the Han Lin Yuan (Imperial Library), the most important intellectual center in all China.

The powerful blaze could not be contained, and soon the walls, along with the floor and roof, were on fire. The library did not escape unscathed. Lancelot Giles, son of the sinologist Herbert Allen Giles, witnessed the events and describes the panic among scholars about the burning of the legendary Yong Lo Da Dia, an encyclopedia with 22,937 divisions covering all things human and divine in 370 million words. Lancelot threw himself into the flames, and in a laconic confession said: "I saved section 13,345 by myself."

It was an almost useless act because, in an early sort of hypertext, all the sections referred to others. It was said that in order to read a paragraph of the encyclopedia it was necessary to know all dialects of Chinese and venture into the exploration of astronomy and zoology. When it was finished, scholars compared it to the universe, because it was assumed no one would ever read it through. Like the Great Wall, the encyclopedia was a vast construction in defense of

Chinese identity. We should note that the encyclopedia was never printed and always kept in manuscript. It disappeared for the first time in a fire in 1449; the only extant copy, restored from memory, was the one burned in 1900. The Han Lin Yuan library lacked a reliable catalog, though it did contain, among other things, an encyclopedia that had been ordered by the second Ming emperor. It was completed in 1407, after 2,000 learned men worked on it. The British blamed the Chinese for burning their own culture, and the Chinese protested that the British had caused the fire to change course. The result was the same: the destruction of the grand encyclopedia.

In the same fire, other extraordinary books were burned. The library contained copies of a collection of 3,640 classics transcribed in 36,000 exotic volumes compiled between 1773 and 1782. It was the equivalent of 4.7 million pages and required the work of 300 scholars and 4,000 calligraphers. This collection, the Siku Quanshu, explored all the orders of life in the world, but it only disappeared in part. Some volumes had already disappeared in 1860, during the Second Opium War.

The number of Chinese libraries destroyed during the war that ran from 1937 until 1945 was huge. Since 1905, with the founding of a public library in the province of Hunan, China had begun a notable increase in its print collections. In 1909, for example, a law was promulgated to create public libraries in all provincial capitals. The same year the National Library of Beijing was founded, and by 1936, it contained 500,000 books in Chinese and 117,000 in foreign languages. By 1911, there were libraries in the provinces of Anhui, Guangdong, Heilongjiang, Hubei, Jiangsu, Jilin, Liaoning, Shandong, Shaanxi, Tianjin, Yunnan, Zhejiang, and in Nanjing. In 1912, the public library in Beijing had two branches.

Insofar as we know, there were a total of 51 libraries and 239 free libraries for a population of 433 million. By 1925, the number jumped to 552, and in 1928, there were 643. But in 1934, there were 2,818, and by 1936, there were 4,041 libraries. It was a pinnacle that had been achieved because of the literary revolution, the May 4 Movement of 1919, and the arrival of large-scale public education.

The Japanese invasion and occupation had a devastating effect. Librarians did manage to save foreign-language texts in the Nankai Library, but a brutal bombing raid accompanied by artillery fire reduced more than 224,000 books to ash. In the Paoting region, the Heipei Institute of Technology, the Peiyang National College of Engineering, the Normal School for Women, the College of Commerce and Law were all obliterated. Aside from the sacking, the 350,000 books in the Tsinghua National University suffered such damage that 200,000 books were lost.

Given the policy of erasing the adversary's memory we've seen so often over the course of this history, the Japanese destruction of the libraries in Shanghai, Nanjing, Suzhou, and Hangzhou comes as no shock. A news article quoted a Japanese military man saying that "China will be cleansed of its corrupt thought." In Shanghai, the Japanese used artillery to cleanse, destroying the municipal library. Another 15,000 books were lost in the National Chi Nan University library.

The libraries of the Grand China University, the University of Shanghai, and the University Music Conservatory as well as private collections were hauled into the street and burned. Antique shops were looted under the impassive gaze of the Japanese authorities.

Resistance in Nanjing did not stop this atrocious persecution. The sacking of the Sinological Library of Kiangsu, where some of the nation's most important manuscripts were housed, rendered the collection useless. Some 300,000 books were lost in Nanjing and the surrounding region.

Out of 4,041 libraries, at least 2,500 were destroyed. Some 92 institutions of higher learning were devastated. In all, it's thought China lost almost three million books during the war. But perhaps a more serious threat to the country's cultural patrimony came from within, as it often does, two decades later.

The Red Guard

On August 18, 1966, the world learned of the existence of the Red Guard, an army of militant fanatics in the People's Republic of China. These young people gathered in Beijing's Tiananmen Square shouting quotations from Chairman Mao's *Little Red Book* and demanding a radical transformation of the country. Alongside them, their heads bowed down, walked intellectuals and former political leaders draped with signs describing their counterrevolutionary misdeeds and crimes.

By 1966, Mao knew he had to change his strategy because his enemies had taken over important military and political spaces. Also, the failures and errors of the Great Leap Forward, which had forced him to abandon public appearances, demanded a rapid initiative. On August 8, during the Eleventh Plenary Session of the Eighth Committee of the Chinese Communist Party, he engineered the promulgation of the Great Proletarian Cultural Revolution in a document that would come to be known as the Sixteen Points.

Days later, he met with the Hongweibing (Red Guard), young people between the ages of twelve and thirty who were organized in divisions and detachments with provincial and municipal barracks. Thus Mao revealed his new weapon to his adversaries, and to show his solidarity with these rebels, he wore a red flag pin. The Red Guard, which would eventually have millions of members, guaranteed his ability to thwart any dissident through surveillance and intimidation.

The Cultural Revolution began. In essence, it was an attempt to impose a Marxist analysis on society in order to destroy centers of intellectual and popular resistance and to extirpate "capitalist" inclinations from the populace and the Communist Party. Mao wanted to diminish what he called the Four Old Men: customs, habits, culture, and thought. The objective was to create a new country using the premise that there can be no construction without destruction and that "it is just to rebel against reactionaries." The magnitude of the Cultural Revolution was not known until arrests and attacks against teachers began. Starting in 1967, it was obvious that terror would characterize this process.

Mao's wife Jiang Qing, a former actress, assumed control of the Beijing Opera and transformed it. Traditional Chinese subjects were treated with contempt in favor of ideological songs and stories. Within a short time, intellectuals classified as "opportunists" were attacked and jailed. In the streets, millions of Red Guards, all in uniform, struck fear into moderate leaders and bullied any writer who did not dedicate his or her work to the revolution. Book burning had been quite popular since 1949, but it increased radically in 1967. The University of Beijing suffered confiscation and destruction of all books considered damaging to the awareness of the people. The hysteria was so great that one author, Ba Jin, confessed: "I destroyed books, magazines, letters, and manuscripts that I'd kept for years. . . . I completely denied myself, literature, and beauty." Gao Xingjian, who won the Nobel Prize for Literature in 2000, was sent to a reeducation camp and had to burn a suitcase containing all his unpublished writing. Thousands of writers were jailed or ended their days abused and forgotten.

Chinese book destruction also extended to Tibet, where, beginning in 1950, scores of texts were condemned to incineration. After 1966, the number went up at an alarming rate, and if a monk were caught with certain books, it could cost him imprisonment or death, as E. M. Neterowicz confirms. At least 6,000 monasteries and more than 100,000 monks were attacked.

The Soviet Union

The birth of the Soviet Union was one of the twentieth century's major political and social events. With regard to culture, the state distinguished itself as a sponsor of censorship and book destruction. But it began differently.

On March 3, 1917, the Provisional Government restored freedom of the press, as part of its complete break with the past: between 1803 and 1916, more than 20,000 books and newspapers had been destroyed or proscribed. In barely five days, the Russian Revolution—between March 8 and March 12, 1917—brought down Czar Nicholas Romanov, ended centuries of monarchical rule, and a new era began.

Freedom was short-lived. Lenin's wife, Nadezhda Krupskaja, in charge of the Department of Public Education, swept libraries clean of works on czarism and capitalism (unless they were condemnatory). She burned books by Kant and Descartes. The director of the feared Cheka (Extraordinary Commission to Fight Counterrevolution), Felix Dzerzhinsky, a lover of flowers and a noted hiker, condemned scores of writers to death. On June 6, 1922, the new government established an Office of Press Control, called Glavit, with jurisdiction over all government agencies. The Russian National Library, in its Special Repository, kept all works this office forbade. In 1989, with perestroika in full swing, the number of works in that collection of the damned was revealed: some 27,000 books in Russian, a quarter million in foreign languages, and over a half million periodicals.

In 1923, a constitution created the Union of Soviet Socialist Republics. In 1928, authors were obliged to subscribe to communist theses. In 1932, socialist realism, the literature of the proletariat, was established as an aesthetic criterion, and the Writers Union was established to keep any writer from forgetting that literary canon. It was a terrible period for public and private libraries, and many intellectuals fled to avoid incarceration or death. The assassination of Sergei Kirov in 1934, supposedly at the instigation of Joseph Stalin, was the beginning of an era of persecution. The 1930s saw the systematic purging of Communist Party members, veterans of the 1917 revolution. More than four million people were put on trial and at least 800,000 executed. Many writers were sent to gulags, or forced-labor camps, in remote regions of Siberia, the finishing touch to the terror of the Stalin era. There were more than a thousand proscribed writers. Yevgeny Zamyatin (1884–1937), who died in exile, went so far as to say: "In Russia, what honors a writer most is to have his books in the catalog of forbidden titles."

Asaf Rustamov, a writer, recounts a story of just one Stalinist outrage. When he was ten years old, in July 1928, he lived in a village in Azerbaijan, which had been annexed by the Russians. Government agents ordered everyone to gather up their books. Anyone who defied the order would die; anyone who didn't turn in their books at 5:00 P.M. that day would die. At the end of the day, the agents brought the people together, urged them to practice collective freedom, and burned the books. Rustamov doesn't end his story there. In 1949, when he was a soldier in the Russian army, he burned his own books. Warned by a friend in the KGB that he was under surveillance, he burned his entire library.

Among the authors whose works were burned or who were jailed themselves are Isaac Babel, the great short-story author. At dawn on May 15, 1939, two members of the NKVD (People's Commissariat for Internal Affairs) arrested Babel without explaining the accusations against him. Surprised, Babel blurted out: "They didn't let me finish." In 1940, he was executed. In 1958, Boris Pasternak won the Nobel Prize for Literature, but the Writers Union would not let him receive it. His work was forbidden in the Soviet Union until 1989, and several editions were burned or confiscated. In 1945, Alexander Solzhenitsyn was tried and sent to prison for eight years for criticizing the Stalin regime. In 1969, he was expelled from the Soviet Writers Union. In 1970, he won the Nobel Prize for Literature. His *Gulag Archipelago, 1918–1956*, in which he exposed to the world the conditions imposed on political prisoners in his country, was regularly burned or confiscated in his homeland. Joseph Brodsky, winner of the 1987 Nobel Prize for Literature, was exiled in 1972. Anatoli Kuznetzov (1929–1979) went into exile to avoid being murdered. His works disappeared from all libraries.

In the aftermath of Stalin's death in 1953, a strange episode took place regarding the *Great Soviet Encyclopedia*. Lavrentiy Beria, the chief of Soviet security, died nine months later, and shortly thereafter the publishers of the encyclopedia sent letters to subscribers informing them that they should remove the article on Beria and replace it with a postcard of the Bering Sea, included with the letter. This kind of total censorship is characteristic of the twentieth century.

Occupied Lands

In November 1940, Soviet troops occupied Latvia, Estonia, and Lithuania. They massacred the civilian population and established an extensive apparatus of state censorship. Soldiers confiscated books and burned them. The occupation of Estonia was rapid: the Soviets immediately prohibited 212 periodicals as well as works by any author considered an enemy of the regime. A decree by the Ministry of Education's Section for Internal Affairs stipulated that libraries were to remove any books containing anti-Soviet, bourgeois, chauvinist, and theological material. An honorable commission of bibliophiles chose 1,552 titles to be removed from libraries, but about 200,000 volumes were destroyed. By 1953, more than 1.5 million books had been destroyed. By 1966, the list of prohibited books in Estonia had reached 9,300.

On May 28, 1940, agents of the Glavit examined 71 libraries and 52 bookshops in Lithuania. In November 1944, a general order facilitated the confiscation of all fascist and anti-Soviet books. More than 220,000 Lithuanians, including hundreds of intellectuals, were sent to Siberia between 1947 and 1949. Between 1946 and 1950, some 150,000 books disappeared from the Tallinn Central Library as a consequence of the cultural purge. Another order proposed the destruction of all foreign books, and in 1949 a contractor was paid 19,000 rubles to eradicate thousands of books.

Between 1944 and 1945, scores of libraries were destroyed in Budapest. In Romania, the same acts were repeated, and 300,000 books disappeared in 1945. The division of Germany allowed the Soviets to build a wall to keep the West from knowing about the cultural purges in East Germany, where, in 1953, the Communists confiscated and destroyed five million books.

The fall of the Soviet Union in 1989 did not mark an end to censorship, as so many hoped it would. In 1998, in Ekaterinburg, Bishop Nikon Mironov of the Russian Orthodox Church joined a long line of distinguished book burners when he ordered the burning of scores of theological treatises proposing that the Orthodox faith interact with other religious credos. Works by John Meyendorff, Alexander Men, Nikolai Anansiev, and Alexander Schmemann were publicly destroyed. Anti-Semitism continues as well, as does the concomitant destruction of Jewish cultural heritage: in March 1999, the synagogue Congregation B'nai Israel in the Siberian city of Novosibirsk was attacked. Precious relics, religious texts, and worst, the library was completely destroyed, along with dozens of videos on Jewish history, the Holocaust, and rabbinical traditions.

One of the great unresolved scandals involving the Soviet Union is the fate of millions of art objects, books, and archives confiscated after World War II. In the official warehouses millions of registers and books from England, France, Germany, the Ukraine, Belgium, Liechtenstein, Poland, and Hungary are stored away. The collections confiscated by the Nazis from Jewish families were scattered to Moscow, Saint Petersburg, and elsewhere. Thousands of boxes from the libraries of the Gestapo, Goebbels, Ribbentrop, and the Saxon kings of Morizburg were transported to the Soviet Union, where they were warehoused. Some texts, of course, disappeared.

Chapter 22

Spain, Chile, and Argentina

Even before the Spanish Civil War ended in 1939, Franco outlawed opposition parties and separatist groups. Over the succeeding years, laws authorized repression of "masons and communists," and political dissidents of varying stripes, termed "traitors to the homeland." All over Spain, jails were established to hold the defeated groups, whose number exceeded 200,000. The Franco dictatorship would last until 1975.

Between 1939 and 1944, more than 100,000 republicans were executed or died in prison as a result of the appalling conditions there. The regime took maximum advantage of the 1938 Law of Press and Publishing to control publishers and communication media. The state closed the centers of the Popular Front and all other political organizations that opposed Franco. Libraries were confiscated and burned. Certain authors—Marx, Engels, and Mao for instance—were absolutely prohibited, but so was erotic literature—a definition that extended to authors such as Henry Miller and D. H. Lawrence. Thousands of texts were incinerated or pulped.

Once the armed conflict was over, the devastating occupation of cities began. In Barcelona, in 1939, teams conducted 1,500 searches of businesses and homes, and an office was created to coordinate confiscation. From innocent photographs to copies of newspapers like *La Veu de Catalunya*, everything was seized. Almost 3,000 sacks were sent by train to Salamanca. The same procedure prevailed in the Basque region.

The degree of censorship and destruction was so severe that as late as 2004 the governments of Catalonia and the Basque region were demanding the return of original documents taken by Franco's troops. The Commissió de la Dignitat, made up of representatives from various groups interested in recovering archives, pointed out in 2002 that, even though sixty years had gone by, the General Archive of the Civil War in Salamanca had yet to answer their requests.

The mind behind this censorship was Ramón Serrano Súñer, Franco's brother-in-law, who admired Hitler and collected Goebbels's speeches. In the General Directorate of Press and Propaganda, a team of intellectuals applied themselves to prepublication censorship.

As late as 1966, works by José Miguel Ullán were sequestered and destroyed. The next year, Isaac Montero, author of *Alrededor de un día de abril* ("Concerning a Day in April"), was jailed. The novels of the Duchess of Medina Sidonia were prohibited. In 1968, the entire edition of *El poder está en la calle* ("Power Is in the Street") by Servio Vilar was confiscated and destroyed. Authors like Juan Marsé and Juan Goytisolo were menaced. Their books were published abroad, but if their works turned up in Spain, they would instantly disappear. Even books by Spanish American authors such as the Cuban writers Alejo Carpentier and Guillermo Cabrera Infante were expurgated before being allowed to circulate. And that took place during Franco's most flexible period.

Chile

After the military coup of September 11, 1973, in Chile, the junta led by Augusto José Ramón Pinochet Ugarte persecuted all sectors of society that had supported President

Salvador Allende. Perhaps no one at the time understood the symbolic meaning of the attack on the Palacio de la Moneda, in the course of which Allende was killed and a historic document destroyed: Chile's original declaration of independence from Spain. Immediately thereafter, special laws were passed: the National Congress was dissolved, along with the Constitutional Tribunal. All political parties that had participated in the Popular Unity government were declared illegal. Using the excuse that they were extirpating incipient communism, the junta created organisms intended to purge the country of Soviet influence and Marxist ideas. According to a report made by Monsignor Sergio Valech, who brought about an investigation of the consequences of the Pinochet regime, a partial figure suggests there were 28,459 victims of political incarceration and torture and 34,690 arrests. Of those arrested, 1,244 were under eighteen years of age, and among those, 176 were under thirteen.

During what became known as the "cultural blackout," the Quimantú Publishing Company was attacked just days after the coup, and five million books intended for Cuba were cut into pieces. Quimantú, a Quechua name that combines the words *mapudungun kim*, meaning "knowing," and *antu* or "sun," was the government publishing house. In the history of Chile, there were no precedents for Quimantú's massive production of books. Standard editions ran to an astonishing 50,000 copies; there were also minibooks, with four titles a month, almost always novellas or short stories by famous authors. In the face of international outrage, Quimantú was renamed Gabriela Mistral Publishing Company after Chile's first Nobel laureate, and editorial control was given to General Diego Barros Ortizpero. It was a failure.

Books by Pablo Neruda, Gonzalo Drago, and Leonardo Espinoza were destroyed. Censors shut down the PLA (Latin American Press) bookstore and press and the

UDA distributors. The plan of the junta was to exercise absolute control over publishing, though confiscation of socialist works was common as well. During the Pinochet dictatorship, that is, between 1973 and 1990, thousands of books were seized and destroyed. On November 28, 1986, for example, the authorities of the port of Valparaíso, following the orders of Admiral Hernán Rivera Calderón, burned 14,846 copies of Gabriel García Márquez's nonfiction text *Clandestine in Chile: The Adventures of Miguel Littin*. Works by Jorge Edwards and Ariel Dorfmann, as well as editions of poets like Neruda or texts on Allende, were destroyed.

In 2006, the Concrete Gallery of the Matucana Cultural Center presented an exhibit entitled "In Memory of the Books: Memory Exhumed," including photos of soldiers carrying books to the fires in 1973. The show also included private memoirs of those who burned their own books in order to survive. Before patrols came looking for compromising texts, hundreds of Chileans had to make bonfires in their backyards, their toilets, or their fireplaces.

The confiscation of archives was a common practice in Pinochet's Chile. Over the years, it became one of the means whereby memory itself was confiscated. Some archives were in universities, other in political organizations, and even in institutions where Allende had collaborators.

Argentina

For much of the twentieth century Argentina has endured dictatorship; only since 1983 has a democratic regime been in place. But the greatest damage to books took place after the death of Juan Domingo Perón on July 1, 1974.

Perón's party split, and it was clear that the faction which would come to be known as Los Montoneros would never yield to the growing right wing. Every five hours during 1976, there was a politically motivated assassination. Every three hours, a bomb went off. Naturally, this played well for the military, and on March 24 of the same year, there was a coup against Isabel Perón. A military junta took control.

A strategy of repression was put into practice: intimidation by means of state terrorism. All political activity was suspended, unions were held in check, strikes forbidden, congress dissolved, the supreme court eliminated, nightclubs closed, and so on. The world watched with indifference while Argentina lived through the bloodiest period of authoritarianism in its modern history. Professors, students, union members, and writers were kidnapped and murdered. The era of the *desaparecidos*—the disappeared—had begun, and thousands fled into exile.

On April 26, 1976, military officers organized an exemplary event to combat immorality and communism. On the drill ground of the Third Army Division, books the army had confiscated from bookshops and libraries in the city of Córdoba were burned. A proclamation was read denouncing Freud, Hegel, Marx, Sartre, and Camus. In their 2003 book *Un golpe a los libros* (A Coup Against Books), Hernán Invernizzi and Judith Gociol provide the best analysis of what transpired with regard to censorship and book destruction. They show that dictatorships do not repress culture simply to subjugate one sector of society but in fact carry out systematic purges to modify historical memory. In the coup's aftermath, the Argentinean admiral Emilio Massera, for example, spoke about "a war between cultures and countercultures."

In its last years the junta was no less adamant in stamping out errant culture. On August 30, 1980, trucks dumped 1.5 million books and pamphlets published by Centro Editor de América Latina (CEAL) on some vacant lots in the Sarandí neighborhood in Buenos Aires. Minutes later, as ordered by La Plata federal judge Héctor Gustavo de la Serna, police agents doused the books with gasoline and set them on fire. Photos were taken because the judge was afraid people might think the books were stolen and not burned. José Boris Spivacow, founder of CEAL and an organizer of cultural events, watched in horror, unable to intervene.

Spivacow created whole book lines at Eudeba, the University of Buenos Aires press, that educated generations of intellectuals in the Spanish-speaking world: imprints such as Cuadernos, Ediciones Previas, and Serie del Siglo. He was also behind *Historia de América Latina en el Siglo XX* ("Latin American History in the Twentieth Century"), *Historia del Movimiento Obrero* ("History of the Workers Movement"), *El País de los Argentinos* ("The Country of the Argentines"), and *Los Hombres de la Historia* ("The Men of History"). He shook up the entire continent by publishing Erich Fromm's *Escape from Freedom*. He directed Eudeba from 1958 until 1966 and published 802 titles, republished 281, and printed 11,461,032 books.

Graciela Cabal recreates the atmosphere during the dictatorship:

> At first we were very afraid. Each time I got ready to go to the CEAL, I would tell my upstairs neighbor that if I wasn't home by a certain time she should take my three children to my mother's house. But at the same time we got used to working in that context of terror. My office—for example—had a hole in it left from one of the bombs thrown at the publishing house. I would lean papers just to one side of it. One day, they called from a warehouse to tell us they'd been raided and that police were coming to the editorial offices. We got ready: We threw away portfolios, hid agendas in the backyard, burned papers. We told the neighbors we were going to have a cookout and burned papers in the bathroom, which turned black from the smoke.

The bathrooms in our houses were just as black. I tore up and burned many books, and that was one of the things I could never get over. I did it, and I wept because I didn't want my children to see me. I didn't want them to talk about it in school, didn't want them to know their mother was capable of destroying books. . . . I was so ashamed. The books from the Sarandí warehouse burned for three days.

Book burning by the authorities was accompanied by actions no less intimidating. The offices of Siglo XXI were sealed and the publishers arrested. The bookshop To Be, owned by Omar Estrella in Tucumán, was sacked. The Galerna Publishing Company, owned by Guillermo Schavelzon, was attacked with explosives. On March 24, 1976, Horacio González and Isabel Valencia, owners of the prestigious Trilce Bookstore, were kidnapped. The list of the disappeared grew daily, as writers, publishers, editors, booksellers, and even proofreaders were taken away.

Daniel Luaces, one of the editors of the CEAL, was viciously murdered; the secretary to the publisher, Graciela Mellibovsky, disappeared, as did Héctor Abrales, technical editor of CEAL, Diana Guerrero, a translator for CEAL, and many more men and women. House by house, the military searched for compromising books, which they immediately destroyed.

In 1983, President Raúl Alfonsín's National Commission on the Disappeared (CONADEP) published a report under the title *Never Again*.

With sadness, with pain, we have carried out the mission assigned us by the Constitutional President of the Republic. This was an arduous task because we had to reassemble an obscure puzzle many years after the events had taken place, when evidence had been deliberately erased, all documentation burned, and even buildings demolished.

In 2000, for example, archives which had escaped incineration by the the junta's Ministry of the Interior were found in a building basement. Four thousand pages' worth of documents attest to the cultural damages wrought by the dictatorship—an archive of crimes. The destruction was of such magnitude in Argentine publishing that an entire industry was swept away.

Chapter 23

A Particular Kind of Hatred

More thorough than conquering armies, battling ethnicities have done their utmost to eradicate all traces of their enemies. In recent times, egregious examples include the following: On the night of May 31, 1981, a group of fanatics set fire to the Jaffna library, founded in 1841 and housed at the time in a magnificent 1950 building containing almost 100,000 books and manuscripts relevant to the Tamil culture. One of the works it held was a unique copy of the *Yalpanam Vaipavama*, a historical chronicle about Jaffna.

In February of 1992, during the capture of the city of Khojali, Azerbaijian, by Armenian separatists, more than 1,000 people, mostly women and children, were murdered. Armenian troops subsequently invaded Shusha in 1992 and attacked more than 927 libraries and 22 museums. The result: 4,600,000 books lost, including ancient philosophical and musical treatises, as well as 40,000 rare books.

In 1998, a French bookseller whose name was expunged from news articles was handed a two-year suspended sentence for destroying Muslim and Arabic texts from a municipal library in Paris. The fanatic hid the Arabic books and brought them home, where he burned them.

But these are dwarfed by the scale and intensity of the Bosnian War, 1992–1995.

Bosnia

"There's nothing left here," declared Vjekoslav, a librarian. "I saw a column of smoke and papers flying everywhere. I wanted to cry, to shout, but I stayed on my knees with my hands on my head. For the rest of my life, I'll have the burden of remembering how they burned the Sarajevo National Library." A Bosnian writer, Ivan Lovrenović, tells how the century-old Vijecnica, the tall, imposing, colorful building that was the National Library of Bosnia-Herzegovina in Sarajevo, was shelled on the night of August 25, 1992.

The library contained 1.5 million volumes, 155,000 rare texts, 478 manuscripts, and millions of periodicals from around the world. The Serbian general Ratko Mladić gave the order to burn the library using twenty-five incendiary shells fired over three days, even though the building was marked with blue flags to indicate its status as cultural patrimony. Sarajevan friends of books formed a long human chain to pass the books to a safe place, and they did save some. Firemen attempted to extinguish the fire, but the intensity of the attacks did not allow it. Finally, the Moorish columns burned, and the windows exploded outward, letting the flames escape. The roof caved in, and scattered over the floor were the remains of manuscripts, works of art, chunks of walls and staircases. A volunteer fireman, Kenan Slinić, asked by journalists why he risked his life for a library, said: "I was born in this land, and what burned was part of me."

Bosnian poet Goran Šimić wrote "Lament for Vijecnica" in 1993:

> The National Library burned for three days last August and the city was choked with black snow.
> Set free from the stacks, characters wandered the streets, mingling with passers-by and the souls of dead soldiers.

"The attack lasted less than half an hour," wrote Kemal Bakaršić, the chief librarian of the National Museum of Bosnia and Herzegovina (founded in 1888). He wrote:

> The fire lasted into the next day. The sun was obscured by the smoke of books, and all over the city sheets of burned paper, fragile pages of grey ash, floated down like a dirty black snow. Catching a page you could feel its heat, and for a moment read a fragment of text in a strange kind of black and grey negative, until, as the heat dissipated, the page melted to dust in your hand.

How did this barbarism begin? The old Yugoslavia was united by Joseph Tito's iron hand. When he died, the leaders who followed were unable to maintain that unity and Yugoslavia began to disintegrate. Problems long held in check began to surface: ethnic differences between the Serb minority and the Bosnian majority, poor communication, contentious territorial divisions, and the militarism that had been imposed on the entire society. Soon the country fragmented into a series of independent states. The wealthier parts of the country decided to go it alone, and declared themselves republics—and were quickly recognized by the West. Croatia, for example, proclaimed itself a republic on June 25, 1991, after a referendum in which 85 percent of the people voted in its favor.

Repression by the Yugoslav army was tremendous, but that did not stop Croatian sovereignty from being recognized by the entire world on January 15, 1992. Meanwhile, a war began without anyone's having to declare it. And one of its worst consequences was that the Serbs put into practice a policy of cultural annihilation and genocide. The ancient strategy of *damnatio memoriae*, or memory erasure, was carried out in a horrifying way. They burned millions of books and devastated an entire people.

In eastern Slavonia, the Municipal Library of Vinkovci, founded in 1875, was the first library to fall, on September 17, 1991, with a loss of 85,000 books, jewels of literature and thought, manuscripts by notable local authors. According to witnesses, people went around picking up pieces of books, trying to reconstruct them. The public library of Pakrac, founded in 1919, was shelled, but its 22,000 books were evacuated.

The advancing Serbian troops did not stop when they reached the University of Osijek. They destroyed nearly half of the 30,000 books in the Central Library for Agriculture, just finished in 1990. Osijek also lost its historical archives and rare book collection.

The municipal museum of the town of Vukovar, an eighteenth-century village, contained 32,513 historical objects, 515 rare books dating from the sixteenth century on, and 13,000 books. Between August 25 and 16, 1991 it was shelled, and on September 20, a plane bombed the building several times, leaving it in flames. The few rare books saved were left to looters, who sold them on the black market.

Vukovar's public library, founded in 1947, with 76,000 books and thousands of cassettes and videos, was destroyed around the same time. Only its bibliographic jewels were saved. The library of the historical museum and the Lavoslav Ruzicka Museum were annihilated. The Franciscan monastery in Vukovar, with four incunabula and 7,000 books published between the fifteenth and twentieth centuries, was also ruined. No one knows what, if anything, survived. On November 18, 1991, the Serbs occupied Vukovar, expelled its 50,000 inhabitants (mostly women and children), and burned every undesirable book they could find.

The heart of Yugoslavia was said to be Dalmatia, which may explain why it was attacked so savagely. In Zadar, the scientific library, a precious monument from 1850, was destroyed by artillery fire on October 5, 1991. The Serb soldiers stole whatever they could of its 600,000 works, thirty-three incunabula, 1,080 manuscripts, 370 parchments, 1,350 rare books, 1,500 musical scores, 5,566 periodicals, 929 magazines, 1,200 maps, 2,500 photos, and 60,000 miscellaneous documents. Unfortunately, the Serbs had to retreat and had no idea what to do with 200,000 stolen books. The officers came up with an ideal solution: they kept all books in Latin and Cyrillic characters and burned the rest.

The municipal library of Zadar, built in 1857, with 60,000 books, was bombed on October 9, 1991. Only the collection of musical scores and music books from the music school were seriously damaged.

The famously lovely city of Dubrovnik, where the first pharmacy in Europe was created, part of the cultural patrimony of humanity, was destroyed over the course of 1991. On December 6, 800 shells abolished everything. Incendiary shells hit the library of the Interuniversity Center, and 20,000 books disappeared forever. The science library, founded in 1950, contained 200,000 volumes, 922 manuscripts, 77 incunabula, almost 10,000 rare books, and 7,783 periodicals. It was hit by more than sixty shells on November 19, 1991, and five more on June 8, 1992.

In Bosnia-Herzegovina some of the most radical acts of violence in European cultural history were perpetrated. I have already described how the National Library in Sarajevo was destroyed, but there were other cultural targets. On May 17, 1992, the Oriental Institute of Sarajevo was bombarded. "The loss cannot be measured or ever repaired," wrote Bakaršić, the chief librarian of the Bosnian national museum. "In less than two hours, five thousand unique manuscripts, Turkish, Persian and Arabic, over a hundred plat books from Ottoman times (books that can no longer show that Slavs professing Islam have lived in Bosnia for many centuries), other records of the Ottoman rule numbering some two hundred thousand pages, three hundred microfilm files of Bosnian writings from other manuscript libraries, the ten thousand volumes of the Institute's research library, and three hundred sets of periodicals. . . . All lost in flame."

András Riedlmayer, director of Harvard's Aga Khan Program for Islamic Architecture, reported, "The Oriental Institute had clearly been singled out. According to interviews with eyewitnesses, the building had been hit with a barrage of incendiary munitions, fired from positions on the hills overlooking the town center. No other buildings in the densely built neighborhood were hit." The Municipal Library of Sarajevo, with 300,000 books, was left with half its collection. The National Museum of Bosnia, with 400,000 books, lost much of its holdings. The Franciscan library in Nedjarici was looted. In Mostar, 50,000 books were burned, along with the library of the archive. The library of the University of Mostar was destroyed along with the municipal library, though in the latter case, the bravery of the librarians saved more than half the books.

The writer Lovrenovic confessed that he had to flee, leaving his library, made up of classics, manuscripts, diaries, essays, and stories to the mercies of the Serbs. They burned it all.

Between 1993 and 1994, while the United Nations argued over whether to conduct trials for crimes perpetrated during the wars in Bosnia, militias made up of Croat nationalists from Bosnia mercilessly attacked Muslim monuments. Naturally, they destroyed public and private libraries. The library of the Muslim community in Stolac was burned in July 1993. Hundreds of books disappeared, along with forty manuscripts dating from the seventeenth to the nineteenth century. The library of the Emperor's Mosque (mosque of Sultan Selim I, built in 1519), containing a number of ancient manuscripts, was also exterminated. Then the ruins were dynamited, making reconstruction impossible. The library of the Pogradska Mosque (founded in 1732) was burned at 11:00 A.M. on July 28, 1993. Private libraries belonging to scores of families were burned, among the more celebrated the libraries of the Behmen, Mahmutcehajic, Mehmedbasic, and Rizvanbegovic families. Between 1992 and the end of the war, 188 libraries were put at risk; forty-three were completely destroyed.

The statements of the Council of Europe talk in terms of "a cultural, European catastrophe of terrifying proportions," and, in a sorrowful, melancholy report, the UN Security Council established that there was "intentional destruction of cultural goods that cannot be justified by military necessity." Not even the Nazis managed to destroy books so efficiently.

In the spring of 2000, the UN Interim Administration Mission in Kosovo (UNMIK), together with specialists appointed by UNESCO, acting for the Council of Europe and the International Federation of Library Associations and Institutions (IFLA), visited Kosovo. They tried to evaluate the damage caused by the Serbian purges and found the situation worse than originally thought. Their summation includes the following statistics: three central libraries destroyed, with 261,000 books burned; 62 provincial libraries destroyed, with 638,000 books burned. The Serbs devastated the culture of Kosovo for ethnic reasons. Between 1991 and 1995, more than 100,000 books were destroyed in the National Library. Another 100,000, along with 8,000 magazines and myriad periodicals, were removed from the library and publicly burned.

Serbian leaders accused Albanian nationalists of destroying two million Serb books in Kosovo. To that they added that the libraries of Pristina, Prizren, Djakovica,

Istok, Glogovac, Srbica, Podujevo, and many other cities under the control of Albanian groups had been decimated. Serbs claimed that 11,000 books from the Vuk Karadzic Library were pulped in Vladicin Han.

Chechnya

The image we must conjure up now is that of Edilbek Kasmagomadov, director of the most important library in the northern Caucasus. Imagine him sitting on the grass of a darkened soccer field in 1995, stiff with cold, watching the doors of the basement where 20,000 books saved from the Russian bombardment of Grozny and its library were stored. In 1994, the collection comprised more than 2.5 million works in more than thirty languages and an index of 800,000 licenses covering the years between 1957 and 1992. "There is nothing to be done," commented the librarian. "Everything has been destroyed." A young man nearby replies, "And this is only the beginning." Not a single library remains intact in the region.

This cultural disaster began when Chechnya declared its independence from the Soviet Union in 1991. In 1994, Russian troops poured in and destroyed Grozny to send a message to the followers of the local leader Dzhokhar Dudayev. Between 1994 and 1996, 80,000 people died and 200,000 became refugees. The Russian army ultimately had to withdraw in humiliation, and a new government took power. Then the counterattacks began. They were defined as terrorism, but much depends on who is defining the term "terrorism."

At the outset of the war, there were more than a thousand libraries in the region and more than eleven million books, library networks in the University of Grozny, the Petroleum Institute, and the Pedagogic Institute. There were fourteen technical libraries and 450 scholarly libraries. Around 1995, the Russians destroyed the National Library, the National Children's Library, the National Medical Library, the university libraries, and the Central Library of Sciences. Most librarians fled, and hundreds of centers were closed.

Millions of texts were looted or destroyed, but no voices have been raised in the West to denounce this barbarism. The black market is well-stocked with artworks and books from this zone.

Chapter 24

On the Natural Enemies of Books

Horace lamented that moths would make his works disappear. It is sad to think that the moth larva has reduced so many thousands of works to dust. Of that species there are some especially destructive varieties, notably *Anobium pertinax*, *A. punctatum*, *A. eruditus*, and *A. Paniceum*. *Xestobium rufovillosum* caused the holes in many texts from the fifteenth to the eighteenth centuries. *Hoffmannophila pseudospretella* opens huge holes in a page and can reduce a book to nothing in a short time. Around 1416, Cincius Romanus wrote to Francesco de Fianna, a disciple of Petrarch, that during a trip to the Monastery of Saint Gall in Germany, he found in the church tower "myriad books kept there like prisoners, and the library neglected and infested with dust, worms, soot, and all kinds of things that cause the destruction of books." Among the Lepidoptera, two varieties are dangerous for books: the small, gray-brown *Tineidae*, whose larvae can devour entire bindings, and the equally destructive *Tinea pellionella*.

In the case of insects, those that devour plants are attracted by the cellulose in paper, wood, fabric, and bookbindings. Certain adhesives used in binding books are vegetable in origin and also attract insects. The list of dangerous insects is long, but these are some of the more interesting.

> *Thysanura*. This order includes *Lepisma saccharina* (silverfish), of a leaden color and scaly exoskeleton. It eats paper, rubber, leather, and textiles.

Blattodea. Many libraries are plagued by cockroaches—black, German, and American. They lay their eggs in the bindings of books. In the tropics, they eat wood and moist paper, cardboard bindings, and labels. Their filth also dirties texts.

Orthoptera. The seemingly innocent cricket can destroy books because it eats paper, cloth, leather, and parchment.

Isoptera. Termites are especially destructive in African or South American libraries.

Ptinidae. The 500 species of spider beetles eat wood, leather, wool, and even skin. They bore holes in paper and lay their eggs.

Corrodentia. An order that includes fleas, bark-lice and booklice that destroy paper. The worst are *Trogium pulsatorium* and *Liposcelis divinatorius.*

Coleoptera. Beetles: they attack leather bindings and parchment. Notable among them is the family of *Cerambycidae*, the 20,000 species (yes) of which eat wood and paper.

Hymenoptera. The ninety families, and tens of thousands of species, in this order of wasps and ants lay eggs after perforating pages. Carpenter ants, *Camponotus,* are incredibly voracious, even boring tunnels through shelved books.

Vespidae. The 5,000 species of wasps in this family are dangerous because they use paper to build nests.

Books stored on compact disks made of aluminum and polycarbonates are not biodegradable and are very long-lasting. However, in 1999 it was discovered that certain mushrooms of the *Geotrichum* variety (used in cheese making) can damage compact disks.

Along with worms and insects, rats cause severe damage. In 45 BCE, Cicero considered the problem; in Book 27 of *De divinatione* he notes: "The rats in my house just gnawed Plato's *Republic*." In the eighteenth century, the Westminster library suffered enormous losses because it was overrun by rats.

Self-Destroying Paper

In antiquity, papyrus and parchment were condemned to an ephemeral existence that could be prolonged or shortened by climate. Paper was thought to be more lasting, but the kind used between 1850 and the end of the twentieth century contained acid (with a pH between three and six) and deteriorated.

Paper made of linen or cotton rags is durable, but the introduction of wood pulp and new bleaching and gluing processes brought with them unstable elements, such as hemicellulose and lignin. Bleaching with alum salts and rosin accelerates the rapid deterioration of paper because it facilitates acidic formation, which breaks up molecular chains. In other words, chains of glucose molecules linked by acetyls in wood-pulp paper are vulnerable to attack by hydrogen ions. Acidic hydrolysis breaks down those acetyl links and alters the structure of cellulose, causing irreversible damage.

The widespread use of paper came about thanks to a French veteran of the American Revolutionary War, Louis-Nicholas Robert. Robert was charged by the National Convention with developing a machine to mass-produce paper, and he did so in 1799 at the papermaking firm of Didot Saint-Léger. At the time, skilled human workers were hard to find, expensive—and essential throughout the papermaking process, which demanded the cleaning, sorting, cutting, and boiling of cotton or linen rags. Until Robert's machine, which made paper in a continuous roll, the final process of sheet-formation was carried out by hand.

Around 1803, Saint-Léger sold the prototype in London to the Fourdrinier brothers. Although the brothers greatly advanced the invention, their research forced them into bankruptcy and it was left to others to derive riches from their machine.

Wood-derived paper was made possible by the isolation of cellulose by Anselme Payen in 1839. Since then, paper manufacturers have treated wood with chemicals to extract cellulose through the elimination of lignin and the resinous material that links the fibers. In 1854, Hugh Burgess and Charles Watt patented the process in the United States. They cooked the wood in caustic soda at high temperatures in order to get fibers. Once these fibers were whitened, they could be made into paper. However, the resultant paper was short-lived, opaque, and soft. These methods were perfected during the nineteenth century: this increased the earnings of publishers, but sentenced books to self-destruction.

The status of these books is a huge challenge to librarians. The International Federation of Library Associations and Institutions (IFLA) points out that in the United States alone there are eighty million books made of perishable paper. The National Library of Paris has millions. One conservator observes:

Of the approximately twenty million books and pamphlets in the Library of Congress, approximately thirty percent are in such critical condition that they cannot circulate. An inspection of the New York Public Library revealed that around fifty percent of its more than five million books are on the brink of disintegration. This phenomenon is observable in the greatest university research libraries. Millicent Abell, at the Yale library, calculates that some seventy-six million books all over the United States are literally turning to dust.

Today's libraries face pinched budgets and more or less permanent crises. The annual rate of deterioration was fixed by one study at 4.66 percent a year. If we imagine a collection of one million books with a substitution price of $10 per volume, it would be worth $10 million, so if we apply the rate of loss, depreciation to the collection would add up to $466,000 a year, or $1,276 per day. Just the 3,400 academic libraries alone in the United States have over 800,000,000 volumes, and there are another 9,000 public libraries holding untold billions of volumes, which means that the cost of counteracting the effects of acid degradation would be many times the nation's annual spending on libraries ($12 billion a year). And this does not take into account the damage to books by use, biological agents, or photocopying.

Several factors accelerate the self-destruction of paper. Improper storage, humidity, bad ventilation, a dry environment, high temperatures, pollution, and too much light. Light, infrared or ultraviolet, contributes to the chemical decomposition of all organic material by means of oxidation. Leave a book near a window and in a short time its pages become discolored and yellowed. Ultraviolet light produces that fragmented condition in cellulose paper.

In his book *Double Fold*, the writer Nicholson Baker condemns many librarians for their policies of "destroying to preserve." Baker notes that in 1950, the CIA and the Library of Congress imposed new technologies and let thousands of books disappear without any guarantee that microfilm would outlast paper.

The Library of Congress has spent enormous sums on microfilming books, and their conservation comes to millions of dollars a year, enough money to buy a huge warehouse where an entire century's worth of newspapers might be stored. Baker has fomented a heated debate. He has revealed to readers a painful situation: libraries (and publishers) regularly destroy books, documents, periodicals, and magazines.

During the final years of the twentieth century and the opening years of the twenty-first, we have witnessed a transformation of book format. Aside from changing the nature of reading and introducing rather comfortable interactive elements, these new kinds of books have generated new problems. We've all used compact disks. Information is stored on a CD by means of a laser that makes coded microscopic holes called pits or hills. The presence of the light from another laser is reflected onto a surface whose final pulses are collected by a diode that turns them into electric impulses.

The importance of a compact disk is easy to understand if we think that all of surviving ancient Greek literature could be stored on a single one—this is the case of the famous *Thesaurus Linguae Graecae*, which includes texts from Homeric times down to the Byzantine empire. A compact disk can hold all the works of Cervantes or Shakespeare, the *Encyclopedia Britannica* or an up-to-date atlas of the world. It can store digitized photographs of thousands of medieval manuscripts, reminding us that when someone destroys a disk containing that kind of information, he or she destroys an entire library. This occurs whenever a disk is scratched or is not readable: it is tossed into the trash.

The book is changing by the hour, and a revolution has begun that has barely shown its first results. Over the past few years, a new kind of book has appeared, the electronic book. There is a wide market for these books, though they have yet to take the place of traditional paper volumes. Each e-book can store millions of facts, and it's thought that in a few years students will go to class with an entire library of fourteen million books in their pockets. That future is barely upon us, but it is clear that the continuous destruction of these books, through accidents or malice, is inevitable. So when future students destroy their electronic books, they may eradicate fourteen million texts.

At the same time, it's important to realize that millions of books have been digitized and made into a virtual library. The University of Virginia and the Gutenberg Project, to mention just two providers of electronic books, offer thousand of classics in different languages over the Internet. But even these libraries are not safe. Hackers constantly attack them in order to destroy their archives. The day is coming when biblioclasts will use computer programs, not fire—clean and devastating.

The Internet has most certainly been the first step toward the globalization of knowledge and will make the task of book destruction harder, but it will not stop censorship or the desire to eradicate stored data. In other words, the destruction of books is far from over.

Chapter 25

Iraq

On May 10, 2003, I arrived in Iraq, a member of an international commission sent to evaluate the damage to the National Library of Baghdad, in Arabic Dar al-Kutub Wal-Watha'q. Exactly seventy years earlier, the great book burnings of 1933 had taken place in Germany. May 10 is a fatal day for culture. I had been warned about what to expect by my colleagues, but what I learned and what I saw left me with insomnia.

The National Library I visited was a large three-story building, with lattice windows all around, built in 1977. There was still a statue of Saddam Hussein at the entrance, his left hand raised in greeting, his right pressing a book to his chest: like so many despots, Hussein, as difficult as this is to believe, was a voracious reader. I understand the statue has since been removed like all the others. Even from a distance, I could see that the façade had suffered fire damage. The blaze had blown out the windows, imprinting a melancholy air on the place. I could see into the building, where scores of workers and experts were working. The light, filtered through the windows, revealed thousands of papers scattered on the floor. The reading room, the card catalog, and the stacks themselves had all been razed.

The structure looked so severely damaged that I thought it precarious: only with luck would it withstand even the slightest earth tremor. An employee commented in a low voice that the library had suffered two attacks, not one, and two sackings. That astonished me, because I hadn't read that information in other reports. There was still ash all over the floor. The metal archives were burned, open, and emptied.

The looting of the library was preceded by some disconcerting events. First came the attack on Baghdad with Massive Ordnance Air Blast (MOAB) bombs and missiles, which destroyed more than 200 public buildings and dozens of markets and businesses. This was the Shock and Awe campaign that took place during the last days of March. On April 3, there was fighting at the Saddam Hussein Airport, six miles from the city center. On April 7, there were tanks in the streets. By April 8, U.S. troops controlled parts of Baghdad. That day, at one of the bends in the Tigris River, between the Al-Jumhuriya and the July 14 bridges, the offensive became more ferocious. Along one side of the river, the Third Infantry Division advanced from the south, while the Iraqis tried to retreat to the north—after placing a bomb on the Al-Jumhuriya Bridge. Ultimately, it was not a bitter battle, and in a few hours, between 7:30 and 9:30 A.M., the streets were packed with M1 Abrams tanks. Simultaneously, the two most important presidential palaces and several government ministries—Foreign Affairs and Information—were attacked. Squads of soldiers were posted at the Ministry of Petroleum, from which not even a pencil was removed.

The main point of resistance was in the southern part of the city, where the fedayeen were entrenched. At a certain moment, the allied artillery blew up a cache of arms and munitions hidden under sand berms on the bank of the Tigris. Along with the information that Saddam Hussein's regime had fallen and that Saddam and his sons had fled, the attacks provoked general confusion. There were no police, and the U.S. soldiers had been ordered not to fire on civilians.

On Wednesday, April 9, the statue of Saddam in the main square was torn down. A soldier draped a U.S. flag over his face, but quickly replaced it with an Iraqi flag. Once pictures of the event were in circulation and the rumor that Saddam was gone spread, a human tidal wave, repressed by ten years of economic blockade and an implacable dictatorship, ran uncontrolled through the streets. The initial looting was directed at the palaces and houses of Iraqi chiefs. The hospitals lost everything, even beds. In stores, shop owners armed with rifles, pistols, and even iron bars, stood guard and scared away the thieves, many of them young boys and girls. Between April 9 and 10, many places considered symbols of the regime succumbed to violence and looting.

On April 10, a crowd gathered in the unprotected library. First they were cautious and swift, then brazen. Anarchy prevailed. Women and children, young and old, took away everything they could. The first group of looters knew where the most important manuscripts were and grabbed them up. Others, hungry and resentful of the old regime, came later and brought on the disaster. The mob ran everywhere with the most valuable books. They took the photocopy machines, the paper, computers, printers, and all the furniture. On the walls they left messages: "Death to Saddam!" "Saddam apostate!" A cameraman was inexplicably allowed to film everything, but he disappeared without a trace.

The looting was repeated a week later. A group arrived in unmarked blue buses. Encouraged by the passivity of the soldiers, they placed white phosphorous stolen from the military in the stacks and set them on fire. (Flames from white phosphorus cannot be extinguished with water.) They also piled up books to burn them. A few hours later, a column of smoke rose up until it was visible from over a mile away. All old machines in the building and some newspapers burned. On the third floor, where the microfilm archives were stored, nothing remained. The heat was so intense that (and this I saw) it cracked the marble floor and damaged the concrete staircases and the roof. The second attack wiped out the Iraqi National Archive, located on the second floor of the library. Ten million documents disappeared, including tomes from the Ottoman period such as registries and decrees.

The journalist Robert Fisk, Middle East correspondent for the *Independent*, witnessed the events and commented in a celebrated article.

So yesterday was the burning of books. First came the looters, then the arsonists. It was the final chapter in the sacking of Baghdad. The National Library and Archives—a priceless treasure of Ottoman historical documents, including the old royal archives of Iraq—were turned to ashes in three thousand degrees of heat. Then the library of Korans at the Ministry of Religious Endowment were set ablaze.

I saw the looters. One of them cursed me when I tried to reclaim a book of Islamic law from a boy of no more than ten. Amid the ashes of Iraqi history, I found a file blowing in the wind outside: pages of handwritten letters between the court of Sharif Hussein of Mecca, who started the Arab revolt against the Turks for Lawrence of Arabia, and the Ottoman rulers of Baghdad.

And the Americans did nothing. All over the filthy yard they blew, letters of recommendation to the courts of Arabia, demands for ammunition for troops, reports on the theft of camels and attacks on pilgrims, all in delicate handwritten Arabic script. I was holding in my hands the last Baghdad vestiges of Iraq's written history. But for Iraq, this is Year Zero; with the destruction of the antiquities in the Museum of Archaeology on Saturday and the burning of the National Archives and then the Koranic library, the cultural identity of Iraq is being erased. Why? Who set these fires? For what insane purpose is this heritage being destroyed?

When the disastrous looting and burning were over, there was literally nothing to be done. "Stuff happens," shrugged Donald Rumsfeld, then secretary of defense. He added that "Freedom's untidy, and free people are free to make mistakes and commit crimes, and do bad things." The former library director lamented: "I can't remember barbarity like this, not even from Mongol times." He was referring to the fact that in 1258, the troops of Hulagu, a descendant of Genghis Khan, invaded Baghdad and destroyed all its books by throwing them into the Tigris. Another library employee quipped: "Caesar destroys the books again."

From the outset there was a debate about the library losses, which still rages. Dr. Taher Khalaf Jabur Al-Bakaa, who worked for the interim government in Iraq in 2004, said at the Frankfurt Book Fair that 17,000 works had been destroyed. Less optimistic, Kamal Jawad Ashur said half the books had been stolen and the other half burned. The new director of the library, Kurdish historian Saad Eskander, wrote:

> We lost about sixty percent of our state records and documents—they were either burned or damaged by water. [The lost documents belonged] to all the ministries, all departments of the state from the late nineteenth century up to Saddam's period. As concerns books, I think we lost some twenty-five percent of them, mostly rare books, the most valuable books.

Based on Iraqi librarian reports and my own observations, I calculate that almost a million books disappeared in the looting and burning. The library was enormous and there were many duplicate volumes. At one time, laws required that five copies of anything printed be donated to the library, though the economic situation during Saddam's final years dramatically reduced that practice. Even so, thousands of donations enriched the collection for decades.

On the street, at bookstalls, volumes from the National Library were being sold for pennies. Every Friday, at the street market on Al-Mutanabbi Street, those works were on sale. I personally saw there a volume of the *Arab Encyclopedia* with the official seal stamped on its cover—still visible, though someone had tried to erase it. I found a volume titled *Meshaf resh* ("The Black Book") about the Yazidi culture, a pre-Islamic religious group that lives in northern Iraq. The library losses also affected the National Archive, where possibly four or five million documents disappeared.

Fortunately, many books were saved because they were hidden far from the library, a confirmation of the immense love Iraqis feel for their culture. Until the end of 2005, thousands of books remained on the first and second floors, just piled up and not classified. Along with those books, al-Sayyid Abdul-Muncim al-Mussawi ordered those faithful to him to rescue almost 300,000 books, which were trucked to the Al-Haqq Mosque, where they were arranged in endless rows that often reached the ceiling. Conditions in the mosque are terrible, and it's entirely possible insects have already started to eat the bindings. Mahmud al-Sheikh Hajim, their protector, says it would have been worse if they'd been lost. The people who saved these books allege that they belonged to a Shiite college of clerics. For those clerics, books are sacred.

Another 100,000 books were stored in a building belonging to the Department of Tourism. And several intellectuals showed me books they'd hidden in their houses, books they will return when order is restored or when the "infidels" leave Iraq. A painter who refused to identify himself bought scores of books just to protect them. Most are stored in what was called Saddam City, now Sadr City, a poor zone with two million people packed into unsightly warrens.

In April 2004, the conservator René Teygeler was sent to save some of the books damaged by the firemen at the National Library. Moisture stimulates the growth of destructive mushrooms, and Teygeler attempted to freeze the books, a process that can take eight hours in Baghdad. One of the basic techniques consists in placing the blocks of frozen books in rooms with open windows so the moisture gradually evaporates. The thawing process, unfortunately, caused further damage: the bindings survived, but the pages were damaged.

Only chance saved other Baghdad book collections from looting. The Qadiriya Mosque, whose library represents the most famous Sufi order in the world, is led by Sajid Abd al-Rahman al-Gilani, sixteenth successor to Abd al-Qadir al-Gilani. I was unable to see the collection, but I learned it contains 6,500 books and 2,000 manuscripts of the work of al-Ustadh Mari al-Krimli. The Maktabat al-Hidaya collection was looted: only half of its 600 manuscripts remain.

The destruction of the National Library did not receive the kind of media attention given to the looting of the Baghdad Archaeological Museum. The museum was a majestic structure near the train station, with two sand-colored towers, guarded, when I saw it, by a tank on whose cannon was written "Greetings from the American People." News of its looting shook the entire world when it was divulged on April 12, 2003, and word spread that more than 170,000 objects had been lost. In fact, twenty-five objects of great importance were lost, among them the Warka Vase (later recovered), along with 14,000 minor works.

The uproar was so great that people entering the museum had to show identification and be searched on leaving.

Working there, in charge of the investigation into what took place and attempting to recover the stolen objects, is Colonel Matthew Bogdanos, a responsible and diligent officer, supported by the archaeologist Donny George, the FBI, the CIA, several Islamic studies groups, and a detachment of soldiers. Bogdanos, a lawyer, had for equipment several tables where recovered objects were placed and classified. The number grew because there was a general amnesty decreed for anyone possessing an object who might want to return it. It was not uncommon to see a young person approach the entry, place a sculpture near the door, and leave.

The display rooms of the museum were not burned the day of the looting, though they were devastated. Hundreds of objects were not stolen but simply smashed, while others, which I examined when I was allowed to look over the museum, were damaged when moved by the looters. In the Hall of National Patrimony, manuscripts and 236 porcelains were removed. Some turned up purely by chance. Of a total of eight storage rooms, the looters managed to enter five. They took some things, didn't manage to unpack others, and were just as happy to steal microscopes, chemicals, and archaeological equipment instead of artifacts. On the second floor, where the galleries are located, scores of objects were removed, leaving chaos. Of 451 display cases, at least twenty-eight were destroyed or damaged. The offices were emptied of documents, books, computers, desks, chairs, and anything else portable.

It's important to note here that the books in the National Library were not the only ones destroyed or looted. In the museum, the library dedicated to Mesopotamian subjects was destroyed, along with some Sumerian clay tablets. Luckily, 100,000 tablets were saved because the looters could not break into the room where they were stored. The monuments from the ancient Babylonian city of Sippar, site of what is thought to be the world's first bank, were also safe.

On May 22, I left Baghdad for Vienna and London, and a month later I found out that the Office of Reconstruction and Humanitarian Assistance (ORHA) had named Piero Cordone, Fergus Muir, and military officers A. J. Kesel, Cori Wegener, Chris Varhola, and Wes Somners members. The officers were from the Army Division of Civil Affairs. The group announced that the museum would be reopened in one or two months and displayed several recovered objects. I noted that no one wanted to talk over what had happened or discuss who the culprits were. On July 3, for example, an absurd two-hour show of the treasures of Nimrud cost the lives of a soldier and a journalist and placed at risk an extremely important cultural legacy. I had no idea that a tragedy was just beginning.

In addition to the museum and the National Library, the cultural disaster reached other centers. Not far away, the Al-Awqaf Library, containing some 5,000 Islamic manuscripts, burned to the ground and was utterly obliterated. The usual looting took place there as well. At least half of the collection disappeared, and the building was a shambles. The 5,300 volumes saved were in the hands of librarians in fear of their lives, depressed because they believed in none of the solutions they were hearing from various organizations. I learned from the very few with enough courage to talk to me that one of the guards had been accidentally shot by U.S. soldiers.

Several witnesses told me that the destruction of the books took place when fifteen or twenty civilians violently broke into the library followed by a young man filming the event. Once the manuscripts were stolen, phosphorous grenades were tossed inside the library. Of thirty-two boxes of books, at least ten were destroyed, along with 800 manuscripts.

The situation of the Iraqi universities was and continues to be critical. I learned that after that fateful April 8, looters attacked the University of Baghdad and carried off everything they could. They brought trucks and fled with air conditioners, laboratory equipment, archives, desks, chairs, computers, printers, photocopy machines. As if that were not enough, they also destroyed the student registries, the database, grade sheets, and degrees. The violence has left an indelible mark in the memory of the students. Some, staring at their burned-out center, recalled that at the beginning of the attacks a missile fell next to the university. The United States admitted that was a mistake.

The rest of the university was desolate. The language center, with a library in Russian and German, was nothing more than ashes. I found a copy of *Faust* burned at the edges but missing pages, which had been torn out. A young woman told me it was students who had burned those books because they thought the Russians and Germans had collaborated with Hussein. The faculty was in turmoil over the firing of supporters of the old regime and the possibility of elections. The professors I spoke to talked of nothing else. It was obvious that resentment had taken control of everyone. Another subject was money for salaries and grants, because no banks were working. Most professors hadn't been paid since the seizing of Baghdad.

The medical library of the Mustansiriya University survived the initial fighting, but the university's central library was looted. The College of Physicians, whose prestigious library possessed a collection of the great medieval Arabic texts on medicine, was emptied. A young man from the University of Baghdad said: "Someday someone will burn the Library of Congress, you know, but they won't lose anything like what's been destroyed here."

The Bayt al-Hikma, or House of Wisdom, was attacked. On April 11, the exhibition of materials related to the Ottoman Empire was destroyed and part of the building burned. The looters entered in the morning and left nothing of value, but they returned that afternoon, convinced the best things were hidden. Myriad documents relevant to foreign powers, World War I and World War II, the 1940 coup, and the Ottoman Empire were lost. On the third floor, the fires eradicated everything the looters hadn't already taken. The Coalition Provisional Authority offered the ridiculous sum of $17,000 to rebuild the collection, where more than seventy people were previously employed.

Al-Majma al-Ilmi al-Iraqi, the Iraqi Academy of Sciences, one of the most prestigious research centers in the Middle East, suffered great losses. Located in Al-Wasiriya, it had manuscripts, periodicals, foreign books, and scientific magazines. There was a laboratory with twenty computers and printers. Everything was lost except the building. The Dar Saddam lil-Makhtutat collection was saved because its director, Usama N. al-Naqshabandi, hid it. In Mosul, the libraries of the museum and the university vanished.

While I slept, or pretended to sleep, in the tent I'd set up at the archaeological site at Isin (Ishan Bakrijat), I suddenly heard a deafening blast followed by continuous gunfire. It was May 19, 2003. When I got up I could see U.S. soldiers running from their Humvee, which had been hit by a roadside bomb. Thirty men in the distance were firing. Some had rocket launchers. Another group broke away, ran into the ruins, and brought out objects. I was frightened to death, I confess, and threw myself to the ground.

Next to me, a sergeant suggested surrounding the vandals. The nearest soldier quipped: "You go. I'm not going to die for some pieces of clay. I didn't come here from New Jersey to babysit ruins. Ask for support." Half an hour of fighting shadows went by with everyone shooting at nothing, and finally a UH-60 Black Hawk helicopter started strafing, though it neither wounded nor killed any of the attackers.

The next day, numb from lack of sleep, I saw that the site was a bottomless pit and understood what was really going on. When I looked down into the hole, I discovered that the excavation had been destroyed. Iraq is one of the countries with the largest number of important archaeological sites in the entire Middle East, and it was in these lands, precisely, where the book was born, where libraries were born, where the first legal codes were created. It was horrifying to think that war and its aftermath could endanger new discoveries that might change our idea of history. These sites hold examples of Sumerian, Assyrian, Babylonian, Greek, and Roman cultures.

And the problem is still with us. Important sites have been looted daily over the past several years: Hatra, one of humanity's cultural patrimonies, Nineveh, Ur. . . . The situation is better in the south than in the north, according to reports from the Chicago Oriental Institute and the National Geographic Society.

At Tell al-Majalla, the supervisor Muzahem Mahmoud and the guard Ibrahim Atta watch over the ancient city of Nimrud, where in 1989 the spectacular Tombs of the Queens were brought to light. Their main concern is a series of tunnels used by looters to enter every night. The thieves are only interested in gold and smash pottery because they think it unimportant. Ancient reliefs are pockmarked with bullet holes.

In Nippur, 124 miles southeast of Baghdad, the looters work day and night. In Ashur (Qal'at Sherqat), named part of the Patrimony of Humanity by UNESCO, looters have ruined the site. At the ruins of Sennacherib's Palace in Nineveh, the deterioration of the site is clear to see.

There is a pattern to the looting. Once a work is taken, the gangs, which are highly organized, hide the objects and then sell them—all on an unprecedented scale. On the Internet there are Web sites for viewing looted objects. Joseph

Braude, respected author of *The New Iraq: Rebuilding the Country for its People, the Middle East, and the World*, was arrested for possessing three cylindrical seals he'd bought for $200. Some objects have been sold in order to finance the insurgency.

It's thought that more than 150,000 clay tablets have disappeared. The newspaper *Al-Sabah*, favorable to the United States, published a report in 2004 stating that the Italian soldiers sent to guard archaeological sites were stealing antiquities. The Hague Convention of 1954 that supposedly protects the cultural patrimony of occupied lands is being openly flouted. In May 2004, at Thee Qar, border police confiscated hundreds of objects found on a truck belonging to the Italian Army. It was on its way to Kuwait.

The destruction and looting of these sites was expected. In January 2003, two months before the U.S. invasion, a group of archaeologists met with Joseph Collins, who, they supposed, would relay their message to Paul Wolfowitz, then adviser to President George W. Bush. The archaeologists requested that the U.S. Army protect museums and archaeological sites. McGuire Gibson, of the Chicago Oriental Institute, presented a document naming five thousand essential sites. Martin Sullivan, President Bush's cultural adviser, contacted the president. But when the looting began, Sullivan resigned in frustration.

The reasons for the scholars' concern were legitimate. There were undeniable precedents. After the Gulf War of 1991, the Bureau for Recovering and Investigating Iraqi Looted Antiquities created two centers to investigate and document damage to cultural patrimony. One center was in Turin and the other in Baghdad. Between 2000 and 2001, the bureau created a list of 2,625 missing objects. Most have not been recovered.

In May 2004, U.S. and Italian troops fought the militia loyal to the cleric Muqtada Al-Sadr and in the ensuing conflict the museum of Nasiriyah and four thousand books burned. The news of that disaster was exacerbated by another, even worse: the murder of Iraqi intellectuals by violent factions. According to the Iraqi Union of University Professors, 1,000 intellectuals were murdered between April 2003 and July 2004.

During the Internet Librarian International conference, celebrated in London in 2004, the director of the National Library of Iraq, Saad Eskander, stated that during the time of Saddam Hussein the library and the National Archive were abandoned because the dictator tolerated no signs of dissidence and never stimulated culture. He accused the former minister of culture, Hamid Yusuf Hammadi, of talking about the library as if it were a cemetery and gave evidence to the effect that the librarians were all members of the Baath Party. In 1987, the Baath Party cut off funding for the library and closed archives and libraries. New acquisitions were of no interest to them. If it hadn't been for donations, Eskander said, the bibliographic enterprise of the library would have collapsed.

He also pointed out that in 2003 there were no conservation programs, and that the restoration laboratories had been closed for ten years. He explained that the losses of 2003 could have been avoided if his predecessor had used nearby mosques to store documents and books.

Eskander stated that U.S. troops were responsible for violating the Hague Convention of 1954 by not protecting cultural institutions during the seizure of Baghdad. He noted that soldiers knocked down a statue of Saddam outside the National Library and then left, leaving the building open to looting and arson. Eskander concluded that a large part of the destruction was spontaneous but that some was planned—specifically, the burning of the archives from the Republican era.

The most surprising thing is that once the disaster was over, no action was taken to save the books stored in the Ministry of Tourism. Hundreds were stolen and the building flooded to cover up the theft. I was profoundly upset to learn that, according to Eskander, none of the promises to help the National Library had been kept.

In 2006, Eskander started a blog of his life as librarian and the horrors he experienced. At the end of February 2007, violence in Iraq had turned into genocide. One of the most violent took place on Al-Mutanabbi Street, killing thirty people and destroying dozens of bookstores and stalls. The poet Jabbar Muhabis lamented: "Light will not shine here again," and bemoaned "the end of cultural life" in Baghdad, once the intellectual center of the Middle East.

It's important to read this text carefully: "Communiqués from Baghdad are inadequate, false, and incomplete. Everything is much worse than what we've been told. Today we are on the brink of disaster." That is not part of any official U.S. report and does not date from 2003. It is a fragment from a letter written in 1920 by Lawrence of Arabia to his superiors in England. His prophetic words are only too apt today.

Iraq was supposed to be a model in the war on terrorism, but it became a paradise for terrorists, a nation lacking direction, impoverished by war, afflicted by religious conflicts and terrorism, in economic crisis: a nation that has lost a large part of its memory. Its books are now ashes, its works of art on the market. Iraq was the first place to fall victim to cultural annihilation in the twenty-first century.

Could the reader, astonished at this chronicle of disasters, have imagined that the twenty-first century would begin with the despoliation and the destruction of the cradle of civilization?

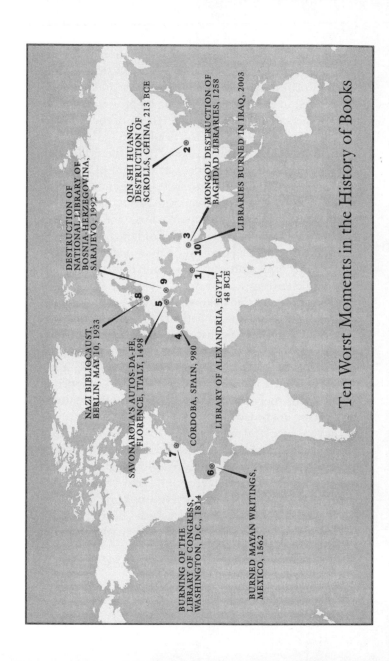

Ten Worst Moments in the History of Books

QIN SHI HUANG,
DESTRUCTION OF
SCROLLS, CHINA, 213 BCE

MONGOL DESTRUCTION OF
BAGHDAD LIBRARIES, 1258

LIBRARIES BURNED IN IRAQ, 2003

DESTRUCTION OF
NATIONAL LIBRARY OF
BOSNIA-HERZEGOVINA,
SARAJEVO, 1992

NAZI BIBLIOCAUST,
BERLIN, MAY 10, 1933

LIBRARY OF ALEXANDRIA, EGYPT,
48 BCE

SAVONAROLA'S AUTOS-DA-FÉ,
FLORENCE, ITALY, 1498

CÓRDOBA, SPAIN, 980

BURNING OF THE
LIBRARY OF CONGRESS,
WASHINGTON, D.C., 1814

BURNED MAYAN WRITINGS,
MEXICO, 1562

Notes

Introduction

p. 5   "Goethe says that when he was young…" Goethe, Johann Wofgang, *Dichtung und Wahrheit*, IV:I, Stuttgart, 1986.

p. 7   "All civilizations, it seems, have postulated their…" By "myth" I mean a sacred story of a people that refers to a primordial time and justifies the ritual meaning of an activity.

p. 8   "Those who attribute destructiveness to instinct…" Sigmund Freud argued for the presence of a destructive instinct. In the first of various works on instincts, *The Instinc~~ts and their Destiny* (1915), Freud states that instinct manifests itself as a unique impulse that is not momentary but drives us constantly. He believed that once established, such a need must be satisfied. It consists of a motive factor, which Freud defined as peremptory, with an objective, and a somatic source. The second relevant text is *Contemporary Considerations on War and Death* (1915), where he returned to instincts to explain the First World War. In *The Malaise of Culture* (1930), Freud gave his final explanation of why men attack culture. He noted that innate passions are more powerful than rational interests, and the repression of the instincts or destructive pulsations by culture, through laws or other factors, provokes a strange human need for liberation and revenge. Even so, years later, Freud called the theory of pulsations or instincts the "mythology of psychoanalysis" because of numerous details that left him displeased.

p. 9   "To the question of whether ancient myths…" Human destructiveness has increased. The number of wars, and their intensity, has kept pace with the advances of civilization. Between 1480 and 1499, there were barely nine major battles, while between 1900 and 1940 there were 892. In the twenty-first century, with the era of two-power confrontation over, tension, fear, and anguish continue to grow.

p. 10   "The appearance of writing presupposes…" While the question of whether Mesopotamian or Egyptian writing came first is still being decided, another issue vexes scholars: Did the first writing system appear in the sixth millennium BCE in Europe? We should recall that after the last ice age, a human wave spread over all the major mountain ranges. According to the late Lithuanian archeologist Marija Gimbutas, those groups developed writing. During the Stone and Bronze Ages, in the Balkans, there existed a center called Vinca, about fourteen kilometers east of Belgrade, on the banks of the Danube. Some 2,000 clay figures and other objects were discovered there incised with marks taken to be ritual writing of religious nature. The most surprising thing is that the signs reappear in Linear A from Crete.

p. 12   "The book is an institution of memory…" Every group or nation has attempted to legitimize its symbols as a form of expression. The 1954 Hague convention popularized the expression "cultural property." With great expectations, a group of UNESCO experts referred to patrimony as "the local, regional, national, continental, or universal totality of moveable or stationary goods, material or immaterial (or not physical) belonging to individuals or institutions or public or semipublic institutions that have exceptional value from a historical, artistic, scientific, economic, or social perspective. Things worthy of being preserved for all nations and for the international community to be known by people for generations to come."

p. 19   "A man as tolerant as David Hume…" *Enquiry Concerning Human Understanding* (1748), Section XII, Part III, 132.

Chapter 1

p. 22   "In Sumer, once Mesopotamia and now southern Iraq…"
Writing developed in Sumer for economic reasons. Denise
Schmandt-Besserat (*Before Writing*, 1992) identifies three
phases before the invention of writing:

- During the Neolithic period, culture moved from
painting to pictograms. In Uruk, balls of clay have
been found that contain tablets marked with figures.
The ball refers to an administrative entity and constituted a form of accounting. The figures on the tablets
resembled animals and geometric figures.

- In the second phase, the books had signs incised on
their exterior. Out of a desire for efficiency, the signs
came to represent internal content.

- Finally came clay tablets, more practical than the balls.
The signs were understood not only as symbols but as
sounds. Writing became more abstract, and around
2000 BCE, the scribes gave each sign a significance
that reduced their number.

p. 23   "Another myth speaks of a king of Uruk…" Orignal text
and transliteration by Herman Vanstiphout, at http://etcsl.
orinst.ox.ac.uk/section1/b1823.htm

p. 23   "Around 2800 B.C.E., the monarchs…" *Man Makes Himself*
(1936) of V. Gordon Childe: "…it was in all likelihood a
magical act whereby a man, departed from the land of the
living for a long time, could still speak from a tablet."

p. 24   "They wrote in cuneiform script…" E. Kämpfer, in 1700,
used the term "cuneiforme" for the first time.

Chapter 2

p. 33   "He governed for sixty-six years…" Isidore of Sevilla
(Etimologías, VI, 10) wrote: "It was in Egypt where
papyrus was used for the first time; it was discovered in
Memphis."

Chapter 3

p. 38   "Partially burned, it is the remains…" The Dervéni Papyrus was discovered in 1962 in Macedonia. Judging by the kind of letters used, scholars like C. H. Roberts date the text to 300 BCE. For further reference, see *Studies on the Dervéni Papyrus* (1997) by André Laks.

p. 39   "The word used for books…" The reader will note that the Phoenician word is at the root of the word "bible."

p. 39   "In the fourth century BCE, the alphabet was transformed…" The hexameter required the existence of long and short vowels.

p. 40   "However, people generally read aloud…" Bernard Knox (*Silent Reading in Antiquity*, 1968) has supported this thesis with two classic examples: the first is from Euripedes' *Hippolytus*, dated by some philologists to 428 BCE. In that text, Theseus observes Phedra holding a small tablet in her hand. He unties the cord binding it, and almost immediately he shouts: "O horror! woe upon woe! and still they come, too deep for words, too heavy to bear! Ah me!" The chorus asks what the tablet contains, and Theseus, still not reading it aloud, summarizes it, showing that he had read it to himself. The second text is in Aristophanes' *Knights*, which is from 424 BCE. Nicia steals an oracle written to Paphlagon, and instead of reading it aloud, decides to read it silently. To these I would add an irrefutable example from Aristophanes' *Frogs*, which dates from 405 BCE. There the character Dionysus says: "[…]when I was on board reading silently *Andromeda*[…]."

Chapter 4

p. 43   "He wrote scores of books…" A catalogue of his books includes the following titles: *Apology for Socrates, Aristides, Aristomacus, Artaxerxes, Assembly, Calcidicus, Letters, Catalogue, Cleon, On Aesop, On Faith, On Fortune, On*

Divine Grace, On the Iliad (two books), *On the Athenian Incursion, On Magnificence, On the* Odyssey (four books), *On Opinion, On Opportunity, On Rhetoric* (two books), *On Old Age, On the Laws of the Athenians* (five books), *On Law, On Marriage, On the Citizens of Athens* (two books), *On Study, On Children, On the Army* (two books), *On Government* (two books), *Dionysus, Exhortations, Fedondas, Homerics, Embassies, Medon, Historical Prologue, On a Column of Light in the Sky.*

p. 48   "Callimachus of Cyrene..." For further information, I recommend these studies on Callimacus: "The Pinakes of Callimachus," *Libr. Quaterly* 28, 2, 1958, by Fr. J. Witty; *Kallimachos* (1975) by A. Skiadas. The prestige of Callmachus has led specialists on Hellenistic culture to conclude he had to be the director of the Library. But on the ancient lists we possess he is not given that title, John Tzetzes called him "*aulicus regius bibliothecarius,*" which only proves the poet had a close relationship with the Library.

p. 48   "The Lexicon of Suda ascribes 800 rolls..." Lexicon, K227: *Callimachus, son of Bato and Mesatma, of Cyrene, grammarian. Disciple of the grammarian Hermocrates of Iasus. Married the daughter of Euphrates of Syracuse; the son of his brother was Callimachus the Younger, who wrote on the islands in epic verse. He was so skillful that he wrote poems in all meters, and composed many prose works. He wrote more than 800 books. He lived during the era of Ptolomey Philadelphus. Before his relationship with the king, he taught grammar in Eleusis, a village near Alexandria. He survived under the reign of Ptolomey, called Evergetes, in Olympiad 127, in whose second year began the reign of Ptolomey Evergetes. His books include:* The Coming of Io, Semele, Founding of Argos, Arcadia, Glaucus, Hopes, Satiric Works, *tragedies, comedies, lyric poems,* Ibis [a deliberately obscure and offensive poem directed at one Ibis, enemy of Callimachus: it concerned Apollonius, author of the *Argonautica*], Museum, Table of Dramatic Writers in Chronological Order from the Earliest Times,

Tables of All Who Were Eminent in Literature in All Genres, On the Glosses and Writings of Democritus, Names of the Months by Nation and City, Founding of Islands and Cities and Their Name Changes, On the Rivers of Europe, Rarities of the Entire World According to Location, On the Changes of Name in Fish, On the Winds, On Birds, On the Rivers of the Uninhabited World, Collection of Marvels from the Entire World According to Location."

p. 53   "After the Zenobia episode, the emperor Diocletian…" Gibbon acidly observed that "the persecution of Diocletian is the first authentic event in the history of alchemy…."

Chapter 5

p. 61   Andronicus: the most rigorous account of his role is perhaps the one by Jonathan Barnes in his "Roman Aristotle," J. Barnes and M. Griffin, Miriam (eds.) *Philosophia Togata II: Plato and Aristotle at Rome*, Oxford University Press, 1999, pp. 1–69.

Chapter 6

p. 67   "In the shadow of the emperor's absolute power stood Li Si…" The Legalist scholars, precursors of some of Machiavelli's ideas, are represented by Shen-Dao, Shen Bu-hai, and Shang Yang. The theses of these three advocates of absolutism were synthesized by Han Fei-zi. Cfr. W.K. Liao, *The Complete Works of Han Fei Tsu, a Classic of Chinese Legalism*, 1939.

p. 70   "Qin Shi Huang's own imperial library…" The stupendous scholarship of Jean-Pierre Drège has documented censorship and biblioclasty in China through the ages: *Les Bibliothèques en Chine au temps des manuscrits jusqu'au Xème siècle*, Paris, 1991.

p. 73 "What allows us to imagine a large number are the *yiwenzhi...*" One work summarizes all the catalogues. William Hong (ed.), *Yiwenzhi ershizhong zonghe yinde* (Combined Indices to Twenty Historical Bibliographies). Harvard Yenching Institute, Index Series no. 10, Beijing, Harvard Yenching Institute, 1933.

Chapter 7

p. 75 "The praetor Quintus Petilius..." There are many studies on this matter, but I would recommend one in particular: Theodor Birt, *Das antike Buchwesen in seinem Verhältniss zur Litteratur, mit Beiträgen zur Textgeschichte des Theokrit, Catull, Properz, und anderer Autoren.* Berlin, W. Hertz, 1882.

p. 76 "On Virgil's deathbed in 19 BCE..." *Virgilio* (1976, p. 91) by Agustín García Calvo. The original sources for this anecdote are: Donatus, *Vita Verg.* 38f; Servius' commentary; Probus' life of Virgil; *Vita Gudiana I*; *Anthol. Lat.* 653 and 672.

p. 82 "The papyri revealed speeches thought lost by the philosopher Epicurus and texts of Philodemus..." Philodemus was a poet and philosopher. The Philodemus Project, coordinated by Prof. Richard Janko of the University of Michigan, is trying to publish the fragments of his books. A good analysis of his thought appears in *La literatura griega de la época helenística e imperial* (1972) by Raffaele Cantarella.

Chapter 8

p. 88 "Among the Greeks, at the beginning, there were few copies of a single text..." This applies to later periods: only one manuscript source exists for the Lexicon of Hesiquius of Alexandria (fifth century CE)—the Marc. Gr. 622, of the fifteenth century. Kurt Latte made an edition in two volumes which appeared in 1953 and 1966. Imagine if such a valuable manuscript had disappeared in a fire.

p. 88   "Nowadays, there are no examples..." *Berol.* 9865, with *The Persians* by Timotheus of Miletus is considered one of the most ancient papyri of Greek literature, along with the Dervéni papyrus.

p. 88   "In fact, despite the labor of libraries..." Cfr. Isidoro de Sevilla (*Etymologiess*, VI, 12): "And it is called a codex by a transposition of the name of tree trunks or vines, as if we were to say *caudex*, because it resembles holding books the way the trunk supports the branches."

p. 89   "Telephos of Pergamon..." From Suda's *Lexicon: Telephos of Pergamon, grammarian, also wrote* On Syntax, *where he reveals how many things a grammarian must know*; On Rhetorical Figures in Homer *in two books*; On the Syntax of Attic Discourse *in five books*; On the Relationship between Homer and Plato; Lives of Tragedians and Authors of Comedy; Book Expertise, *in two books, where he teaches that book acquisition is noble*; On Whether Homer Is the Only Ancient Greek Author Who Wrote Greek Correctly; Description of Pergamon; On the Temple of Augustus in Pergamon, *in two books*; On the Court in Athens; On the Kings of Pergamon *in five books*; On the Wearing of Clothes and other Daily Items *(in alphabetical order)*; On Odysseus' Wanderings; *a collection of practical epithets with the intention of helping better fluidity in sentences, in ten books[...]*

p. 98   "Copies of Sappho..." This assertion is in dispute. Pope Gregory VII ordered copies of Sappho's poems burned in 1073 both in Rome and Byzantium, leading to the conclusion that no other copy survived until the thirteenth century. Even so, D.L. Page (*Sappho and Alceus*, 1955, p. 113) notes that there is a reference to Book 8 of the complete works of Sappho in the library of Photoius, Patriarch of Constantinople from 858 to 867 and from

877 to 886. Miguel Psellos mencioned Sappho in a letter (Sathas, Mes. Bibl. 5, 59 f.) bearing witness to her popularity. In *The Oxford Dictionary of Byzantium* (1991, p. 1841) we find: "After a period of silence, Sappho reappears at the end of the tenth century, when Suda included her biography and passages from her original poems *[...] Sappho was especially popular in the twelfth century, though often Tzetzes (Cramer, Anecd. Gr. Paris. 1: 63. 20-21) claims her works had disappeared[...]Interest in Sappho diminished after the eleventh century, though Planudes, Moscopoulos, and Metoquides were familiar with her verses* [...]

Chapter 10

p. 103   "This magic phase of Irish history..." Heiric de Auxerres wrote in 870 CE: "Almost all Ireland, disdaining the sea, is emigrating toward our shores with a flock of philosophers!"

p. 122   "Some Muslims buried their Korans, but the search was painstaking... " The expulsion of the Moors and Jews obliged, for example, the Sephardic Jews to abandon hundreds of manuscripts. In March of 2003, manuscripts written in Hebrew, among them documents from a notary office, sales contracts, marriage certificates, and versions of the Torah, were found hidden in the bindings of books in Girona, in northeastern Spain. What saved the texts was the strategy of stuffing the book covers with the forbidden manuscripts.

Chapter 14

p. 142   "'The Anabaptists boasted of their innocence ...'" Norman Cohn, *The Pursuit of the Millennium* (1957, revised and expanded 1970).

p. 144   Pinelli's library: I recommend Marcella Grendler, "A Greek Collection in Padua: the Library of Gian Vincenzo Pinelli (1535-1601)," *Renaissance Quarterly* 33, (1980).

Chapter 15

p. 150   John Dee's library is lovingly described in Roberts, Julian and Watson, Andrew, *John Dee's Library Catalogue*, 1990.

Chapter 16

p. 162   "Emile Zola, in a panic, wrote…" I suggest two titles: *Les manuscrits de la Bibliothèque du Louvre. Brûlés dans la nuit du 23 au 24 Mai 1871 sous le règne de la Commune* (1872) by Louis Paris and *Rapport sur les pertes eprouvees par les bibliothèques publiques de Paris en 1870 y 1871* (1871) by M. Baudrillart, as well as Zola's own *La Débacle*.

p. 162   "In October 1873, the young poet Arthur Rimbaud…" Enid Starkie, in *Arthur Rimbaud* (1989, p. 309), suggests that Rimbaud burned his manuscripts, but it is also possible that he burned only the books he had with him at the time. See also the bibliophile's account: Losseau, León, "La légende de la destruction par Rimbaud de l'édition princeps de Une saison en enfer," *Annuaire [pour 1915] de la Société des bibliophiles et iconophiles de Belgique* (1916).

Chapter 17

p. 173   "Philip wanted his library…" There is an extensive bibliography on this subject: Almela, J. A., *Descripción de la Octava Maravilla del Mundo que es la excelente y santa casa de San Lorenzo, el Real, Monasterio de Frailes Jerónimos y colegio de los mismos y seminario de letras humanas y sepultura de reyes y casa de recogimiento y descanso después de los trabajos del gobierno, fabricada por el muy alto y poderoso rey y señor nuestro Don Felipe de Austria, segundo de este nombre. Compuesto por el Doctor Juan Alonso de Almela, medico natural y vecino de Murcia, dirigido a la Real Magestad del*

Rey Don Felipe, 1594; Andrés, G. de, "Entrega de la librería real de Felipe II (1576). Edición, prólogo e identificaciones de obras," *Documentos para la Historia del Monasterio de El Escorial*, Madrid, 1964; Antolín, G., *La librería de Felipe II*, Madrid, 1964; Campos Y Fernández De Sevilla, F. J., *Fondo manuscrito americano de la Biblioteca de San Lorenzo de El Escorial*, San Lorenzo de El Escorial, 1993; Zarco, J. , *La Biblioteca de El Escorial*, Barcelona, 1929.

p. 175 "At least three manuscripts..." An inventory of the losses exists: *Catálogo de los códices griegos desaparecidos de la Real Biblioteca de El Escorial* (1968) de Gregorio de Andrés. See also Gregorio de Andrés, *El incendio del monasterio de El Escorial del año 1671. Sus consecuencias en las artes y las letras*, Madrid, 1976.

p. 184 "...Dutch cartographer Joan Blaeu..." Les Elzevier. *Histoire et annales typographiques*, Bruxelles, 1880. See also Koeman, Cornelis. *Joan Blaeu and his Grand Atlas : Introduction to the Facsimile Edition of Le grand atlas, 1663*, Amsterdam, Theatrum Orbis Terrarum, 1970.

Chapter 18

p. 190 "Only twelve copies of the 1827 edition..." The twelve known copies are located in the Huntington Library (San Marino, California), Harry Ransom Humanities Research Center (University of Texas, Austin), Berg Collection (New York Public Library), Lilly Library (Indiana University), a private collection (purchased at Sotheby's, New York, in January of 1990), The Alderman Library (University of Virginia), the Joseph Regenstein Library (University of Chicago), a private collection (acquired on June 7, 1988 at Sotheby's New York for $198,000), the British Library, the William Andrews Clark Library (University of California), the collection of Richard Gimbel and the Free Library of Philadelphia.

Chapter 19

p. 201   "Armed with that ruined book as my only talisman..."
The dispersion of sources has not made research in this
section any easier, but María Teresa Delgado has supplied
me with a solid bibliography: Escolar Sobrino, Hipólito,
La cultura durante la guerra civil, Madrid, Alhambra,
1987; Turrión Garcia, Maria Jose, "La biblioteca de
la sección guerra civil del Archivo Histórico Nacional
(Salamanca)," *Boletín de la ANABAD 2*, (1997), p.p.
89-113 Gamonal Torres, Miguel Ángel; Herranz Navarra,
Juan Francisco, "Los servicios de bibliotecas en el ejército
popular de la República durante la Guerra Civil," *Boletín
de la Asociación Andaluza de Bibliotecarios* 2, 4, (1986),
pp. 35-39; Ruperez, María, "Bibliografía sobre la guerra
civil," *Claridad* 16, (1986), pp. 99-105.

p. 205   "All Spanish archives were severely damaged..." There
is an extensive bibliography on the destroyed archives:
Conde Villaverde, María Luisa; Andrés Díaz, Rosana
de. "Destrucción de documentos en España: historia,
prevención y reconstrucción," *ARCHIVUM* v. XLII,
(1996), pp. 119-129; San Sebastián, Koldo, "El Exilio
de los Archivos," *X Congreso de Estudios Vascos: archivos,
bibliotecas y museos,* Iruñea, 21-25 abril, 1987. Separata.
Donostia: Eusko Ikaskuntza, 1987. pp. 619-703; Sigalat
Vayá, María José, "La guerra civil y los Archivos munici-
pales. El caso de Carcaixent," *Biblioteques, Arxius i Centres
de Documentaciò, Jornadas sobre Cultura en la Comunitat
Valenciana. II. 1996.* Valencia, 1996, pp. 551-559; Jaramillo
Guerreira, Miguel Ángel. "Los archivos y la Guerra Civil,
1936 a 1939," en *Historia de los archivos y de la archivística
en España*. Valladolid: Secretariado de publicaciones e
Intercambio Científico de la Universidad de Valladolid,
1998. pp. 161-174; Zamora i Escala, Jaume Enric, "El
salvamento de los archivos catalanes durante la Guerra
Civil española (1936-1939)," *Lligall. Revista Catalana
d'Arxivística 16*, (2000), pp. 85-151; Grau Pujol, Josep
M.T.;Güell, Manuel, "La crónica negra de la destrucción

de archivos en la demarcación de Tarragona," *Lligall.*
Revista Catalana d'Arxivística 18, (2001), pp. 65–120.

p. 206 "Then came a decree..." I owe this valuable information to
the librarian (and friend) Emiliano Bartolomé Domínguez.
In all cases, the source used was the *Repertorio cronológico
de legislación*, compiled by Editorial Aranzadi.

p. 206 "But that event was preceded..." The bibliography on
this subject is seemingly infinite. I've read the follow-
ing with great interest in order to complete this section:
Walberer, Ulrich (Ed.), *10 Mai 1933 Bücherverbrennung
in Deutschland und die Folgen,* Frankfurt am Main,
Fischer Taschenbuch Verlag, 1983; A. Graf and H. D.
Kuebler, *Verbrannte Bücher Verbrannte Ideen,* Hamburg,
O. Heinevetter, 1993; Volker Dahm, *Das Jüdische Buch
im Dritten Reich Vol. 1: Die Ausschaltung der Jüdischen
Autoren, Verleger und Buchhändler,* Frankfurt am Main,
Buchhaendler Vereinigung, 1979.

p. 208 "Some of the most prominent philosophers..." Many years
later, Heidegger claimed he did not participate in book
burning. He attempted to explain himself in an interview
with *Der Spiegel* (May 31, 1976):

SPIEGEL: *You know that in this context, some criticism
of you has been raised related to your collaboration with the
NSDAP and similar bodies. It is widely believed you have
never denied these accusations. You have been reproached
for participating in book burning organized by students or
by the Hitler Youth.*

HEIDEGGER: *I prohibited the plan to burn books which was
supposed to take place in front of the university building.*

SPIEGEL: *You have also been reproached for allowing books
by Jewish authors to be removed from the University Library
and the Philosophy Seminar.*

HEIDEGGER: *As director of the seminar, I could only use
the library. I did not give in to the repeated demands that
books by Jewish authors be removed. Former participants*

*in my seminars can testify today to the fact that not only
was no book by a Jewish author withdrawn but that those
authors, especially Husserl, were quoted and commented
on just as before 1933.*

p. 210   "Against the materialist, utilitarian class..." *Gegen
Klassenkampf und Materialismus für Völksgemeinschaft
und idealistische Lebenshaltung. Marx, Kautsky.*

p. 210   "A musical prelude..." Dietrich Aigner. *Die Indizierung
"Schädlichen und Unerwünschten Schrifttums" im Dritten
Reich.* Frankfurt am Main: Buchhändler-Vereinigung,
1971, p. 1018:

p. 218   "According to one scholar, the works of more than 5,500
authors..." W. Jutte, "Volksbibliotheke im Naztionalsozialismus,"
Buch und Bibliothek 39, pp. 345–348, 1987.

A statistical summary appears in Friedman, Philip. "The
Fate of the Jewish Book During the Nazi Era," *Jewish Book
Annual* 13, (1957–58), p. 4. Also worthy of consultation:
Viktor Reimann, *Dr. Joseph Goebbels*, 1971.

p. 210   "... Goebbels explained the reasons..." The text appears
in the *Völkischer Beobachter*, May 12, 1933.

Chapter 21

p. 236   "During the Eleventh Plenary Session..." It is impos-
sible to record here all the publications reviewed for this
entry, but the following texts are essential: Asia Research
Center, *The Great Cultural Revolution in China* (Hong
Kong, Asia Research Center, 1967); William Joseph, ed.
New Perspectives on the Cultural Revolution (Cambridge:
Harvard University Press, 1991); Hongyong Lee, *The
Politics of the Chinese Cultural Revolution* (Berkeley:
University of California Press, 1978); Joan Robinson,
The Cultural Revolution in China (Baltimore: Penguin
Books, 1969).

p. 237 "The hysteria was so great that one author…" Lee-hsia Hsu Ting. *Government Control of the Press in Modern China 1900-1949*, Cambridge: Harvard University Press, 1974.

p. 238 "Thousands of writers were jailed…" Lee-hsia Hsu Ting, "Library Services in the People's Republic of China," *Library Quarterly* 53, 1983, p. 148.

Chapter 23

p. 252 "Bosnian poet Goran Simic…" The essential bibliography on the legacy destroyed and the devastating effects of similar attacks appears in several sources: *The Art Treasures of Bosnia and Herzegovina*. Ed. Mirza Filipovic with text by Djuro Baselr, Sarajevo, Svjetlost, 1987; "Rebuilding Bosnia's Library: Local Scholars Seek Help of Colleagues Worldwide," *Chronicle of Higher Education*, vol. 41 no. 18, 13 January 1995, pp. A35-37; *Council of Europe. Parliamentary Assembly. Information Report on the Destruction by War of the Cultural Heritage in Croatia and Bosnia-Herzegovina*. Strasbourg, 1993; Detling, Karen J. "Eternal Silence: The Destruction of Cultural Property in Yugoslavia," *Maryland Journal of International Law and Trade*, vol. 17 no. 1, Spring 1993, pp. 41-75; Fisk, Robert. "Waging War on History: In Former Yugoslavia, Whole Cultures Are Being Obliterated," *The Independent* (London), 20 June 1994, p. 18; Lovrenovic, Ivan. "The Hatred of Memory." New York Times, 28 May 1994, p. A15.

p. 256 "András Riedlmayer…" The report may be found at http://hague.bard.edu/reports/BosheritageReport-AR.pdf

p. 256 "Between 1993 and 1994…" United Nations Commission on ex-Yugoslavia, 1994, Suppl. VI, paragraphs 183-193, Suppl. XI, paragraphs 17, 22 and 33. Also worthy of note is Kemal Bakaršic's extraordinary essay in *The New Combat*, Autumn 1994 (p. 10).

Chapter 24

p. 260   "In the case of insects..." All entomological references
derive from: Manfrini De Brewer, Mireya-Sosa, Claudio
A. "Insectos en Bibliotecas y Archivos. Principales especies
de insectos perjudiciales para las colecciones de bibliotecas
y archivos y algunos depredadores naturales que ayudan
a controlarlos," Ciencia Hoy 35, 1996.

p. 262   "Paper made of linen or cotton rags is durable..." I
am indebted to Arsenio Sánchez Hernampérez, of the
Laboratorio de Restauración de la Biblioteca Nacional
de España, for this section. He is the author of *Políticas
de Conservación en Bibliotecas*, Madrid, Arco libros,
1999. Almost all the information I present, including
the examples, derives from his disinterested exposition.

p. 262   "Acidic hydrolysis..." Interested readers may find the
following bibliography helpful: Smith, Richard D.
"Paper Deacidification: A Preliminary Report," *Library
Quarterly* 36, 4, (1966), pp. 273-292; Smith, Richard D,
"Deacidification of Paper and Books", American Libraries 6, 2,
(1975), pp. 108-110; Young, Luther. "Librarians Try to Save
Books from Their Own Paper," *The Sun* (London), November
13, (1989), A-1, A-5; Cookson, Clive. "New Chapter Opens
in a Tragic Story," *Financial Times*, March 9, 1990, p. 10;
Turko, Karen. *Mass Deacidification Systems.* Washington,
D.C., Association of Research Libraries, 1990.

Chapter 25

p. 271   "From the outset there was a debate about the library
losses..." Mite, V. "Iraq: Archives, libraries devastated
by war, looting." Radio Free Europe/Radio Liberty, 13
July, 2004.

p. 271   "We lost about sixty percent..." Among the library
catalogues: Naqshabandi, Usamah Nasir, and Zamya
Muhammad 'Abbas. *Makhtutat al-hisab wa-al-handasah*

wa-al-jabr fi maktabat al-mathaf al-'Iraqi, Bagdad, Wizarat al-Thaqafah wa-al-I'lam, al-Mu'assasah al-'Ammah lil-Athar wa-al-Turath, 1980; Behnam Fadil Affadh, *târîkh al-tibâ'a wa la-matbû'ât al-irâqiyya,* Baghdad, 1984; Abd al-Jabbar Abd al-Rahman, *Iraqi national Bibliography,* 1856-1972, 3 vols., Bagdad, 1978; Zâhida Ibrahim, *Kashshâf al-jara'id wa al-majallât al-'irâqiyya,* Baghdad, 1976; Kurkis Awwad, A. *Dictionary of Iraqi Authors during the Nineteenth and Twentieth Centuries* (1800-1969), 3 vols., Baghdad, 1969; Kurkis Awad and Abdul Hamed al-Alouchi, *A Bibliography of Baghdad,* Baghdad, 1962; Abdul Husayn Y. Ali, *A List of Books and References Concerning Basra,* Basra, 1981.

p. 273 "Only chance saved other Baghdad book collections..." McGuire Gibson, "Cultural Tragedy in Iraq: A Report on the Looting of Museums, Archives, and Sites", IFAR Journal, Vol. 6, Nos. 1 & 2, 2003; Jonathan Steele, "Museum's Treasures Left to the Mercy of Looters," *The Guardian* (London), April 14, 2003; David Blair, "Thieves of Baghdad Rob Museums of Priceless Treasure", *Daily Telegraph* (London), April 14, 2003.

p. 273 "The destruction of the National Library..." John M. Russell, "A Personal Account of the First UNESCO Cultural Heritage Mission to Baghdad; May 16-20, 2003." Paper presented to the Archaeological Institute of America.

p. 275 "Not far away, the Al-Awqaf..." Abd Allah Al-Jabbouri wrote a history of this center: *Maktabat al-awqâf al-'amma, târîkhuhâ wa nawâdir makhtûtâtihâ.* Baghdad, 1969.

Bibliography

Adamgy, Yiossuf. *A verdade ácerca da biblioteca de Alexandria*. Loures: Al Furqán, 1989.

Adunka, Evelyn. *Der raub der bücher. Plünderung in der NS-Zeit und Restitution nach 1945*, Vienna: Czernin Verlag, 2002.

Aguirre Beltrán, Gonzalo. *La actividad del santo oficio de la inquisición en Nueva España, 1571–1700*. Mexico City: INAH, 1981.

Ahmad, Salim Abd al-Razzaq. *Fihris makhtutat Maktabat al-Awqaf al-Ammah fi al-Mawsil*. Al-Jumhuriyah al-Iraqiyah, Wizarat al-Awqaf wa-al-Shuun al-Diniyah, 1982.

Aigner, Dietrich. "Die Indizierung: Schädlichen und Unerwünschten Schrifttums," in *Dritten Reich*. Frankfurt: Buchhändler-Vereinigung, 1971.

al-Husayni, Ahmad al-Rajibi. *Fihrist makhtutat Khizanat al-Rawdah al-Haydariyah fi al-Najaf al-Ashraf*. 1971.

Alnander, Samuel Johansson. *Historia librorum prohibitorum in Svecica*. Uppsala: 1764.

al-Rashti, Muhamad ibn Abd al-Husayn; al-Husayni, al-Sayyid Ahmad. *Fihrist makhtutat al-shaykh Muhamad al-Rashti al-muhdah ila Maktabat al-Imam al-Hakim al-'Ammah fi al-Najaf al-Ashraf*. Najaf: Matba'at al-Nu'man, 1971.

Alusi, Numan ibn Mahmud. *Fihrist makatib Baghdad al-mawqufah*. Baghdad: Markaz Ihya al-Turath al-Ilmi, 1985.

Andert, Frank. *Verbrannt, verboten, verbannt—vergessen? Kolloquium zum 60. Jahrestag der Bücherverbrennung von 1933*. Leipzig: Rosa-Luxemburg-Verein, 1995.

Andres, Gregorio de. *El incendio del monasterio de El Escorial del año 1671. Sus consecuencias en las artes y las letras.* Madrid: El Escorial, 1976.

Anonymous. *Inscriptiones Graecae,* Berlin: Brandenburg Academy of Arts and Sciences, 47 vols., 1815.

———. "Germany's Book Bonfire," *Literary Digest* 115 (May 27, 1933): 14–15.

———. "War Situation," *Special Libraries* 62, no. 1 (1971): 32–40.

———. *Nie wieder Faschismus und Krieg: die Mahnung der faschistischen Bücherverbrennung am 10. Mai 1933.* Berlin: Humboldt-Universität zu Berlin, Gesellschaftswissenschaftliche Fakultät, 1983.

Aragón, Henrique de. *Arte cisoria o Tratado del arte del cortar del cuchillo.* Madrid: El Bibliófilo, 1981.

Arndt, Augustinus. *De libris prohibitis commentarii.* Cincinnati: F. Pustet, 1895.

Arnim, H. von. *Stoicorum veterum fragmenta.* Leipzig: B. G. Teubner, 1964.

Arnold, Klaus. *Johannes Trithemius (1462–1516): Zweite, bibliographisch und überlieferungsgeschichtlich neu bearbeite Auflage, Quellen und Forschungen zur Geschichte des Bistums und Nochstifts Würzburg XXIII.* Würzburg: Kommissionsverlag F. Schöningh, 1971.

Arsalan, Ibrahim Khurshid. *Faharis al-ruqayqat li-Maktabat Makhtutat al-Majma al-Ilmi al-Iraqi.* Baghdad: Al-Majma, 1981.

Ascarelli, F. "Le biblioteche italiane e la guerra," *Rivista storica italiana* 60 (1948): 177–182.

Asselineau, Charles. *L'enfer du bibliophile,* 1860. http://ourworld.compuserve.com/homepages/bib_lisieux/enferbib.htm.

Awwad, Kurkis. *Al-Makhtutat al-'Arabiyah fi Maktabat al-Mathaf al-'Iraqi.* Baghdad: Matba'at al-Rabitah, 1957–1959.

———. *Catalogue of the Arabic manuscripts in the Iraq Museum Library.* Baghdad: Ar-Rabita Press, 1957–1959.

———. *Fihrist makhtutat khizanat Yaqub Sarkis al-muhdah ila Jamiat al-Hikmah bi-Baghdad,* al-Hikma University. Baghdad: Matbaat al-Ani, 1966.

Awwad, Mikhail. *Makhtutat al-Majma al-Ilmi al-Iraqi: dirasah wa-fahrasah.* Baghdad: Matbaat al-Majma al-Ilmi al-Iraqi, 1979–1983.

Aymes, Jean-René. *La guerra de la independencia en España (1808–1814)*. Madrid: Siglo XXI, 2003.

Back, E. A. "Bookworms," *Indian Archives* 1, no. 2 (1947): 126–134.

Báez, Fernando. *El Tractatus Coislinianus*. Mérida: Universidad de Los Andes, 2000.

———. *Los fragmentos de Aristóteles*. Mérida: Vicerrectorado Académico de la Universidad de Los Andes, 2002.

———. *Historia de la antigua biblioteca de Alejandría*. Madrid: Vintila Horia, 2003.

———. "Iraq es un libro quemado," *La Vanguardia,* Suplemento Cultural (May 2003) 29–end.

———. *La destrucción cultural de Iraq. Un testimonio de posguerra*. Barcelona: Octaedro, 2004.

Bagnall, R. S. "The Origin of Ptolemaic Cleruchs," *Bulletin of the American Society of Papyrologists* 21 (1984): 7–20.

Bagster, Samuel. *Samuel Bagster of London 1772–1851. An Autobiography*. London: Samuel Bagster & Sons, 1972.

Bakaršić, Kemal. "The Libraries of Sarajevo and the Book that Saved Our Lives," *The New Combat* (Autumn 1994): 13–15.

Baker, H. D., R. J. Matthews, and J. N. Postgate. *Lost Heritage: Antiquities Stolen from Iraq's Regional Museums*. London: British School of Archaeology in Iraq, 1993.

Balbuena, Bernardo de. *Grandeza Mexicana*. Mexico City: 1604.

Banks, Edgard J. *Bismya, or The Lost City of Adab*, New York and London: Knickerbocker Press, 1912.

Barash, David P. *Understanding Violence*. Boston: Allyn & Bacon, 2001.

Baratin, Marc, and Jacob, Christian, eds. *O poder das bibliotecas*. Rio de Janiero: Universidade Federal de Rio de Janiero, 2000.

Barón Fernández, J. *Miguel Servet: Su vida y su obra*. Madrid: Austral, 1989.

Bartlett, Frederic. *Remembering: A Study in Experimental and Social Psychology*. Cambridge: Cambridge University Press, 1964.

Basbanes, Nicholas. *A Splendor of Letters: The Permanence of Books in an Impermanent World*. New York: Harper Perennial, 2004.

Basmah'ji, Faraj. *Kunuz al-Mathaf al-'Iraqi*. Baghdad: Wizarat al-I'lam, Mudiriyat al-Athar al-'Ammah, 1972.

———. *Treasures of the Iraq Museum*. Baghdad: Al-Jumhuriya Press, 1976.

Baudrillart, M. *Rapport sur les pertes éprouvées par les bibliothèques publiques de Paris en 1870 et 1871.* Paris: 1871.

Bauer, Walter. *Orthodoxy and Heresy in Earliest Christianity.* Philadelphia: Fortress Press, 1971.

Beck, Christian Daniel. *Specimen historiae Bibliothecarum Alexandrinarum: quod amplissimi philosophorum ordinis permissu.* Lipsiae: ex officiana Langenhemia, 1779.

Becourt, Daniel. *Livres condamnés, livres interdits.* Paris: Cercle de la Librarie, 1961.

Bégin, E. A. *Histoire des sciences, des lettres, des arts et de la civilisation en pays Messin, depuis les Gaulois jusqu'à nos jours.* Metz: 1829.

Behrendt, Roland. "The Library of Abbot Trithemius," *American Benedictine Review* 10 (1959): 67–85.

Bekker-Nielsen, Hans. *Arne Magnusson: The Manuscript Collector.* Odense, Denmark: Odense University Press, 1972.

Belis, Annie. *Aristoxène de Tarente et Aristote. Le traité d'harmonique.* Paris: Méridiens-Klincksieck, 1991.

Benayahu, Meir. *Sefarim she-nithabru be-Vavel u-sefarim she-neteku bah.* Jerusalem: Yad ha-Rav Nisim, 1993.

Benét, Stephen Vincent. *They Burned the Books.* New York: Farrar & Rinehart, 1942.

Benítez, Fernando. *El libro de los desastres.* Mexico City: Era, 2000.

Benzelius, Adolf. *De censura librorum.* Stockholm: 1743.

Berkovits, Ilona. *Illuminated Manuscripts from the Library of Matthias Corvinus.* Budapest: Corvina Press, 1964.

Bermant, Chaim, and Michael Weitzman. *Ebla: An Archaeological Enigma.* London: Weidenfeld and Nicolson, 1978.

Bernays, Jacob. *Zwei Abhandlungen über die aristotelische Theorie des Drama.* Berlin: 1880.

Bidez, J. *Un singulier naufrage littéraire dans l'antiquité.* Bruxelles: Office de la Publicité, 1943.

Biondo, Flavio. *Historiarum ab inclinatione Romanorum imperii decades.* Venice: Octavianus Scotus, 1483.

Birt, Theodor. *Das antike Buchwesen in seinem Verhältniss zur Litteratur, mit Beiträgen zur Textgeschichte des Theokrit, Catull, Properz, und anderer Autoren.* Berlin: W. Hertz, 1882.

———. *Die Buchrolle in der Kunst.* Leipzig: Teubner, 1907.

Blackman, A. M. *The Story of King Kheops and the Magicians.* Transcript of the Westcar Papyrus (Berlin Papyrus 3033). Edited by W. V. Davies. Reading, PA: J. V. Books, 1988.

Blackmore, Susan. *The Meme Machine.* Oxford: Oxford University Press, 2000.

Blades, William. *The Enemies of Books,* rev. ed. London: Elliot Stock, 1888.

Blanck, Horst. "Un nuovo frammento del Catalogo della biblioteca di Tauromenion," *La Parola del Passato* 52 (1997): 241–255.

Blazina, Vesna. "¿El memoricidio es un crimen contra la humanidad igual que el genocidio?" *Studia Croatica* 134 (1997): 121.

Bloom, Jonathan M. *Paper Before Print: The History and Impact of Paper in the Islamic World.* London: Yale University Press, 2001.

Blum, R. *Kallimachos. The Alexandrian Library and the Origins of Bibliography.* Madison: University of Wisconsin Press, 1991.

Boissier, Gaston. *La fin du paganisme. Étude sur les dernières luttes religieuses en Occident au ive siècle.* Paris: Hachette, 1909.

Bolseé, J. "La protection des archives en temps de guerre," *Archives, Bibliothèques et Musées de Belgique* 16 no. 2 (1939): 116–120.

Borin, Jacqueline. "Embers of the Soul: The Destruction of Jewish Books and Libraries in Poland During World War II," *Libraries and Culture* 28 (1993): 4.

Borque López, Leonardo. *Bibliotecas, archivos y guerra civil en Asturias.* Gijón, Spain: Trea, 1997.

Bosmajian, Haig. *Burning Books.* Jefferson, NC: McFarland, 2006.

Boudinhon, A. *La nouvelle legislation de l'index.* Paris: 1899.

Bowman, Alan K., and Greg Woolf. *Cultura escrita y poder en el Mundo Antiguo.* Barcelona: Gesida, 2000.

Bowring, John. *Conflagration of Åbo.* London: Soho, Howlett & Brimmer, 1828.

Boyd, Clarence Eugene. *Public Libraries and Literary Culture in Ancient Rome.* Chicago: University of Chicago Press, 1915.

Boyer, J. "Insect Enemies of Books," *Scientific American* 98 (1908): 413–414.

Brenner, Hildegard, *Die Kunstpolitik des Nationalsozialismus.* Hamburg: Rowohlt, 1963.

Bridgeman, B. *The Biology of Behavior.* Hoboken, NJ: John Wiley & Sons, 1988.

Briet, Suzanne. *Bibliothèques en détresse.* Paris: UNESCO, 1949.

Brooks, P., "The Bookworm Vanquished," *Philippine Agriculturist* 23 (1934): 171–173.

Browne, Thomas. *The Works of the Learned Sr Thomas Brown, Kt. Doctor of Physick, late of Norwich.* London: Printed for Tho. Basset, Ric. Chiswell, Tho. Sawbridge, Charles Mearn, and Charles Brome, 1686.

Bruce, Lorne D. "A Note on Christian Libraries During the Great Persecution, 303–305 A.D.," *Journal of Library History* 15, no. 2 (1980): 127–137.

———. "A Reappraisal of Roman Libraries in the Scriptores Historiae Auguste," *Journal of Library History* 16, no. 4 (1981): 551–573.

Brugnoli, Giorgio, and Stok, Fabio, eds. *Vitae vergilianae antiquae. Scriptores graeci et latini.* Rome: Istituto Polygraphico, 1997.

Brunet, P. G., and J. M. Quérard. *Livres perdus et exemplaires uniques.* Reprint of the Bordeaux edition of 1872. Bologna: Arnaldo Forni Editore, 1984.

Brunet, Jean-Charles. *Manuel du libraire et de l'amateur de livres.* Paris: Firmin-Didot, 1860–1865.

Büch, Boudewijn. *Boekenpest.* Amsterdam: Arbeiderspers, 1988.

Bujanda, Jésus Martinez de. *Index de l'Université de Louvain, 1546, 1550, 1558,* Sherbrooke, Quebec: University of Sherbrooke, 1986.

———. *Index de Venise, 1549, Venise et Milan, 1554.* Sherbrooke, Quebec: University of Sherbrooke, 1987.

———. *Thesaurus de la littérature interdite au xvie siècle: auteurs, ouvrages, éditions,* Sherbrooke, Quebec: University of Sherbrooke, 1996.

Burton, John Hill. *The Book-hunter.* Edinburgh: 1898.

Burton, Robert. *The Anatomy of Melancholy.* York: J. Cuthell and Co., 1821.

Bury, Richard de. *The Love of Books or Philobiblon.* Lenox, MA: Hard Press, 2006.

Burzachechi, M. "Ricerche epigrafiche sulle antiche biblioteche del mondo greco: II," *Atti della Accademia Nazionale dei Lincei,"* ser. 8, vol. 17 (1963): 75–96.

Busse, Adolf, ed. *Olympiodori Prolegomena et in Categorias commentarium.* Berlin: Walter de Gruyter, 1900.

Buzás, Ladislaus. *German Library History, 800–1945.* Translated by William D. Boyd. Jefferson, NC: Macfarland & Co., 1986.

Cagnat, Rene, et al. *Inscriptiones Graecae ad res Romanas pertinentes.* Rome: L'Erma, 1964.

Canart, Paul. *Les Vaticani Graeci, 1487–1962: Notes et documents pour l'histoire d'un fonds de manuscrits de la Bibliothèque vaticane.* Citta del Vaticano: Biblioteca apostolica vaticana, 1979.

Canfora, Luciano. *Conservazione e perdita dei classici.* Padova: Antenore, 1974.

———. *The Vanished Library: A Wonder of the Ancient World.* Trans. Martin Ryle. Berkeley: University of California Press, 1990.

———. *Une profession dangereuse. Les penseurs grecs dans la cité.* Paris: Desjonquères, 2001.

———. ed. *Libri e biblioteche.* Palermo, Italy: Sellerio, 2002.

Cantarella, Raffaele. *La letteratura greca dell'Età Ellenistica e Imperiale.* Florence: Sansoni, 1968.

Capaldi, Nicholas. *Censura y libertad de expresión.* Buenos Aires: Ediciones Libera, 1976.

Carreño, Alberto María. "La primera biblioteca pública del continente americano," *Divulgación Histórica* 8, no. 4 (June 15, 1943).

Casamassima, E. "La Nazionale di Firenze Dopo il 4 novembre 1966," *Associazione Italiana per le Biblioteche* 7, no. 2 (1967): 53–66.

Casanova, Paul. *Mohammed et la fin du monde, étude critique sur l'Islam primitif.* Paris: 1911.

———. "L'incendie de la Bibliothèque d'Alexandrie par les Arabes: Communication faite à l'Académie des Inscriptions et Belles-Lettres le mercredi 28 mars 1923," *Revue des bibliothèques* 33 (1923): 253–264.

Castillo Gómez, Antonio, ed. *Historia de la cultura escrita. Del Próximo Oriente Antiguo a la sociedad informatizada.* Gijón, Spain: Ediciones Trea, 2002.

Cavallo, G., and H. Maehler. *Greek Bookhands of the Early Byzantine Period: A.D. 300–800.* London: University of London Institute of Classical Studies, 1987.

Cerny, Jaroslav. *Paper and Books in Ancient Egypt, An Inaugural Lecture Delivered at University College London, 29 May 1947.* London: H. K. Lewis, 1952.

Chalbaud Zerpa, Carlos. *Historia de Mérida.* Merida: Talleres Gráficos, 1983.

Champollion, Jean-François. *Lettres et journaux écrits pendant le voyage d'Égypte.* Paris: Christian Bourgois, 1986.

Chartier, Roger. *The Order of Books: Readers, Authors, and Libraries in Europe Between the 14th and 18th Centuries*. Palo Alto, CA: Stanford University Press, 1994.

Chimalpahin Cuauhtlehuanitzin, Domingo Francisco de San Antón Muñón. *Primera, Segunda, Cuarta, Quinta y Sexta Relaciones de las Différentes Histoires Originales*. Edited by Josefina García Quintana, Silvia Limón, Miguel Pastrana, and Víctor M. Castillo. Mexico City: Instituto de Investigaciones Históricas, UNAM, 2003.

Chroust, A. H. "The Miraculous Dissapearance and Recovery of the Corpus Aristotelicum," *Classica et Mediaevalia* 23 (1963): 50–67.
———. *Aristotle. New Light on His Life and on Some of His Lost Works*, 2 vols. London: Routledge & Kegan Paul, 1973.

Clanchy, M. T. *From Memory to Written Record: England 1066–1307*. London: Arnold, 1979.

Clark, Albert Curtis. *The Descent of Manuscripts*. Oxford: Clarendon Press, 1918.

Clark, Stephen P. H., and David H. Clark. *Newton's Tyranny: The Suppressed Scientific Discoveries of Stephen Gray and John Flamsteed*. New York: W. H. Freeman, 2001.

Clarke, G. W. "Books for the Burning," *Prudentia* 4, no. 2 (1972): 67–82.

Cleator, P. E. *Lost Languages*. Denver, CO: Mentor Books, 1959.

Clowes, William Laird. *Bibliotheca Arcana seu Catalogus Librorum Penetralium*. London: George Redway, 1885.

Coeuré, Sophie. *La mémoire spoliée. Les archives des francais, butin de guerre nazi puis soviétique*. Paris: Payot, 2007.

Collins, Nina L. *The Library in Alexandria and the Bible in Greek*. Leiden, Boston, and Cologne: E. J. Brill, 2000.

Conde Villaverde, María Luisa, and Rosana de Andrés Díaz. "Destrucción de documentos en España: historia, prevención y reconstrucción," *Archivum* 42 (1996): 119–129.

Cotton, P. E. "Fire Tests of Library Bookstacks," *National Fire Protection Association Ouarterly* 84, no. 15 (1960): 288–295.

Craig, Alec. *The Banned Books of England*. Foreword by E. M. Forster. London: Allen & Unwin, 1937.

Cramer, F. H. "Bookburning and Censorship in Ancient Rome," *Journal of the History of Ideas* 6 (1945): 157–196.

Cribiore, Raffaella. *Writing, Teachers, and Students in Graeco-Roman Egypt*. Atlanta: Scholars Press, 1996.

Cunha, George Martin. *Métodos de evaluación para determinar las necesidades de conservación en bibliotecas y archivos: un estudio RAMP con recomendaciones prácticas*. Paris: UNESCO, 1988.

Curless, M. "Fire Protection and Prevention in Libraries," *New York Library Association Bulletin* 2 (1964): 91–93.

Curtius, E. R. *Literatura Europea y Edad Media Latina*. Mexico City: Fondo de Cultura Económica, 1955.

Curwen, Henry. *A History of Booksellers, the Old and the New*. London: Chatto & Windus, 1873.

Cuthbertson, David. *A Tragedy of the Reformation, Being the Authentic Narrative of the History and Burning of the Christianismi Restitutio, 1553*. Edinburgh and London: Oliphant, Anderson & Ferrier, 1912.

Dadson, Trevor J. *Libros, Lectores y Lecturas: Estudios sobre Bibliotecas Expanolas del Siglo de Oro*. Madrid: Arco Libros, 1998.

Dahan, Gilbert. *Le brûlement du Talmud à Paris, 1242–1244*. Paris: Le Cerf, 1999.

Dahl, Sven, *Historia del libro*. Madrid: Alianza, 1999.

Dahm, Volker. *Das Juedische Buch im Dritten Reich* I: *Die Ausschaltung der Juedischen Autoren, Verleger und Buchhaendler*. Frankfurt: Buchhändler-Vereinigung, 1979.

Dainard, J. "From Agamemnon to Alexandria: The Libraries of Classical Antiquity," *Pacific Northwest Library Association Quarterly* 65 (2001): 28–32.

Dalby, A. "Sumerian Catalogs." *Journal of Library History* 21, 3 (1986): 475–487.

Daraul, Arkon. *A History of Secret Societies*. New York: Citadel Press, 1989.

Daywahchi, Said. *Makhtutat al-Maktabah al-Markaziyah fi al-Mawsil*. Baghdad: Matbaat al-Majma al-Ilmi al-Iraqi, 1967.

De Camp, L. Sprague. "Books That Never Were," *Fantasy and Science Fiction* 43, no. 6 (1972): 78–85.

Defourneaux, Marcelin. *L'Inquisition espagnole et les livres français au xviiie siècle*. Paris: Presses Universitaires de France, 1963.

Delia, Diana. "From Romance to Rhetoric: The Alexandrian Library in Classical and Islamic Traditions." *American Historical Review* 97, no. 5: (1992): 1449–1467.

Delon, Michel, ed. *La bibliothèque est en feu*. Nanterre: Centre de Recherches du Département de Français de Paris, 1991.

Dempsey, D. "Operation Booklift: Restoring the Library at the Jewish Theological Seminary of America." *Saturday Review* 50 (1969): 39–41.

Denis, Philippe. *Jean Morély et l'utopie d'une démocratie dans l'Église*. Geneva: Librarie Droz, 1993.

Depons, François. *Viaje a la parte oriental de tierra firme*. Caracas: Tipografía Americana, 1930.

Déroche, F., ed. *Manuel de codiciologie des manuscrits en écriture arabe*. Paris: Bibliothèque Nationale de France, 2000.

Déroche F., A. Gacek, and J. J. Witkamp. eds. *Manuscripts of the Middle East*. Leiden: TerLugt Press, 1990.

Deschner, Karlheinz. *Historia criminal del cristianismo*, vol. 3. Madrid: Martínez Roca, 1992.

De Vleeschauwer, Herman Jean. *Les bibliothèques ptoléméennes d'Alexandrie*. Pretoria: Unisa Press, 1955.

Dewhirst, Andrei, and Robert Farrell, ed. *The Soviet Censorship*. Lanham, MD: Scarecrow Press, 1973.

Dickinson, Donald G. *Dictionary of American Book Collectors*. New York: Greenwood, 1986.

Diels, H. *Die Fragmente der Vorsokratiker*, 6th ed. Rev. by Walther Kranz. Berlin: 1952.

Dietrich, A. "Ibn al-Kifti," in M. T. Houtsma et al., eds., *The Encyclopædia of Islam: A Dictionary of the Geography, Ethnography and Biography of the Muhammadan Peoples,* 4 vols. and Suppl. Leiden and London: E. J. Brill / Luzac, 1913–1938.

Diez Macho, Alejandro. *Apócrifos del antiguo testamento*, vol. 2. Madrid: Cristiandad, 1983.

Diller, Aubrey. *The Textual Tradition of Strabo's Geography*. Amsterdam: Hakkert, 1975.

Dilts, M. R. *Claudii Aeliani Varia historia*. Leipzig: Teubner, 1974.

Diodorus Siculus, *Library of History*, 12 vols. Translated by C. H. Oldfather. Cambridge: Harvard University Press, 1933.

Dion Cassius. *Histoire romaine*. Paris: Les Belles Lettres, 1992–2002.

Dioscorides. *De materia medica*. Translated by Manuela García Valdes. Madrid: Gredos, 1998.

Diringer, D. *The Illuminated Book: Its History and Production*. London: Faber & Faber, 1955.

————. *The Book Before Printing. Ancient, Medieval and Oriental.* New York: Dover, 1982.

Ditchfield, Peter H. *Books Fatal to Their Authors.* London: Eliot Stock, 1903.

Dittenberger, W. *Sylloge inscriptionum Graecarum,* vols. 1–4. Leipzig: 1915–1924.

Dix, T. Keith. "Books and Bookmaking," in Bruce M. Metzger and Michael D. Coogan, eds., *The Oxford Companion to the Bible,* 1993, pp. 93–95.

————. "Public Libraries at Rome: Ideology and Reality," *Libraries and Culture* 29, no. 3 (1994): 282–296.

————. "Libraries in Roman Baths?" With George Houston. *Balnearia* 4, no. 1 (1996): 2–4.

————. "Pliny's Library at Comum," *Libraries and Culture* 31 (1996).

————. "Ovid Strikes Out: Tristia 3.1 and the First Public Libraries at Rome," *Augustan Age* 7 (1996): 27–35.

————. "The Library of Lucullus," *Athenaeum* 88 (2000): 441–46.

Doblhofer, E. *Rutilius Claudius Namatianus. De reditu suo sive Iter Gallicum,* 2 vols. Heidelberg: Carl Winter Universitätsverlag, 1972.

Dombrovskii, Kirill. "Vsya pamyat' mira," *Bibliotekar* Year XII, vol. 2 (1982): 60–63.

Donini, P. L. *Tre studi sull'aristotelismo nel II secolo d.C.* Turin: Paravia, 1974.

Dosa, Marta L. *Libraries in the Political Scene.* Westport, CT: Greenwood Press, 1974.

Doucet, R. *Les bibliothèques parisiennes au xvi siècle.* Paris: Editions A. et J. Picard et Cie, 1956.

Drège, Jean-Pierre. *Les bibliothèques en Chine au temps des manuscrits jusqu'au xe siècle.* Paris: École Française d'Extrême-Orient, 1991.

Drogin, Marc. *Biblioclasm: The Mythical Origin, Magical Power and Perishability of the Written Word.* Lanham, MD: Rowman & Littlefield, 1989.

Drossaart Lulofs, Hendrik Joan. "Neleus of Scepsis and the Fate of the Library of the Peripatos," *Tradition et traduction. Les textes philosophiques et scientifiques grecs au moyen age latin. Hommage à Fernand Bossier.* Ancient and Medieval Philosophy, ser. 1, vol. 25, 1999.

Drujon, Fernand. *Catalogue des ouvrages, écrits et dessins de toute nature poursuivis, supprimés ou condamnés depuis le 21 octobre 1814 jusqu'au 31 juillet 1877.* Paris: Libraire Ancienne et Moderne, 1879.

———. *Essai bibliographique sur la destruction volontaire des livres ou bibliolytie.* Paris: Quantin, 1889.

———. *Destructarum editionum centuria.* Paris: Academie de beaux livres, 1893.

Du Camp, Maxime. *Souvenirs littéraires.* Paris: Libraire Hachette, 1882.

Dudbridge, Glen. *Lost Books of Medieval China.* London: British Library, Panizzi Lectures, 2000.

Dunton, John. *The Life and Errors of John Dunton, Citizen of London.* London: J. Nichols & Son Bentley, 1818.

Durán, Diego. *Historia de las Indias de Nueva España e islas de Tierra Firme,* vol. 1. Mexico City: Porrúa, 1967.

———. *Tratado Segundo: Libro de los ritos y ceremonias en las fiestas de los dioses y celebración de ellas.* Mexico City: Porrúa, 1995.

Düring, Ingemar. *Aristotle in the Ancient Biographical Tradition.* London: Taylor & Francis, 1987.

Ebling, F. J. *Historia natural de la agresión.* Mexico City: Siglo XXI, 1966.

Eche, Youssef. *Les Bibliothèques arabes publiques et semi-publiques en Mésopotamie, en Syrie et en Égypte au Moyen Âge.* Damascus: Institut Français de Damas, 1967.

Eco, Umberto. "Desear, poseer y enloquecer," *El Malpensante* 31 (June 16–July 31, 2001): 55–58.

Eisenberg, Daniel. "Cisneros y la quema de los manuscritos granadinos," *Journal of Hispanic Philology* 16 (1992): 107–124.

Eliade, Mircea. *El mito del eterno retorno.* Buenos Aires: Emecé, 1968.

———. *Mito y realidad.* Barcelona: Labor, 1983.

Elschenbroich, Erika. *Wissenschaft und Kunst im Exil: Vorgeschichte, Durchführung und Folgen der Bücherverbrennung: eine Dokumentation.* Osnabrück: Wurf, 1984.

Elzevier, Les. *Histoire et annales typographiques.* Brussels: 1880.

Ermolaev, Herman. *Censorship in Soviet Literature, 1917–1991.* Totowa, NJ: Rowman & Littlefield, 1996.

Ernesti, Johann. *Ueber das Recht, besonders das der Hierarchie auf Censur und Bücherverbote und über die sich anmaßende Abgaben-Befreiung der katholischen Geistlichkeit in weltlichen Dingen.* 1829.

Escolar Sobrino, Hipólito. *La cultura durante la guerra civil.* Madrid: Alhambra, 1987.

———. *Historia universal del libro.* Madrid: Gredos, 1993.

———. *La biblioteca de Alejandría.* Madrid: Gredos, 2001.

Eusebius. *Chronici canones latine vertit . . . Hieronymus.* London: I. K. Fotheringham, 1923.

———. *The Church History.* Translated and commentary by Paul Maier. Nashville, TN: Kregel Academic & Professional, 2007.

Eustratius. *In ethica nicomachea i commentaria,* in G. Heylbut, ed., *Eustratii et Michaelis et Anonyma in Ethica Nicomachea Commentaria.* Berlin: Reimer, 1892.

Farrer, James Anson. *Books Condemned to Be Burnt.* London: Elliot Stock, 1904.

Febvre, Lucien, and Henri-Jean Martin. *The Coming of the Book: The Impact of Printing 1450–1800.* Los Angeles: Verso, 1997.

Fehrle, R. *Das Bibliothekswesen im alten Rom: Voraussetzungen, Bedingungen, Anfänge.* Wiesbaden: Ludwig Reichert-Verl, 1986.

Feijoo, Benito Jerónimo. *Teatro crítico universal o Discursos varios en todo género de materias, para desengaño de errores comunes.* Edited, with introduction and notes, by Giovanni Stiffoni. Madrid: Castalia, 1986.

Fernandez, Stella Marie. *Muerte y resurrección del libro.* Buenos Aires: Universidad de Buenos Aires, 1977.

Fernandez Areal, Manuel. *El control de la prensa en España.* Madrid: Guardania, 1973.

Fernández de Retana, Luis. *Cisneros y su siglo: Estudio histórico de la vida y actuación pública del Cardenal.* Madrid: El Perpetuo Socorro e Imprenta Clásica, 1929.

Fernández Soria, Juan Manuel. *Educación y cultura en la Guerra Civil (1936–1939).* Barcelona: NAU Libres, 1984.

Ferrer, Joaquim, Josep M. Figueres, and Josep M. Sans Travé. *Els papers de Salmanca. Història d'un boti de guerra.* Barcelona: Libres de l'Índex, 1996.

Ferris, José Luis. *Miguel Hernández: Pasiones, cárcel y muerte de un poeta.* Madrid: Temas de Hoy, 2002.

Ferruti, Francesco. "Su alcuni recenti studi riguardanti la biblioteca attalide di Pergamo," *ArchClass* vol. 51, n.s. 1 (1999–2000): 305–327.

Fessler, Joseph. *Das kirchliche Bücherverbot.* Vienna: Carl Gerold, 1858.

Festa, N. *I frammenti degli stoici antichi*, vol. 1. Bari, Italy: Zenone, 1971.

Fierro Bello, María Isabel. *La heterodoxia en al-Andalus durante el período omeya*. Madrid: Instituto Hispano-Arabe de Cultura, 1988.

Flashar, H. *Die Philosophie der Antike*, vol. 3. Basel, Switzerland: Schwabe & Co., 1983.

Fleming, P. *The Siege at Pekin: The Boxer Rebellion*. New York: Dorset Press, 1959.

Fonvielle, Bernard-François. *Voyage en Espagne*. Paris: 1823.

Forbes, Clarence A. "X.—Books for the Burning," *Transactions of the American Philological Society* 67 (1936): 114–25.

Forster, Edward Morgan. *Alexandria: A History and a Guide*. Oxford: Oxford University Press, 1986.

Fortenbaugh, William W., ed. *Peripatetic Rhetoric After Aristotle*, Piscataway, NJ: Transaction Publishers, 1994.

Fortenbaugh, William, W., and Schütrumpf, Eckart, eds. *Demetrius of Phalerum: Text, Translation, and Discussion*. Piscataway, NJ: Transaction Publishers, 2000.

Fortson-Jones, Judith. "Fire Protection for Libraries," *Catholic Library World* 53, (1981): 211–213.

Fragnito, Gigliola, ed. *Church, Censorship and Culture in Early Modern Italy*, Cambridge: Cambridge University Press, 2001.

Frankfort, H., H. A. Frankfort, J. A. Wilson, and Thorkild Jacobsen. *El pensamiento prefilosófico*. Mexico City: Fondo de Cultura Económica, 1954.

Franklin, Alfred. *Histoire de la Bibliothèque Mazarine et du palais de l'Institut*. Paris: H. Welter, 1901.

Fraser, Peter M. *Ptolemaic Alexandria*, 3 vols. Oxford: Oxford University Press, 1972.

Fraxi, Pisanus. *Bibliography of Prohibited Books*. New York: Jack Brussel, 1962.

Frazer, James George. *Folklore in the Old Testament: Studies in Comparative Religion, Legend and Law*. London: Macmillan, 1918.

Frías León, Martha. *El libro y las bibliotecas coloniales mexicanas*. Mexico City: UNAM, 1977.

Friedrich, Thomas. *Das Vorspiel. Die Bücherverbrennung am 10. Mai 1933: Verlauf, Folgen, Nachwirkungen Eine Dokumentation*. Berlin: LitPol Verlagsgesellschaft, 1983.

Fromm, Erich. *The Anatomy of Human Destructiveness*. New York: Holt, 1992.

Fu'adi, Abd al-Hadi. *Nusus al-madrasiyah al-qursiyat al-shakl*. Baghdad: Republic of Iraq, Ministry of Culture and Arts, State Organization of Antiquities, 1979.

Fujii, Hideo, and Kazumi Oguchi. *Lost Heritage: Antiquities Stolen from Iraq's Regional Museums*, fasc. 3. Tokyo: Institute for Cultural Studies of Ancient Iraq, Kokushikan University, 1996.

Fulton, John Farquhar. *Michael Servetus, Humanist and Martyr. With a Bibliography of His Works and Census of Known Copies by Madeline E. Stanton*. New York: H. Reichner, 1953.

Furlani, Giuseppe. "Sull'incendio della biblioteca di Alessandria," *Aegyptus: Rivista Italiana di Egittologia e di Papirologia* 5 (1924): 205–212.

Gaiser, K. "Plato's Enigmatic Lecture on the Good," *Phronesis* 25 (1980): 69.

Galeano, Eduardo. *Memorias del Fuego,* vol. 1. Buenos Aires: Siglo XXI, 2000.

Gamboni, Dario. *The Destruction of Art*. London: Reaktion Books, 1997.

Gamillscheg, E., and B. Mersich. *Matthias Corvinus und die Bildung der Renaissance*, Wien: Österreichische Nationalbibliothek, 1994.

Garbelli, Filippo. *Le biblioteche in Italia all'epoca romana*, Milan: 1894.

García Icazbalceta, Joaquín. *Bibliografía mexicana del siglo* XVI. Mexico City: Fondo de Cultura Ecónomica, FCE, 1954.

García Martínez, Florentino. *Textos de Qumrán*. Madrid: Trotta, 1992.

Gardiner, Alan H. *The Royal Canon of Turin*. Oxford: Griffith Institute. 1997.

Garin, E. *Giovanni Pico della Mirandola. Vita e dottrina*. Florence: 1937.

Gassendi, Pierre. *Viri Illustris Nicolai Claudii Frabricii de Peiresc, Senatoris Aquisextiensis vita*. Paris: 1641.

Gassert, Philipp, and Daniel S. Mattern. *The Hitler Library: A Bibliography*. Westport, CT: Greenwood Press, 2001.

Gavrilov, A. K. "Reading Techniques in Classical Antiquity," CQ 47 (1997): 56–73.

Gay, Jules. *Bibliographie des ouvrages relatifs á l'amour, aux femmes, au marriage et des livres facétieux pantagruéliques, scatologiques, satyriques, etc*. Paris: J. Lemonnyer, 1894/1900.

Geanakoplos, D. J. *Greek Scholars in Venice.* Cambridge: University of Cambridge Press, 1962.

Gellrich, J. M. *The Idea of the Book in the Middle Ages.* Ithaca: Cornell University Press, 1985.

Gertz, Elmer. *Censored Books and Their Right to Live.* Lawrence: University of Kansas Libraries, 1965.

Giannini, A. *Paradoxographorum Graecorum Reliquiae.* Milan: Istituto Editoriale Italiano, 1965.

Gibson, Ian. *Erotomaniac: The Secret Life of Henry Spencer Ashbee.* New York: Da Capo, 2001.

Gil Fernández, Luis. *Panorama social del humanismo español (1500–1800)*, 2d ed. Madrid: Editorial Tecnos, 1997.

Giles, Lancelot. *The Siege of the Peking Legations: A Diary.* Nedlands, Australia: University of Western Australia Press, 1970.

Gillett, Charles Ripley. *Burned Books: Neglected Chapters in British History and Literature*, 2 vols. New York: Kennikat Press, 1974.

Gilliard, Frank D. "More on Silent Reading in Antiquity: *Non Omne Verbum Sonabat*," *Journal of Biblical Literature* 112 (1993): 689–696.

Gimeno Blay, Francisco M. "Quemar libros . . . ¡qué extraño placer!," *Eutopías. 2a Época: Documentos de Trabajo,* no. 104. Valencia: Episteme, 1995.

Gleig, George R. *Narrative of the Campaigns of the British Army at Washington.* London: John Murray, 1821.

Gneuss, Helmut. *Books and Libraries in Early England.* Aldershot, UK: Ashgate Publishing Ltd., 1996.

Gómez de Castro, Álvar. *De las hazañas de Francisco Jiménez de Cisneros.* Translated by José Oroz Reta. Madrid: Fundación Universitaria Española, 1984.

Goody, J. *La lógica de la escritura y la organización de la sociedad.* Madrid: Alianza, 1990.

Gordon Childe, V. *Man Makes Himself.* London: Rationalist Press Association, 1936.

Graf, A., and Kuebler, H. D. *Verbrannte Buecher Verbrannte Ideen.* Hamburg: O. Heinevetter, 1993.

Grätz, Heinrich. *Geschichte der Juden von del ältesten Zenten bis auf die Gegenwart*, XI vols. Lepizig: Leiner, 1863–76.

Greenlea, F., and E. Richard. *La inquisición en Nueva España S. XVI.* Mexico City: Fondo de Cultura Ecónomico, 1981.

Grendler, Paul F. "The Destruction of Hebrew Books in Venice, 1568," *Proceedings of the American Academy for Jewish Research* 45 (1978): 103–130.

Gretser, Jacob. *De jure et more prohibendi expurgandi et abolendi libros hæreticos et noxios.* Ingolstadt: 1653.

Gronovius, Johannes Frederici. *De Museo Alexandrino: Exercitationes Academicae . . . post Caniculares Ferias, ab Filio Ejus Exceptae, et Nunc Primim Editae.* Lugduni Batavorum: P. Vander, 1699.

Guy, Kent. *The Emperor's Four Treasuries: Scholars and the State in the Late Qianlong Period.* Cambridge: University of Cambridge Press, 1987.

Haarmann, Harald. *Historia universal de la escritura.* Madrid: Gredos, 2001.

Haarmann, Herman, et al. "Das War ein Vorspiel Nur—," in *Bücherverbrennung Deutschland 1933: Voraussetzungen und Folgen,* Ausstellung der Akademie der Kunste, May 8–July 3, 1983. Berlin: Medusa, 1983.

Hadas, M. *Aristeas to Philocrates.* New York: Harper and Brothers, for the Dropsie College for Hebrew and Cognate Learning, 1951.

Haddad, Butrus. *Makhtutat al-Suryaniyah wa-al-Arabiyah fi Khizanat al-Rahbaniyah al-Kaldaniyah fi Baghdad.* Baghdad: al-Majma al-Ilmi al-Iraqi, 1988.

Haddad, Gérard. *Les biblioclastes.* Paris: Grasset, 1990.

———. *Manger le livre: Rites alimentaires et fonction paternelle.* New York: Hachette, 2005.

Haddaw, Hamid Majid. *Makhtutat Maktabat al-Alamat al-Hijjat al-Sayid Abbas al-Husayni al-Kathani fi Karbala.* Karbala Matbaat Ahl al-Bayt, 1966.

Haight, Anne Lyon. *Banned Books, 387 b.c. to 1978 a.d.* New York: R. R. Bowker, 1978.

Halivni, David. *The Book and the Sword: A Life Of Learning in the Shadow of Destruction.* New York: Farrar, Straus & Giroux, 1996.

Hamel, Christopher de. *A History of Illuminated Manuscripts.* London: Phaidon Press, 1986.

Hamilton, Robert M. "The Library of Parliament Fire," *Bulletin of the Canadian Library Association* 9 (1952): 73–77.

Hamlin, Arthur T. "The Libraries of Florence, November 1966," ALA *Bulletin* (1967): 141–150.

———. "The Library Crisis in Italy," *Library Journal* (1967): 2519.

318   *A Universal History of the Destruction of Books*

Handover, Phyllis Margaret. *Printing in London from 1476 to Modern Times*. London: Allen & Unwin, 1960.

Hansen, E. V. *The Attalids of Pergamon*. Ithaca: Cornell University Press, 1971.

Harper, Henry Howard. *Library Essays about Books, Bibliophiles, Writers and Kindred Subjects*. Boston: Privately Printed, 1924.

Hart, William Henry. *Index Expurgatorius Anglicanus: Or, A descriptive catalogue of the principal books printed or published in England, which have been suppressed, or burnt by the common hangman, or censured, or for which the authors, printers, or publishers have been prosecuted*. London: John Russell Smith, 1872.

Havelock, E. *The Muse Learns to Write. Reflections on Orality and Literacy from Antiquity to the Present*. New Haven and London: Yale University Press, 1986.

Heartman, Charles F., and James R. Canny, *A Bibliography of First Printings of the Writings of Edgar Allan Poe*. Hattiesburg, Miss.: Book Farm, 1943.

Heisterbach, Caesarius. *Dialogus Miraculorum*. Cologne: H. Lempertz, 1851.

Heller, Agnes. *Instinto, agresividad y carácter*. Barcelona: Ediciones Península, 1980.

Heller-Roazen, Daniel. "Tradition's Destruction: On the Library of Alexandria," *October* 100 (Spring 2002): 133–153.

Hendrickson, G. L. "Ancient Reading," *Classical Journal* 25 (1929): 192–196.

Hermeias. *Kommentar zu Plantons "Phaidros."* Tuebingen, Germany: Mohr Siebeck, 1997.

Herrman, Wolfgang. "Prinzipelles zur Säuberung der öffentlichen Bücherein," *Börsenblatt für den deutschen Büchhandel* 100 (May 16, 1933): 356–358.

Herrmann-Mascard, Nicole. *La censure des livres à Paris à la fin de l'Ancien Régime: 1750–1789*. Paris: Presses Universitaires de France, 1968.

Higman, Francis. *Censorship and the Sorbonne: A Bibliographical Study of Books in French Censured by the Faculty of Theology of the University of Paris, 1520–1551*. Geneva: Droz, 1979.

Hochhuth, Rolf. "Verbrannte Bucher: Verbrannte Menschen. Uberlegungen zur Bucherverbrennung," *Die Zeit* 20 (May 20, 1943): 15.

Hoepfner, Wolfram. *Zu griechischen Bibliotheken und Bücherschränken*. Berlin: de Gruyter, 1996.

Hoeven, Hans van der, and Joan van Albada. *Memory of the World. Memory Lost: Libraries and Archives Destroyed in the Twentieth Century.* Paris: UNESCO, 1996.

Hollweck, Joseph. *Das kirchl. Bücherverbot. Ein Commentar zur Constitution L.sXIII. Officiorum ac munerum.* Mainz: 1897.

Hong, William, ed. *Yiwenzhi ershizhong zonghe yinde. Combined Indices to Twenty Historical Bibliographies,* Index Series no. 10. Beijing: Harvard Yenching Institute, 1933.

Horsfall, Nicholas. "Empty Shelves on the Palatine," *Greece and Rome* 40, no. 1 (1993): 58–67.

Horton, Carolyn. "Saving the Libraries of Florence," *Wilson Library Bulletin* 41, no. 10 (1967): 1034–1043.

Houston, George W. "A Revisionary Note on Ammianus Marcellinus 14.6.18: When Did the Public Libraries of Ancient Rome Close?" *Library Quarterly* 58, no. 3 (1988): 258–264.

Howes, Wright. *U.S.-Iana (1700–1950): A Descriptive Check-List of 11,450 Printed Sources Relating to Those Parts of Continental North America Now Comprising the United States.* New York: R. R. Bowker, 1954.

Huby, P. M. "The Transmission of Aristotle's Writings and the Places Where Copies of His Works Existed," *Classica and Medievalia* 30 (1969): 241–247.

Hunter, R. L. *Eubulus: The Fragments.* Cambridge: Cambridge University Press, 1983.

Hurley, Timothy. *A Commentary on the Present Index Legislation.* Dublin: Browne and Nolan, 1907.

Ibrahim, Zahidah. *Fihrist al-makhtutat al-Arabiyah al-musawwarah fi al-Iraq wa-al-majdudah fi al-Maktabah al-Markaziyah li-Jamiat Baghdad.* Jamiat Baghdad, 1970.

Invernizzi, Hernán. *Los libros son tuyos.* Buenos Aires: Eudeba, 2005.

Invernizzi, Hernán, and Judith Gociol, *Un golpe a los libros.* Buenos Aires: Eudeba, 2003.

Isidore de Seville. *Etimologías,* 2 vols., Latin text, Spanish translation and notes by José Oroz Reta and Manuel Marca Casquero; introduction by Manuel C. Díaz y Díaz. Madrid: Ediciones Católica, 1982–1983.

Jacks, Leonard. *The Great Houses of Nottinghamshire and the County Families.* Nottingham: 1881.

Jackson, H. "Aristotle's Lecture Room and Lectures," *Journal of Philology* 35 (1920): 191–200.

Jackson, Holbrook. *The Fear of Books.* New York: Soncino Press, 1932.

Jacoby, F. *Die Fragmente der griechischen Historiker*, 16 vols. Berlin: 1923–1958.

James, M. R. *The Wandering and Homes of Manuscripts.* New York: Macmillan, 1919.

Jammes, André. "De la destruction des livres," in *Le livre et l'historien: études offertes en l'honneur du professeur Henri-Jean Martin.* Geneva: Droz, 1997, pp. 813–817.

Jammes, Paul. *Le bucher bibliographique. Collection de livres condamnés, poursuivis et détruits.* Paris: Librarie Paul Jammes, 1968.

Jianzhong, W. "The Destruction of Books and Libraries in Shanghai During World War II," *Journal of Information, Communication, and Library Science* 2 (1996): 9–14.

Jiménez Gómez, Santiago. *Guía para el estudio de la Edad Media Gallega (1100–1480).* Santiago: Servicio de publicaciones de la Universidad de Santiago de Compostela, 1973.

Johnson, David Ronald. "The Library of Celsus, An Ephesian Phoenix," *Library Bulletin* (1980): 651–653.

Johnson, I. M. "The Impact on Libraries and Archives in Iraq of War and Looting in 2003: A Preliminary Assessment of the Damage and Subsequent Reconstruction Efforts," *International Information and Library Review* 37 (2005): 209–271.

Jones, Derek, ed. *Censorship: A World Encyclopedia.* London: Fitzroy Dearborn, 2001.

Jones, Horace L., ed. and trans. *The Geography of Strabo*, 8 vols. Cambridge: Harvard University Press, 1917–1932.

Joveini, Ata-ol Molk. *Tariq-e Jahangosha, Nashr-e Ketab.* Teheran: 1367.

Juburi, Abd Allah. *Fihris al-makhtutat al-Arabiyah fi Maktabat al-Awqaf al-Ammah fi Baghdad, al-Jumhuriyah al-Iraqiya.* Riasat Diwan al-Awqaf, 1973.

Juburi, Abd Allah, and Hasan al-Ankurii. *Fihris makhtutat Hasan al-Ankurli al-muhdah ila Maktabat al-Awqaf.* Riasat Diwan al-Awqaf, 1967.

Jünger, Ernst. *Diario de guerra y ocupación.* Barcelona: Plaza y Janes Editores, 1972.

Justice, Steven. *Writing and Rebellion: England in 1381.* Berkeley: University of California Press, 1994.

Kantorowicz, Alfred. "Why a Library of the Burned Books," *Library Journal*, 59 (June 1, 1934): 470.

———. "The Burning of the Books," *Free World* 5, no. 5 (May, 1943).

Kebric, R. B. "In the Shadow of Macedon: Duris of Samos," *Historia Einzelschrift 29*, Wiesbaden: 1977.

Keeney, Philip O. "Japanese Libraries Are War-Damaged," *Library Journal 73*, no. 9 (May 1, 1948): 681–684, 698.

Kelly, Stuart. *The Book of Lost Books*. New York: Viking, 2006.

Knesebeck, Harald Wolter von dem. *Zur Ausstattung und Funktion des Hauptsaales der Bibliothek von Pergamon*. London: Boreas, 1995.

Khaqani, Ali. *Makhtutat al-Maktabah al-Abbasiyah fi al-Basrah*. Baghdad: 1962.

Kibre, Pearl. *The Library of Pico della Mirandola*. New York: Columbia University Press, 1936.

Kindstrand, J. F. *Bion of Boristhenes: A Collection of Fragments*. Uppsala: 1976.

Klippel, Georg H. *Ueber das Alexandrinische Museum*. Göttingen: Vandenhoeck & Ruprecht, 1838.

Knuth, Rebecca. *Libricide: The Regime-Sponsored Destruction of Books and Libraries in the Twentieth Century*. Westport, CT: Praeger, 2003.

Koeman, Cornelis. *Joan Blaeu and His Grand Atlas: Introduction to the Facsimile Edition of Le Grand Atlas, 1663*. Amsterdam: Theatrum Orbis Terrarum, 1970.

Kornicki, P. *The Book in Japan. A Cultural History from the Beginnings to the Nineteenth Century*. Leiden: Brill, 1998.

Koster, W. J. W. *Scholia in Aristophanem*, pars I. fasc. I A, *Prolegomena de comoedia*, Groningen, the Netherlands: 1975.

Krehl, C. L. E. *Ueber die Sage von der Verbrennung der alexandrinischen Bibliothek durch die Araber*. Florence: 1880.

Kroller, F., and Reinitzer, S. "Schaden an Kroatischen Bibliotheken durch die Kampfhandlungen 1991–1992." *Mitteilungen der Vereinigung Oesterreichischer Bibliothekare 45*, no. 3–4 (1992): 74–78.

Krug, Antje, ed. *Archive in Heiligtümern. From Epidaurus to Salerno*. Rixensart, Belgium: Pact Belgium, 1992.

Krummsdorf, Juliane, and Ingrid Werner. *Verbrannt, Verboten, Verbannt, Vergessen? Zur Erinnerung an die Bücherverbrennung, 1933*. Dresden: Bibliothek beim Landesvorstand der PDS, 1993.

322   *A Universal History of the Destruction of Books*

Kuster, Ludolf. *Ludolphi Neocori de museo alexandrino diatribe, nunc primum edita*. Lugduni Batavorum: P. Vander, 1699.

Labowsky, L. *Bessarion's Library and the Biblioteca Marciana. Six Early Inventories*. Rome: Edizioni di Storia e Letteratura, 1979.

Laks, André, and Glenn W. Most. *Studies on the Derveni Papyrus*. Oxford: Oxford University Press, 1997.

Lapidge, Michael. *The Anglo-Saxon Library*. New York: Oxford University Press, 2006.

Lara Peinado, Federico. *Himnos sumerios*. A Coruña: Tecnos, 1988.

———. *Poema de Gilgamesh*. A Coruña: Tecnos, 1997.

Lazinger, Susan S. "The Alexandrian Library and the Beginnings of Chemistry," *Library History Review*, vol. 2 no. 3 (1984): 36–47

Lemerle, P. *Le premier humanisme byzantin. Notes et remarques sur enseignement et culture à Byzance des origines au Xe siècle*. Paris: Presses Universitaires de France, 1971.

Lemmons, Russel. *Goebbels and Der Angriff*. Lexington, KY: University Press of Kentucky, 1994.

Lengyel, Alfonz. "The Library of the Humanist King Mathias Corvinus of Hungary," *Fifteenth Century Studies* 1 (1978).

Leo, Friedrich. *Die griechisch-römische Biographie nach irer litterarischen Form*. Hildesheim: G. Olms, 1965.

Lewis, N. *Papyrus in Classical Antiquity*. Oxford: Clarendon Press, 1974.

Li, Meng-jinn. "Book Disasters in Chinese History," *Journal of the Hong Kong Library Association* 5 (1980): 77–87.

Liao, W. K. *The Complete Works of Han Fei Tsu, a Classic of Chinese Legalism*. London: Probsthain, 1939.

Liu Guo, Jun, and Zheng Yicheng. *The Story of Chinese Books*. Beijing: Foreign Languages Press, 1985.

Lloyd Jones, H. "Lost History of the Lost Library," *New York Review of Books*, June 14, 1990, pp. 27 ff.

López-Baralt, Luce. *Huellas del Islam en la literatura española. De Juan Ruiz a Juan Goytisolo*. Madrid: Hiperión, 1985.

Lord, L. E. "The Early History of the Aristotelian Corpus," *American Journal of Philology* 107 (1986): 137–161.

Lorkovic, Tatjana. "National Library in Sarajevo Destroyed; Collections, Archives Go Up in Flames," *American Libraries* 23, no. 9 (1992): 736, 816.

———. "Destruction of Libraries in Croatia and Bosnia-Herzegovina," *International Leads* 7, no. 2 (1993): 1–2.

————. "Wounded Libraries in Croatia." *Libraries and Culture* 30 (1995): 205–206.

Ludwich, Arthur. *Aristarchs homerische Textkritik nach den Fragmenten des Didymos*. Leipzig: Teubner, 1884–1885.

Lünzner, E. *Epaphroditi grammatici quae supersunt*. Bonn: Dissertatio, 1866.

Lydus, Johannes. *De Mensibus.*, Edited by R. Wuensch. Leipzig: Teubner, 1898.

Lyon, Haight. *Banned Books*. New York: Bowker, 1955.

Mackensen, Ruth S. "Moslem Libraries and Sectarian Propaganda," *American Journal of Semitic Languages and Literatures* 51 (1934–35): 83–113.

Maillard, Firmin. *Les Passionnés du livre*. Paris: Emile Rondeau, 1986.

Mair, A. W. *Callimachus and Lycophron*. Cambridge: Harvard University Press, 1921.

Maiuri, Amedeo. *Nuova silloge epigrafica di Rodi e Cos*. Florence: Felice Le Monnier, 1925.

————. *Herculaneum and the Villa of the Papyri*. Rome: Instituto Geografico de Agostini, 1977.

Maktabat al-Imam al-Hakim al-Ammah fi al-Najaf. *Min nawadir makhtutat Maktabat Ayat Allah al-Hakim al-Ammah*. al-Najaf: Matbaat al-Najaf, 1962.

Manfrini de Brewer, Mireya, and Claudio A. Sosa. "Insectos en bibliotecas y archivos. Principales especies de insectos perjudiciales para las colecciones de bibliotecas y archivos," *Ciencia Hoy* 35 (1996): 39–45.

Manganaro, G. "Una biblioteca storica nel Ginnasio di Tauromenion e il P. Oxy. 1241," *PP* 29 (1974): 389–409.

Manganaro, Jean-Paul. *La véritable histoire de la bibliothèque d'Alexandrie*. Paris: Desjonquères, 1986.

Manguel, Alberto. *A History of Reading*. New York: Penguin, 1997.

————. "Las bibliotecas y sus cenizas," *Letra Internacional* 63 (1999): 18–20.

————. *La biblioteca de noche*. Madrid, Alianza, 2007.

Mansur, Mehmet. *Meshur Iskenderiye kutuphanesine dair risaledir / muellifi Mehmet Mansur*. Istanbul: Ceride-yi Askeriye Matbaası, 1300.

Maracchi Biagiarelli, R. "Si Studia a Firenze Dopo l'Alluvione?" *Bibliofilia* 69, no. 1 (1967): 103–111.

Marcellin, Ammien. *Histoire de Rome*, 3 vols. Clermont-Ferrand: Paléo, 2002.

Marshack, A. *The Roots of Civilization: The Cognitive Beginnings of Man's First Art, Symbol and Notation.* New York: Moyer Bell Ltd, 1992.

Martin, James J. *An American Adventure in Bookburning: In the Style of 1918.* Colorado Springs, CO: Ralph Myles, 1989.

————. "Other Days, Other Ways: American Book Censorship, 1918–1945," *Journal of Historical Review* 10, no. 2 (1990): 133–141.

Mathaf al-'Iraqi, Mudiriyat al-Athar al-'Ammah. *Guidebook to the Iraq Museum.* Baghdad: Directorate General of Antiquites, 1966.

Matthai, Robert A. *Protection of Cultural Properties during Energy Emergencies.* New York: Arts/Energy Studio and American Association of Museums, 1978.

Medina, José Toribio. *Historia del tribunal del santo oficio de la inquisición en México.* Mexico City: Fuente Cultural, 1952.

Meijer, A. C., and R. M. Rijkse. "Het Vacoumvriesdrogen van Grote Hoeveelheden Natte Boeken in Zeeland," *Open* 17, no. 3 (1985): 121–127.

Mendham, Joseph. *The Literary Policy of the Church of Rome exhibited in an Account of Her Damnatory Catalogues or Indices.* London: J. Duncan, 1826.

Merlini, Marco. *La scrittura e' nata in Europa?* Rome: Avverbi Edizioni, 2004.

Merton, Reginald. *Cardinal Ximenes and the Making of Spain.* London: Trubner, 1934.

Metacalf, C. L., and W. P. Flint. *Insectos destructivos e insectos útiles: sus costumbres y su control.* Madrid: Continental, 1965.

Mielsch, Harald. "Die Bibliothek und die Kunstsammlung der Könige von Pergamon," *American Archivist* 4 (1995): 765–779.

Mier, Servando Teresa de. *Apología* o *Memorias*, 2 vols., in *Colección de Escritores Mexicanos # 37.* Mexico City: Porrúa, 1942.

Migne, Jacques Paul. *Patrologie.* Paris: 1689.

Milkau, Fritz. *Handbuch der Bibliothekswissenschaft.* Leipzig: Harrassowitz, 1952–1965.

Millares Carlo, Agustín. *Introducción a la historia del libro y de las bibliotecas,* 3d. ed. Mexico City: Fondo de Cultura Económica, 1986.

Ministère de la Justice War Crimes Commission (Belgium). *War Crimes Committed During the Invasion of the National Territory, May, 1940: The Destruction of the Library of the University of Louvain.* Liège: 1946.

Ministero della Pubblica Istruzione. *La ricostruzione delle biblioteche italiane dopo la guerra, 1940–1945,* 2 vols. Rome: Palombi, 1951, 1953.

Momigliano, Arnaldo. *Les origines de la biographie en Grèce ancienne.* Barcelona: Circé, 1998.

Montanari, Franco. *Pergamo. Lo spazio letterario della Grecia antica: 1, La produzione e la circolazione del texto: 2. L'ellenismo.* Rome: Salerno, 1993.

Moraux, Paul. *Der Aristotelismus bei den Griechen,* vol. 1. Berlin: Walter de Gruyter, 1973.

———. *Les listes anciennes des ouvrages d'Aristote.* Louvain: Éditions universitaires de Louvain, 1951.

Moreau, Édouard de. *La bibliothèque de l'Université de Louvain, 1636–1914.* Louvain: Éditions universitaires de Louvain, 1918.

Moreau, Michael. "Putting It Back Together: Los Angeles Central Library," *Wilson Library Bulletin* 61, no. 7 (1987): 35–39.

Moreri, Luis. *Gran diccionario histórico o miscelánea de curiosidades de la historia sagrada y profana,* vol. 1. Paris: León de Francia, 1753.

Moritz Schwarcz, Lilia. *A longa viagem da Biblioteca dos Reis. Do terremoto de Lisboa à Independência do Brasil.* São Paulo: Companhia das Letras, 2002.

Mudiriyat al-Athar al-'Ammah and Mathaf al-Mawsil, *Guidebook to the Mosul Museum.* Baghdad: Government Press, 1966.

Muhamad, Mahmud Ahmad. *Fihrist makhtutat Maktabat al-Awqaf al-Markaziyah fi al-Sulaymaniyah.* Al-Jumhuriyah al-Iraqiyah, Wizarat al-Awqaf wa-al-Shuun, al-Diniyah, 1982.

Müller, Carl. *Oratores Attici . . . et fragmenta oratorum Atticorum,* vol. 2. Paris: Didot, 1858.

Najaf, Mohammed Mehdi. *Fihrist makhtutat Maktabat al-Imam al-Hakim.* Najaf: Maktabat al-Imam al-Hakim al-Ammah fi al-Najaf, 1969.

———. *Catalogue Manuscripts, Al-Emam Al-Hakim Public Library.* Najaf: Maktabat al-Imam al-Hakim al-Ammah fi al-Najaf, 1979.

Naqshabandi, Usamah Nasir. *Al-'Iraq, Al-makhtutat al-Islamiyah fi al-'alam, al-juz' al-thalith.* Translated by Geoffrey Roper. London: Mu'assasat, 2001.

Naqshabandi, Usamah Nasir, and Amir Ahmad Qishtayni. *Makhtutat al-fiqhiyah*. Baghdad: al-Jumhuriyah al-Iraqiya, Wizarat al-Ilam, Mudiriyat al-Athar al-Ammah, 1976.

Nelson, Dale. "A Holocaust at LC?" *Wilson Library Bulletin* (1982): 356–357.

Nichols, Charles L. *The Library of Rameses the Great*. Berkeley: University of California Press, 1964.

Nichols, John. *Biographical and Literary Anecdotes of William Bowyer*. London: Printed by author, 1782.

———. *Literary Anecdotes of the Eighteenth Century*, 9 vols. London: Nichols, Son, and Bentley, 1812–1816.

Noblecourt, A. *Les techniques de protection de biens culturels en cas de conflit armé*. Paris: UNESCO, 1958.

Nuño, Juan. "Libros en la hoguera." Included in *La escuela de la sospecha*. Caracas: Monte Avila, 1990.

Nuovo, Angela. "Il corano arabo ritrovato (Venezia, Paganino, e Alessandro Paganini, tra l'agosto 1537 e l'agosto 1538)," *La Bibliofilia* vol III (1987): 237–271.

Nwafor, B. U. "Recorded Knowledge: A War Casualty—An Account of Library Devastation During the Nigerian Civil War," *Library Journal* 96, no. 1 (1971): 42–45.

O'Gorman, Edmundo. "Bibliotecas y librerías coloniales, 1585–1694," *Boletín del Archivo General de la Nación* 10, no. 4 (1939): 661–1006.

Olschki, Leo S., and Giuseppe Fumagalli. *Biblioteche immaginarie e roghi di libri*. Campobasso: Palladino, 2007.

Oluwakuyide, Akinola. "Nigerian Libraries After the War," *Wilson Library Bulletin* 46, no. 10 (1972): 881–882, 947.

Ortlob, J. *De ephesinorum libris curiosis combustis*. Leipzig: 1708.

Ossa, Felipe. *Historia de la escritura y la letra impresa*. Bogotá: Planeta, 1993.

Otsuka, Kinnosuke. *Index Librorum Prohibitorum in Pre-War Japan: List of Books and Periodicals in Prof. Otsuka's Collection Burned Secretly by Himself in 1940–1941 Under the Pressure of the Toko (Special Higher Police) and the Kempei (Military Police)*. Tokyo: Musashino, 1959.

Ouaknin, Marc-Alain. *Le livre brûlé: Philosophie du Talmud*. Paris: Le Seuil, 1993.

Page, Denis L. *Sappho and Alceus*. Oxford: Clarendon Press, 1955.

———. *Poetae melici Graeci*. Oxford: Clarendon Press, 1962.

Palau i Dulcet, Antonio. *Manual del librero hispanoamericano,* 2d. ed.,
    28 vols. Barcelona: Palacete Palau Dulcet, 1948–1977.

Pardo Tomás, José. *Ciencia y censura: la inquisición española y los libros
    científicos en los siglos XVI y XVII.* Madrid: Consejo Superior de
    Investigaciones Científicas, 1991.

Paris, Louis. *Les manuscrits de la Bibliothèque du Louvre Brûlés dans
    la nuit du 23 au 24 Mai 1871 sous le règne de la Commune.* Paris:
    Bureau du Cabinet Historique, 1872.

Parpola, S. "Assyrian Library Records," *Journal of Near Eastern Studies*
    42 (1983): 1–29.

Parrot, André. *Trésors du Musée de Baghdad des origines à l'Islam: Musée
    du Louvre Galerie Mollien.* Paris: Réunion des Musées Nationaux,
    1966.

Parthey, Gustav. *Das Alexandrinische Museum: eine von der Königl.
    Akademie der Wissenschaften zu Berlin im Juli 1837 gekrönte
    Preisschrift.* Berlin: Akademischen Buchdruckerei, 1838.

———— *Ptolemaeus Lagi, der Gründer der 32sten aegyptischen Dynastie.*
    Berlin: 1861.

Paschini, Pio. *Domenico Grimani cardinale di S. Marco.* Rome: Edizioni
    di Storia e Letteratura, 1943.

Pearcy, Lee. "Galen's Pergamun," *Archaeology* 38, no. 6 (1985): 33–39.

Pearson, Lionel, and Susan Stephens. *Didymi in Demosthenem com-
    menta.* Stuttgart: B. G. Teubner, 1983.

Pease, Arthur. "Notes on Book-burning," in *Munera Studiosa: Studies
    in Honor of W. H. P. Hatch.* Cambridge, Mass.: The Episcopal
    Theological School, 1946, pp. 145–160.

Pedersen, Olof. *Archives and Libraries in the Ancient Near East,
    1500–300 B.C.* Bethesda: CDL/University Press of Maryland, 1998.

Pedram, Latif. "Afganistán: La biblioteca arde," *Auto da fé* 1 (Fall
    2000).

Peignot, Étienne Gabriel. *Dictionnaire critique, littéraire, et bibli-
    ographique des principaux livres condamnés au feu, suprimés ou
    censurés: Précédé d'un discours sur ces sortes d'ouvrages.* Paris: A. A.
    Renouard, 1806

————. *De Pierre Aretin. Notice sur sa fortune, sur les moyens qui la
    lui ont procurée et sur l'emploi qu'il en a fait.* Paris: A. A. Renouard,
    1836.

————. *Essai historique sur la liberté d'écrire chez les Anciens et au
    Moyen Âge; sur la liberté de la presse depuis le quinzième siècle, et*

sur les moyens de répression dont ces libertés ont été l'objet dans tous les temps; avec beaucoup d'anecdotes et de notes . . . Paris: Crapelet, 1832.

Pelissier, R. *Les bibliothèques en Chine pendant la première moitié du XXe siècle*. Paris: 1971.

Pelland, Lionel. *S. Prosperi Aquitani Doctrina der Praedestinationes et Voluntate Dei Salvifica: De Ejus in Augustinismum Influxu*. Montreal: 1936.

Petersson, Robert T. *Sir Kenelm Digby, the Ornament of England*. Cambridge: Harvard University Press, 1956.

Pettinato, Giovanni. *Ebla, una ciudad olvidada*. Barcelona: Trotta, 2000.

Pfeiffer, Rudolf, *Callimachus*, 2 vols. Oxford: Oxford University Press, 1953.

———. *Hymni et epigrammata*. Oxford: Oxford University Press, 1953.

———. *History of Classical Scholarship*, vol. 1. Oxford: Oxford University Press, 1968.

———. *Historia de la filología clásica*, vol. 1. Madrid: Gredos, 1981.

Pia, P. *Les livres de l'enfer. Bibliographie critique des ouvrages érotiques dans leurs différentes éditions du XVIe siècle à nos jours*. Paris: C. Coulet et A. Faure, 1978.

Pichon, Jean-Charles. *Histoire universelle des sectes et des sociétés secretes*. Paris: Lucien Souny Editions, 1969.

Picón, Juan de Dios. *Estadística y Descripción geográfica, política, agrícola e industrial de todos los lugares de que se compone la Provincia de Mérida de Venezuela*. Mérida: 1832.

Pinto Crespo, Virgilio. *Inquisición y control ideológico en la España del siglo XVI*. Madrid: Taurus, 1983.

Platthy, Jenö. *Sources on the Earliest Greek Libraries with the Testimonia*. Amsterdam: Adolf M. Hakkert, 1968.

Plomer, Henry Robert, et al. *A Dictionary of the Printers and Booksellers Who Were at Work in England, Scotland and Ireland from 1726 to 1775*. London: Bibliographical Society, 1932.

Plumbe, Wilfred J. *The Preservation of Books in Tropical and Subtropical Countries*. Hong Kong: Oxford University Press, 1964.

Pococke, Richard. *Contextio Gemmarum, Sive, Eutychii Patriarchæ Alexandrini Annales*. Oxford: Excudebat H. Hall, 1656.

Polk, Milbry, and Angela Schuster. *The Looting of the Iraq Museum, Baghdad: The Lost Legacy of Ancient Mesopotamia*. New York: Harry N. Abrams, 2005.

Pollux, Julius. *Onomastikon*, 10 vols. Amsterdam: Officina Wetsteniana, 1706.

Popper, William. *The Censorship of Hebrew Books*. Whitefish, MT: Kessinger Publishing, 2007.

Porete, Marguerite. *Le miroir des âmes simples et anéanties qui seulement demeurent en vouloir et désir d'amour*. Introduction, translation, and notes by Max Huot de Longchamp. Paris: Albin Michel, 2000.

Potocki, Jean. *Le manuscrit trouvé à Saragosse*. Paris: Le Livre de Poche, 1993.

Prescott, Andrew. "Their Present Miserable State of Cremation: The Restoration of the Cotton Library," in *Sir Robert Cotton as Collector: Essays on an Early Stuart Courtier and His Legacy*. London: British Library, 1997.

Quevedo, Francisco de. *Antología poética*. Bogotá: Editorial Oveja Negra, 1984.

Quincey, Thomas de. *The Caesars* and *The Avengers*, 2 vols., Boston: J. R. Osgood, 1873.

Ramsden, Charles. *London Bookbinders, 1780–1840*. London: Batsford, 1956.

Rashid al-Din Tabid. *Djami el-tévarikh: Histoire générale du monde, Tarikh-i moubarek-i ghazani: histoire des Mongols*, 2 vols. Edited by Edgar Blochet. Leyden: E.J. Brill, 1911.

Rauf, Imad Abd al-Salam. *Athar al-khattiyah fi al-Maktabah al-Qadiriyah fi Jami al-Shaykh Abd al-Qadir al-Kilani bi-Baghdad*. Baghdad: 1974.

Raynaudus, T. *Erotemata de malis ac bonis libris deque justa aut injusta eorum confixione*. Lyons: 1653.

Reale, Giovanni. *Platone: Alla ricerca della sapienza segreta*. Milan: Giovanni Reale Rizzoli, 1998.

Réau, Louis. *Histoire du vandalisme*. Paris: Robert Laffont, 1994.

Reuchlin, Johannes, *Recommendation Whether to Confiscate, Destroy and Burn All Jewish Books* (reprint edition of 1510 original). Mahwah, NJ: Paulist Press, 2000.

Reyes, Alfonso. *Obras completas*, vol. 13. Mexico City: Fondo de Cultura Económica, 1961.

Ribera y Tarragó, Julián. *Bibliófilos y bibliotecas en la España musulmana*. Zaragoza: 1896.

Riedlmayer, András. *Destruction of Cultural Heritage in Bosnia-Herzegovina, 1992–1996: A Post-War Survey of Selected Municipalities*, 2002, http://hague.bard.edu/reports/BosHeritageReport-AR.pdf.

Rivera, I. R. de. "Sobre la destructividad humana: Un instinto o Una Carencia," in *Memorias,* vol. 2. Mexico City: 1982, pp. 532–550.

Rivolta, Adolfo. *Catalogo dei codici Pinelliani dell'Ambrosiana latini*. Milan: 1933.

Roberts, C. H., and T. C. Skeat. *The Birth of the Codex*. London: British Academy, 1983.

Roberts, Julian, and Andrew Watson. *John Dee's Library Catalogue*. London: Bibliographical Society, 1990.

Robinson, J. M., ed. *The Nag Hammadi Library in English*. Translated by members of the Coptic Gnostic Library Project of the Institute for Antiquity and Christianity. San Francisco: Harper and Row, 1977.

Rodríguez-Miñón, Rafael. *La vida y la obra del bibliófilo y bibliógrafo extremeño D. Antonio Rodríguez-Moñino*. Mérida: Editora Regional de Extremadura, 2000.

Rose, Jonathan. *The Holocaust and the Book: Destruction and Preservation*. Amherst: University of Massachusetts Press, 2001.

Rowell, H. T. "Protection of Libraries in Italy During the War," *Between Librarians: Journal of the Maryland Library Association* 13 (1946): 7–9.

Roy, David T., and Tsuen-Hsuin Tsien. *Ancient China: Studies in Early Civilization*. Hong Kong: Chinese University Press, 1978.

Rubinstein, Nicolai. "Libraries and Archives of Florence," *Times Literary Supplement*, December 1, 1966, p. 1133.

Rufo, Quinto Curcio. *Historia de Alejandro Magno*. Madrid: Gredos, 1985.

Ruperez, María. "Bibliografía sobre la guerra civil," *Claridad* 16 (1986): 99–105.

Ruhken, David. *Rutilius Lupus*. 1768.

Sable, Martin H. "The Protection of the Library and Archive: An International Bibliography," *Library and Archival Security* 5, no. 2–3 (1983): 1–183.

———. "Warfare and the Library: An International Bibliography," *Library and Archival Security* 7, no. 1 (1985): 25–97.

Saenger, Paul. *Space Between Words: The Origins of Silent Reading.* Palo Alto, CA: Stanford University Press, 1997.

Safranski, Rüdiger. *Martin Heidegger: Between Good and Evil.* Cambridge: Harvard University Press, 1999.

Salih, Qahtan Rashid. *Al-Kashshaf al-athari fi al-'Iraq.* Baghdad: Al-Jumhuriyah al-'Iraqiyah, Wizarat al-Thaqafah wa-al-I'lam, al-Mu'assasah al-'Ammah lil-Athar wa-al-Turath, 1987.

Salman, Isa, Usama al-Naqshabandi, and Najat al-Totonchi. *Arabic Texts,* Part 1. *Texts on Wood, Stone, and Other Building Materials.* Baghdad: Ministry of Information, Directorate General of Antiquities, 1975.

San Sebastián, Koldo. "El exilio de los archivos," *X Congreso de Estudios Vascos: Archivos, Bibliotecas y Museos,* Iruñea (April 21–27, 1987): 619–703.

Sánchez Hernampérez, Arsenio. *Políticas de conservación en bibliotecas.* Madrid: Arco Libros, 1999.

Sauder, Gerhard. *Die Bücherverbrennung zum 10 Mai 1933.* Munich: Hanser, 1983.

Savage, Ernest A. *Old English Libraries,* 1911. http://www.gutenberg. org/etext/1615.

Scheffel, Josef Viktor von. *Ekkehard.* Stuttgart: K. Thienemann Verlag, 1930.

Schelhorn, Johann Georg. *Amoenitates literariæ, quibus variæ observationes, scripta item quædam anecdota and rariora opuscula exhibentur,* vol. 11. Leipzig: 1730.

Scherer, Jacques. *Le "livre" de Mallarmé.* Paris: Gallimard, 1978.

Schmandt-Besserat, Denise. *Before Writing,* 2 vols. Austin: University of Texas Press, 1992.

———. *How Writing Came About.* Austin: University of Texas Press, 1996.

Schmelzer, Menahem. "Fire and Water: Book Salvage in New York and Florence," *Special Libraries* 59, no. 8 (1968): 620–625.

Schmidt, Friedrich. *Die Pinakes des Kallimachos.* Berlin: E. Ebering, 1922.

Schmidt, Moritz. *Didymi chalcenteri grammatici Alexandrini fragmenta quae supersunt omnia.* Stuttgart: F. Teubneri, 1854.

Schnabel, P. *Berossos und die babylonisch-hellenist Literatur.* Leipzig and Berlin: 1923.

Schöffling, Klaus von. *Dort wo man Bücher verbrennt: Stimmen der Betroffenen.* Frankfurt: Suhrkamp, 1983.

Schöne, Albrecht. *Göttinger Bücherverbrennung 1933. Rede am 10. Mai 1983 zur Erinnerung an die "Aktion wider den undeutschen Geist."* Göttingen: Vandenhoeck & Ruprecht, 1983.

Schuchner, Silvina. "La familia que enterró sus libros y tardó 18 años en recuperarlos," *Clarín*, March 23, 2001.

Schwartz, Eduard. *Griechische Geschichtschreiber.* Leipzig: Koehler und Amelang, 1957.

Sebald, W. G. *On the Natural History of Destruction.* London: Penguin Books Ltd., 2004.

Servet, Miguel. *Restitución del Cristianismo.* Translation by Ángel Alcalá and Luis Betés. Introduction and notes by Ángel Alcalá. Madrid: Fundación Universitaria Española, 1980.

Shapiro, B. J. *John Wilkins: An Intellectual Biography.* Berkeley: University of California Press, 1969.

Sharpe, Kevin. *Reading Revolutions: The Politics of Reading in Early Modern England.* New Haven: Yale University Press, 2000.

Shaughnessy, Edward. *Before Confucius: Studies in the Creation of the Chinese Classics.* Albany: SUNY Press, 1997.

Shavit, David. *Hunger for the Printed Word: Books and Libraries in the Jewish Ghettos of Nazi-Occupied Europe.* Jefferson, NC: McFarland & Company, 1997.

Sherman, William H. *John Dee: The Politics of Reading and Writing in the English Renaissance.* Amherst: University of Massachusetts Press, 1997.

Shubert, Steven Blake. "The Oriental Origins of the Alexandrian Library," *Libri* 43 no. 2 (1993): 142–172.

Shipley, A. E. "Enemies of Books," *Tropical Agriculture* 2 (1925): 223–224.

Simic, Goran. *Sorrow of Sarajevo.* Cornwall UK: Cargo Press, 1996.

Simpson, Elisabeth, ed. *The Spoils of World War II and Its Aftermath: The Loss, Reappearance and Recovery of Cultural Property.* New York: Harry Abrams, 1997.

Sinova, Justino. *La censura de prensa durante el franquismo.* Madrid: Espasa Calpe, 1989.

Slusser, Michael. "Reading Silently in Antiquity," *Journal of Biblical Literature* 111 (1992): 499.

Smith, Joshua Toulmin. *English Gilds: The Original Ordinances of More than One Hundred Early English Gilds.* Ontario: 1870. (Via the McMaster University Archive for the History of Economic Thought.)

Snell, Bruno. *Tragicorum graecorum fragmenta.* Gottingen: Vandenhoeck & Ruprecht, 1971.

Solinus. *Collectanea Rerum Memorabilium.* Berlin: 1895.

Speyer, Wolfgang. "Buechervernichtung," *Jahrbuch fuer Antike und Christentum* 13 (1970): 123–154.

Ssu-ma Ch'ien, *The Grand Scribe's Record.* vol. 1. *The Basic Annals of Pre-Han China.* Edited by William H. Nienhauser Jr. Bloomington IN: Indiana University Press, 1995.

Stadmüller, Georg. *Michael Choniates Metropolit von Athen.* Dissertation, 1934.

Stalemo, Emilie. "Svenska Brandskyddsforeningens Bibliotek," *Tidskrift för Dokumentation* 18, no. 6 (1962): 73–76.

Stavraki, Emmanuel. *La convention pour la protection des biens culturels en cas de conflit armé.* Athens: Ant. N. Sakkoulas, 1996.

Stern, Guy. *Nazi Book Burning and the American Response.* Lecture. Detroit: Wayne State University, 1991. Simon Wiesenthal Center Annual 2.

Stipcevic, Aleksandar. "Biblioteche distrutte e roghi di libri in Croazia 1991," *Il bibliotecario* 31 (Jan.–Mar., 1992): 157–160.

Stradling, John. *Epigrammata.* London: 1607.

Streck, M. *Assurbanipal und die letzten assyrischen Könige bis zum Untergange Ninivehs.* Leipzig: 1916.

Strong, C. H. *A Brief Sketch of the Waldenses.* Lawrence, Kan.: J.S. Boughton, 1893.

Strong, Gary E. "Rats! Oh No, Not Rats!" *Special Libraries* 78, no. 2 (1987): 105–111.

Sueiro, Daniel, and Bernardo Díaz Nosty. *Historia del franquismo.* Madrid: Sarpe, 1986.

Talas, Muhamad Asad. *Kashshaf an makhtutat khazain kutub al-Awqaf.* Baghdad: Matbaat al-Ani, 1953.

Tellegen, B. D. H. *De provinciale Bibliotheek van Zeeland.* Middelburg, The Netherlands: U. F. Auer and Son, 1892.

Thomas, Donald S. *A Long Time Burning: The History of Literary Censorship in England.* London: Routledge & Kegan Paul, 1969.

Thomas, R. *Oral Tradition and Written Record in Classical Athens.* Cambridge: Cambridge University Press, 1990.

Thompson, James Westfall. *The Medieval Library.* Chicago: University of Chicago Press, 1939.

———. *Ancient Libraries.* Berkeley: University of California Press, 1940.

Thomson, I. "Manuel Chrysoloras and the Early Italian Renaissance," *Greek, Roman and Byzantine Studies* 7, no. 1 (1966): 63–82.

Timperley, Charles Henry. *Dictionary of Printers and Printing.* London: H. Johnson, 1839.

Ting, Lee-hsia Hsu. *Government Control of the Press in Modern China, 1900–1949.* Cambridge, MA: Harvard University Press, 1974.

Todorov, Tzvetan. *The Conquest of America: The Question of the Other.* Norman: University of Oklahoma Press, 1999.

———. *Memoria del bien, tentación del mal.* Barcelona: Península, 2002.

Toman, Jirí. *La protection des biens culturels en cas de conflit armé.* París: UNESCO, 1994.

Torre Revello, José. *El libro, la imprenta y el periodismo en América durante la dominación española.* Buenos Aires: Casa Jacob Peuser, 1949.

Tosi, R. *Studi sulla tradizione indiretta dei classici greci.* Bologna: CLUEB, 1988.

Tourneux, Maurice. *Bibliographie de l'histoire de Paris pendant la Révolution française*, vol. 4. Paris: Imprimerie Nouvelle, 1890.

Tov, Emanuel, ed. *Discoveries in the Judaean Desert*, vols. 1–10. New York: Oxford University Press, 1955–1992.

Tovar, Antonio, and M. de la Pinta. *Procesos inquisitoriales contre Francisco Sánchez de las Brozas.* Madrid: Instituto Antonio de Nebrija, 1941.

Treu, Max. *Der sogenannte Lampriaskatalog der Plutarchschriften.* Waldenberg in Schlesien: 1873.

Tsien, Tsuen-Hsuin. *Written on Bamboo and Silk: The Beginnings of Chinese Books and Inscriptions.* Chicago: University of Chicago Press, 2004.

Tuleja, Tad. *The Catalog of Lost Books: An Annotated and Seriously Addled Collection of Great Books That Should Have Been Written but Never Were.* New York: Columbine Trade, 1989.

Tumah, Salman Hadi. *Makhtutat al-Sayyid Muhamad Baqir al-Tabatabai fi Karbula.* Kuwait: al-Munazzamah al-Arabiyah lil-Tarbiyah wa-al-Thaqafah wa-al-Ulum, Mahad al-Makhtutat al-Arabiyah, 1985.

Tzetzes, Jean. *Historiarum variarum chiliades.* Leipzig: T. Kiessling, 1826.

U.S. Department of the Treasury. *Letter from the Secretary of the Treasury, in relation to the destruction of official books and papers by the fire in the building occupied by the Treasury Department.* Early American Imprints, Series 2, no. 1501, 1990.

University of Oxford, *Judicium and Decretum Universitatis Oxoniensis Latum in Convocatione Habita August 19, Anno Dom. 1690.*

Valette-Cagnac, E. *La lecture à Rome: Rites et pratiques.* Paris: Bellin, 1997.

Vallejo, Juan de. *Memorial de la vida de Fray F. Jiménez de Cisneros.* Madrid: [s.n.], 1913.

Vernet, Juan. *Literatura árabe.* Barcelona: Labor, 1968.

Veyrin-Forrer, Jeanne. *La lettre et le texte: Trente années de recherches sur l'histoire du livre.* Paris: Rue d'Ulm, 1987.

Vila, Samuel. *Historia de la Inquisición.* Terrassa: CLIE, 1977.

Villehardouin, Geoffrey de. *Memoirs or Chronicle of the Fourth Crusade and the Conquest of Constantinople.* Translated by Frank T. Marzials. London: Dent, 1908.

Virgilio, Biagio. *Gli Attalidi di Pergamo: Fama, eredità, memoria.* Pisa: Giardini, 1993.

Vries, Willem de. *Einsatzstab Reichsleiter Rosenberg, Sonderstab Musik: The Confiscation of Music in the Occupied Countries of Western Europe During World War II.* Ann Arbor: University of Michigan Press, 1997.

Wachsmuth, C. *Sillographorum Graecorum Reliquiae, Rec. et Enarravit C. Wachsmuth; Praecedit Commentatio de Timone Philiaso Ceterisque Sillographis, 'Corpusculum Poesis Epicae Graecae Ludibundae.'* Leipzig: 1885.

Walberer, Ulrich. *10 Mai 1933: Bücherverbrennung in Deutschland und die Folgen.* Frankfurt: Fischer Taschenbuch, 1983.

Walford, Cornelius. "Chronological Sketch of the Destruction of Libraries by Fire in Ancient and Modern Times and of Other Severe Losses of Books and Manuscripts, by Fire and Water," Appendix 5. *Transaction and Proceedings of the Second Annual Meeting of the Library Association of the United Kingdom.* London: 1879, 149–154.

———. *The Destruction of Libraries by Fire Considered Practically and Historically.* London: Chiswick Press, 1880.

Wang-Toutain, Françoise. *Le Bodhisattva Ksitigarbha en Chine du ve au xiiie siècle.* Paris: École Francaise d'Extrême-Orient, 1998.

Weiss, Harry B., and Ralph H. Carruthers. "The More Important Insect Enemies of Books and a Bibliography of the Literature," *New*

York Public Library Bulletin 40, no. 9 (1935): 739–752, 827–841, 985–995, 1049–1056.

———. *Insect Enemies of Books.* New York, New York Public Library, 1945.

Weniger, Ludwig. *Das Alexandrinische Museum; eine Skizze aus dem gelehrten Leben des Alterthums: Vortrag gehalten zu Eisenach.* Berlin: 1885.

Wessely, Karl. "De Callimacho bibliothecario." In *Studies Presented to F. Ll. Griffith.* London: Egypt Exploration Society, 1932.

Wiesner, Margot. *Verbrannte Bücher, Verfemte Dichter: Deutsche Literatur, 1933–1945 Unterdrückt und Verboten, Heute Lieferbar.* Frankfurt: Buchhändler-Vereinigung, 1983.

Wilamowitz-Moellendorff, Ulrich von. *Antigonos von Karystos,* vol. 2. Berlin and Zurich: 1881/1966.

Willems, Alphonse. *Les Elzevier. Histoire et annales typographiques.* Brussels: 1880.

Williams, Gareth D. *Banished Voices: Readings in Ovid's Exile Poetry.* Cambridge: Cambridge University Press, 2007.

Wilson, N. "The Libraries of the Byzantine World," *Greek, Roman, and Byzantine Studies* 8 (1967): 53–80.

Winckelmann, Johann Joachim, *Critical Account of the Situation and Destruction by the First Eruptions of Mount Vesuvius of Hercula- neum, Pompeii, and Stabia.* London: T. Carnan and F. Newbery, 1771.

Wood, Anthony. *The History and Antiquities of the University of Oxford,* 2 vols. Oxford: John Gutch, 1796.

Wulf, Joseph. *Literatur und Dichtung im Dritten Reich: Eine Dokumen- tation.* Reinbek: Rowohlt, 1966.

Zarco Cuevas, Julian. *Catálogo de los manuscritos castellanos de la Real Biblioteca de El Escorial.* Madrid: Imp. Helénica, 1924.

———. *La biblioteca de El Escorial.* Barcelona: Madrid: Imp. Helénica, 1929.

Zeno, Apostolo. *Dissertazione sopra le bibliothece antiche.* Venice: 1697.

Zintzen, Clemens, ed. *Suda. Damascii Vitae Isidori Reliquiae.* Hildesheim: Olms, 1967.

Zorzi, M. "La circolazione dei libri a Venezia nel Cinquecento: Biblio- teche private e publiche," *Ateneo Veneto,* n.s. 28 (1990): 117–189.

Index

"If anyone in the United States, or anywhere else in this world, asks about the national differences between Serbs and Muslims, please tell them this kind of story. We are really mixed in a very special way. Like the books in my library. They have no ethical background, no cultural background, no racial or geographic backgrounds. They are simply one by one. Alphabetical, perhaps. The only differences are the size, the cover, and the things they say. I think that is the story."

— Kemal Bakaršić, chief librarian of the National Museum of Bosnia and Herzegovina, writing after the destruction of the National Library in Sarajevo